IMAGES
of America

ALLEGAN

On the cover: Surrounding a 1918 Case touring automobile are newsboys, from left to right, Howard Osmun, Clair McOmber, Harold Bostwich, and Otto Schmitz. They are prepared to deliver the *Allegan News* to subscribers around town. Now known as the *Allegan County News*, the weekly newspaper continues to inform citizens of local and state issues as it has for the past 149 years. (Courtesy Allegan County Historical Society.)

IMAGES
of America

ALLEGAN

Nancy J. Ingalsbee and Carol B. Garofalo
for the Allegan County Historical Society

ARCADIA
PUBLISHING

ISBN 978-0-7385-5073-2

Published by Arcadia Publishing
Charleston, South Carolina

Printed in the United States of America

Library of Congress Catalog Card Number: 2007924633

For all general information contact Arcadia Publishing at:
Telephone 843-853-2070
Fax 843-853-0044
E-mail sales@arcadiapublishing.com
For customer service and orders:
Toll-Free 1-888-313-2665

Visit us on the Internet at www.arcadiapublishing.com

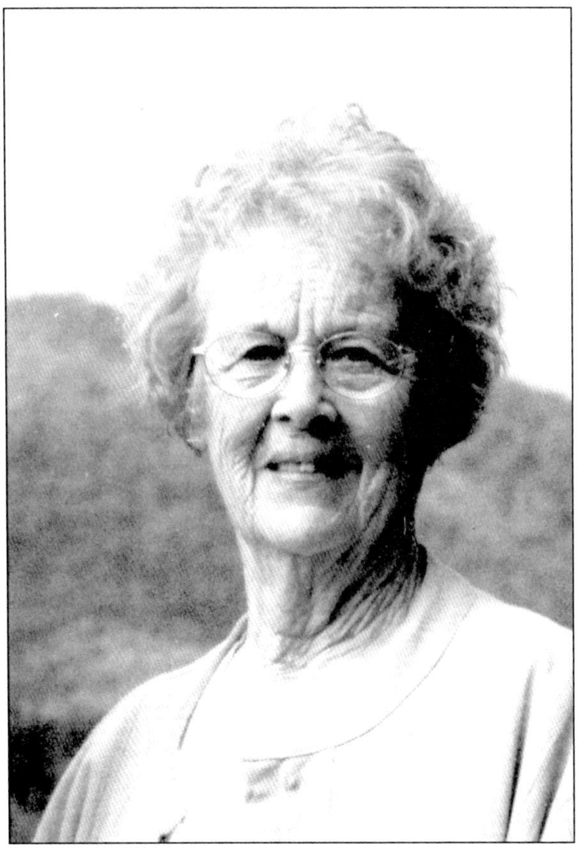

This book is dedicated to Marguerite Miller, director of the Old Jail Museum from 1981 to 2006. Marguerite liked to say that she "courted" in the old jail because in the 1930s the sheriff's family lived there. She married Bart Miller, son of sheriff Fred Miller, in 1939. Under her direction a cadre of volunteers cleaned, organized, and staffed the museum. We miss her every day.

Contents

ACKNOWLEDGMENTS

Many individuals contributed to the production of this book, and we are so grateful to them. First, had it not been for Marguerite Miller and her dedication to the Old Jail Museum, the photographs we needed might not have been available. The Old Jail Museum is still a reality because of her hard work and commitment. To John Pahl and Larry Massie, our local historians, we appreciate the hours they spent in helping us to be both accurate and interesting. Their assistance made this book so much better. Thanks to my reliable museum teen volunteer James Flynn for his technical expertise and assistance. We thank Marian Luttrell Smith, Webster Fiock, Shari Fiock, and Walter Smith, for helping us identify photographs and for giving us other historical assistance, and the staff of the Allegan Public Library who were so helpful in our quest for information. Carol's husband Tony Garofalo's unstinting support and encouragement during this entire process were so appreciated. We thank the Perrigo family, Ruth Berkin, and Nan Hunter for loaning family photographs. We also owe a great debt of gratitude to the Allegan County Historical Society for allowing us access to its Old Jail Museum archives of historical photographs. This book would never have become a reality without those wonderful images.

INTRODUCTION

The first known dwellings on the site of what is now called the city of Allegan were the dome-shaped bark wigwams of a Pottawatomi village. They chose this "big horseshoe bend" in the river as their home because the river, eventually named Kalamazoo (boiling waters), was not only their highway and food source but its wooded banks were their refuge and hunting grounds.

When title to the wilderness called Michigan was secured, a survey was needed. In 1831, the newly platted county was home to only four permanent white families within its 837 square miles. Land speculators from New York soon were sending scouts to investigate the potential of this up-for-grabs land. Elisha Ely of Rochester, New York, was first to check it out for a group that would be called the Boston Company. His report back to the principals—Alexander Ely (his son), Edward Monroe, Samuel Hubbard, Pliny Cutler, and Charles C. Trowbridge—mentioned first and foremost the advantageous eight-foot drop in the river at this attractive bend. Combined with the vast surrounding virgin forests, the site was perfect for harnessing waterpower for a profitable logging industry. The establishment of Allegan as county seat in 1835 further stimulated their interest in investing in its future. Although some towns have seen their county seat status moved to other more desirable venues, Allegan remains the seat of Allegan County to this day. By 1837, the company had erected a dam and proceeded to build a gristmill, sawmill, and 10 homes for workers who had arrived in town. The village of Allegan was on its way.

While most new towns in the territory were being named for prominent citizens or Native American chiefs, the name Allegan apparently was born of the imagination of the governor's good friend Henry L. Schoolcraft. For reasons known only to him, this north country Indian agent apparently joined two native words together to come up with the name Allegan. Loosely translated, the phrase "lake of the Algonquins" seems to have been his inspiration. The fact that there is no other town called Allegan in the world is testimony to the originality of the name.

From the outset, Allegan became home to a remarkable group of interesting historical characters. Col. Joseph Fisk arrived in 1835 to oversee the initial building of the town for the Allegan Company and was the first to purchase a lot. So enthralled was he with his new home that he named his firstborn son Joseph Allegan Fisk. The colonel became widely known as one of the country's leading builders of bridges and railways, and in 1852, he successfully took on the task of constructing the Chicago breakwater. Gen. Benjamin Pritchard, whose Civil War fame is forever tied to the capture of Jefferson Davis, president of the Confederacy, also called Allegan home. After the war, Pritchard and fellow Union officer Gen. Elisha Mix would eventually become neighbors on the high bluff of Davis Street (known at that time as Civil War Alley) overlooking the town of Allegan where they prosperously lived out their days. The Old

Jail Museum in downtown Allegan has devoted a room to Pritchard, and many fascinating items relating to his moment in history are on display.

Allegan is proud of the contribution its surrounding forests made to the rebuilding of Chicago after the 1871 fire. Virgin timber was cut and the logs floated down the river to the sawmill and across the lake to Chicago. Having contributed to Chicago's rebirth, Allegan soon had to deal with its own "great fire," which destroyed a good portion of the business district in 1884. Prior to the fire downtown, Allegan consisted of mostly three-story buildings. The grading of rubble and ash provided a base for rebuilding, leaving the post-fire two-story buildings to comingle with some of the original three-story survivors of the fire. Today there is an underground Allegan resting under the present streets and buildings, with some areas accessible and others long abandoned. Other fires over the years have altered the Allegan skyline, but with improved firefighting methods and equipment, some luck, and a bit of divine providence, no fire has since raged like the great fire of 1884.

In this 21st century, one of Allegan's oldest companies, the Perrigo Company, remains one of the largest employers in town. Founded in 1887, when Luther Perrigo answered a need for home-sized packages of drugs and chemicals, which at that time were almost exclusively available in bulk, it boasts seven plants around Allegan, including the 1921 building adjacent to the 1886 iron bridge. The modern-day Perrigo Company remains a generous benefactor to the city and has become the world's largest manufacturer of over-the-counter pharmaceutical and nutritional products for the store brand market.

Another important part of Allegan's industrial history for at least two generations was Blood Brothers Machine Company, which became a part of Rockwell International before closing its doors in 1992. In its early days, Blood Brothers produced a classic automobile in Allegan called the Cornelian. Allegan's automotive fame was rather short-lived, however, as manufacturing costs escalated and the company found it impossible to continue production. Its 1914 venture into the automotive industry would never again resurface, and the Cornelian became another chapter in Allegan's history.

Throughout the years, Allegan has been blessed with many individuals with a true sense of history and a passion to preserve it. John C. Pahl, Allegan's resident historian, and the late Marguerite Miller, whose name has been synonymous with the Old Jail Museum for the past quarter-century, kept Allegan history alive for as long as many can remember. James J. Green also made contributions in the way of historical research and authored many books on various aspects of Allegan history. In addition, Allegan's own Larry Massie is widely known and respected as a talented author and historian. Through their efforts, and that of their contemporaries, Allegan boasts not only a fine museum and historical village to be proud of, but also an extensive and accurate collection of photographic and written history.

This book is not an attempt to tell the definitive history of Allegan, for that has already been told most eloquently. It is rather an addendum of visual vignettes of places in time, of people who lived, loved, and labored in a place called Allegan.

One

Cameos of the Past

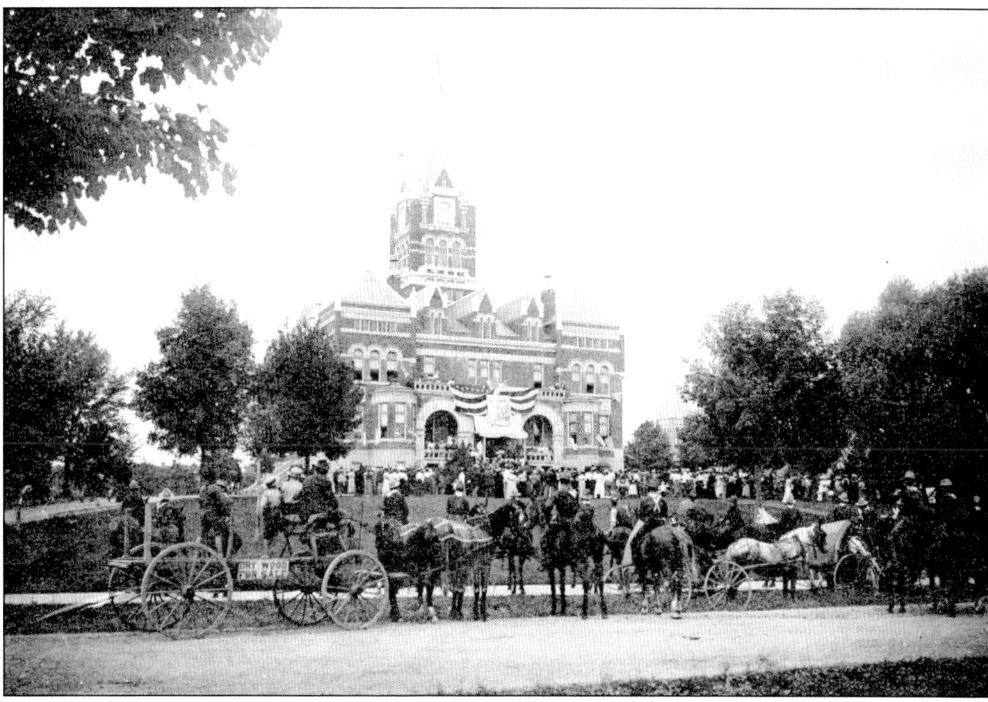

Teddy Roosevelt visited Allegan in 1900, campaigning for soon-to-be president William McKinley. The graceful old county courthouse looms in the background, and horse-drawn buggies are parked along Hubbard Street. Crowds gathered near the decorated courthouse entrance, listening to the man who would become vice president, and then eventually president in 1901 upon the assassination of McKinley.

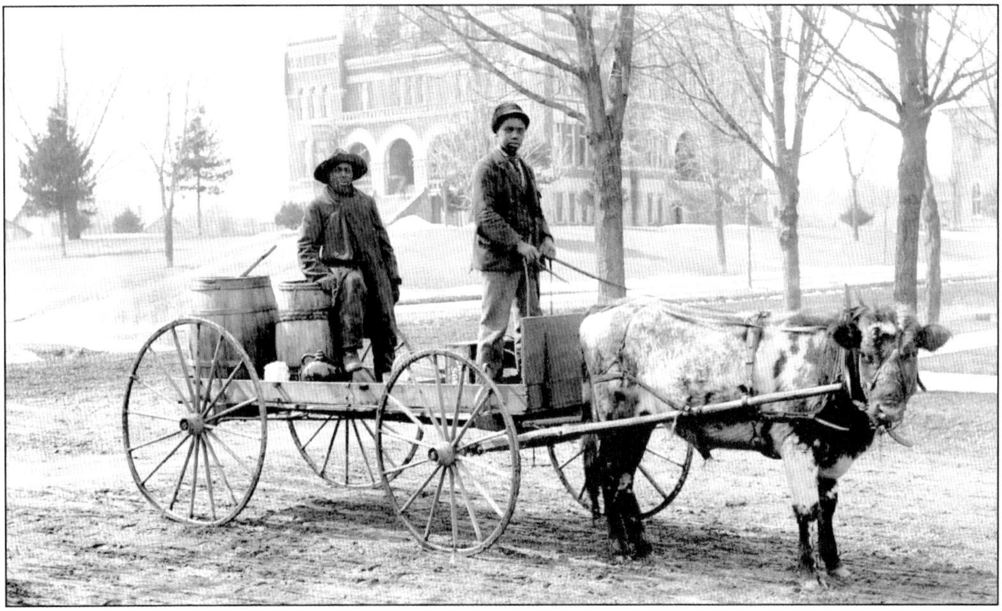

The industrious Mr. Parker was well known around town as Allegan's first department of sanitation. This c. 1900 photograph shows Parker and his assistant in their ox-drawn cart, posing in front of the courthouse at the intersection of Trowbridge and Chestnut Streets. He made good use of the pigs on his farm to dispose of the edible refuse he collected.

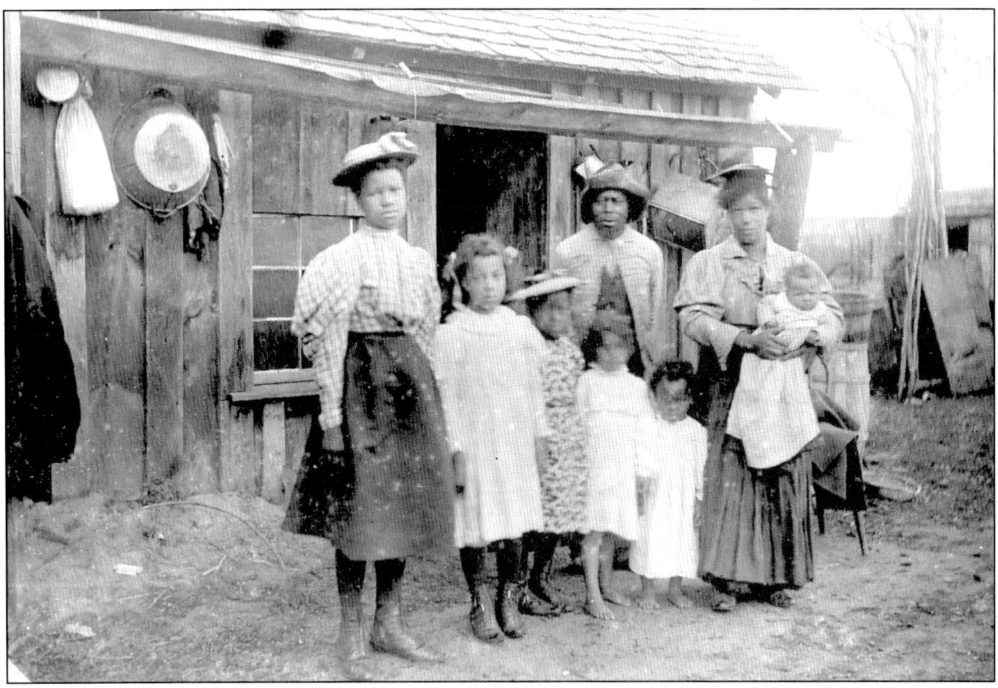

This photograph shows Parker's family in their Sunday best, possibly in front of a building on their farm. The Grace Temple Church on Robinson Avenue, which shared his daughter Grace's name, was where they worshiped. Grace is the first person on the left. The other members of the family are unidentified, although it is known that Grace had a sister Minnie and a sister Rose.

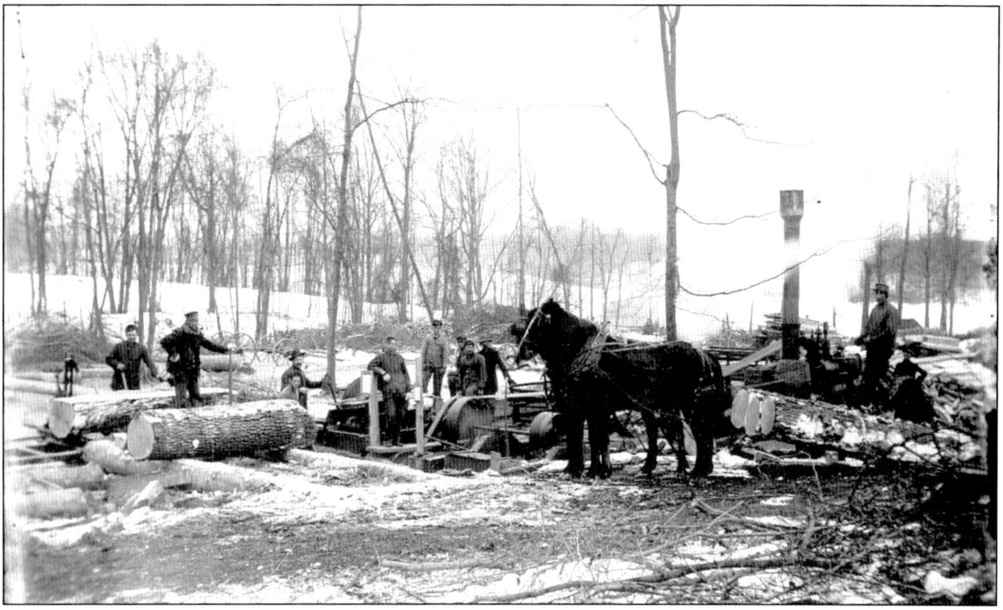

Allegan's old-growth timber was a drawing card that brought early settlers to the area. After the Great Chicago Fire of 1871, some of the timber used to rebuild the city came from the forests surrounding Allegan. The frenetic "timber era" lasted from 1850 to 1880, during which time logs were skidded to the Kalamazoo River and floated to sawmills along the riverbank. Lumber was then loaded on ships for the trip across Lake Michigan.

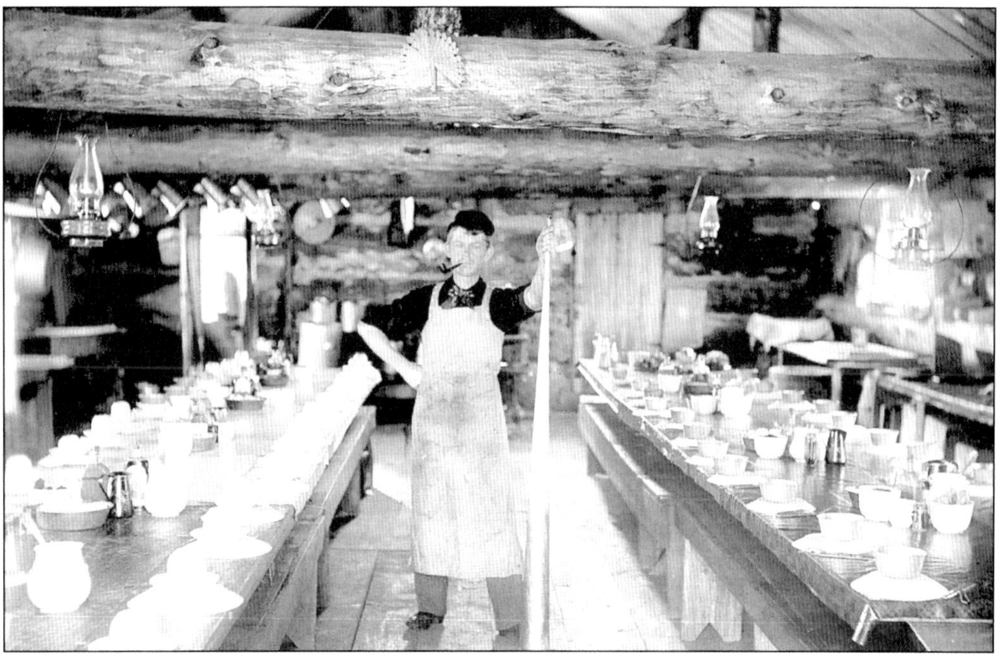

Logging in the 1880s was a physically demanding job. Hand-sawing huge logs and loading horse-drawn skids produced hungry loggers. Above is an unidentified cook in an Allegan area logging camp. The bowls on the table suggest that he may have been about to serve a hearty meal, fueling the men for a day of hard work.

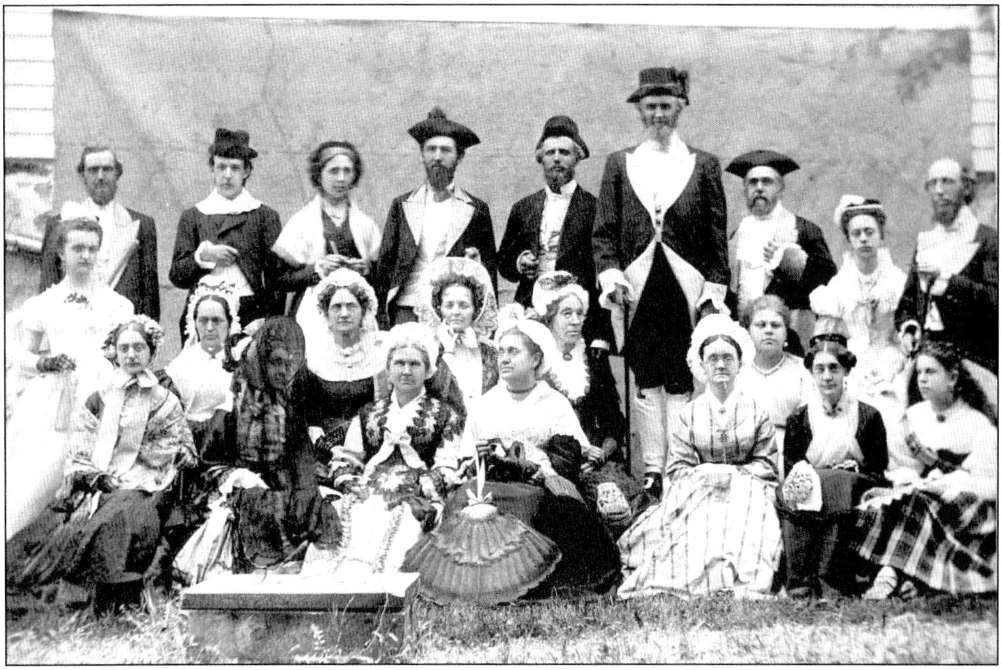

Pictured here is one of the earliest photographs, from about the 1870s, of Allegan's social elite. Of special note are (third row) first on left, grocer C. W. Hall; seventh on left, W. C. Jenner; and ninth on left, Rev. J. D. McCord. Jenner was chairman of the Allegan County Board and a proponent of construction of the courthouse. He was also Allegan's first shoemaker.

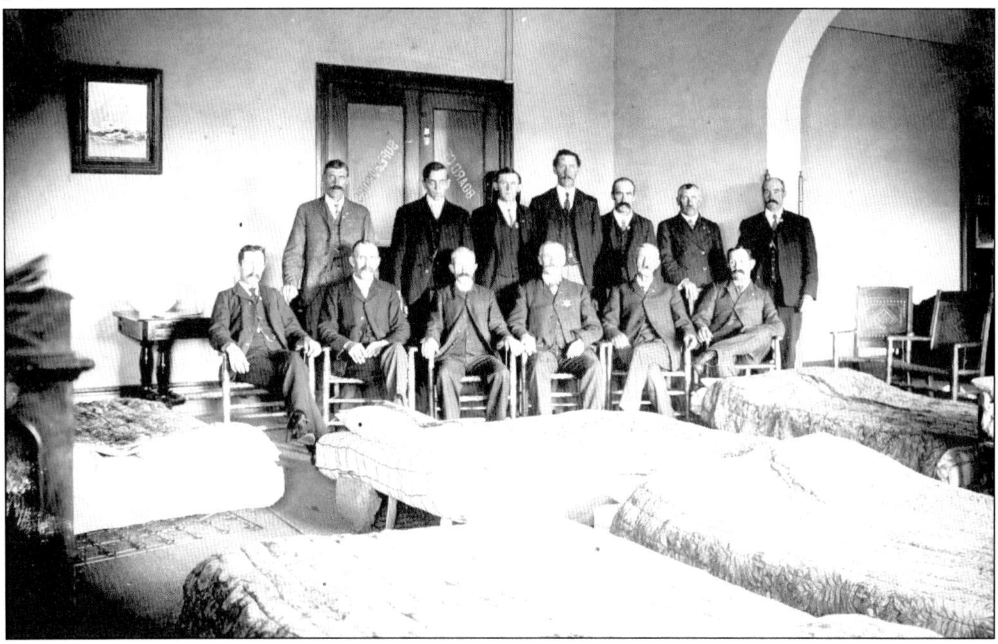

Getting a jury together in the early days was sometimes problematic. Many would be forced to travel from afar in horse-drawn buggies on bumpy roads. When a trial lasting more than one day was in progress, as in this 1906 photograph, cots would be set up in the board of supervisors room and the jurors would find it necessary to stay until the trial was completed.

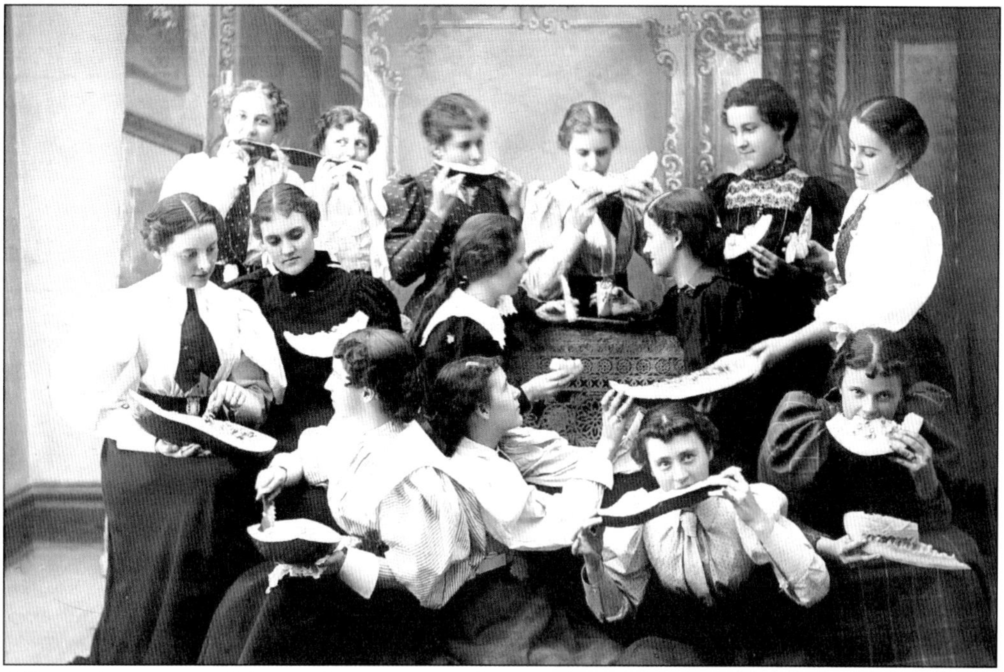

Allegan County is well known for its summer fruit crops, and this early-20th-century photograph shows ladies enjoying the bounty. Identified in no particular order are Leila Stockdall, Clara Coykendall, Mabel Grice, Grace Morse, Bess Adams, Mabel Stark, Maude Blain, Flora Koons, Ella Blain, Sadie Scott, Belle Barton, Gertrude Young, Ruth Packard, and Edith Perrigo.

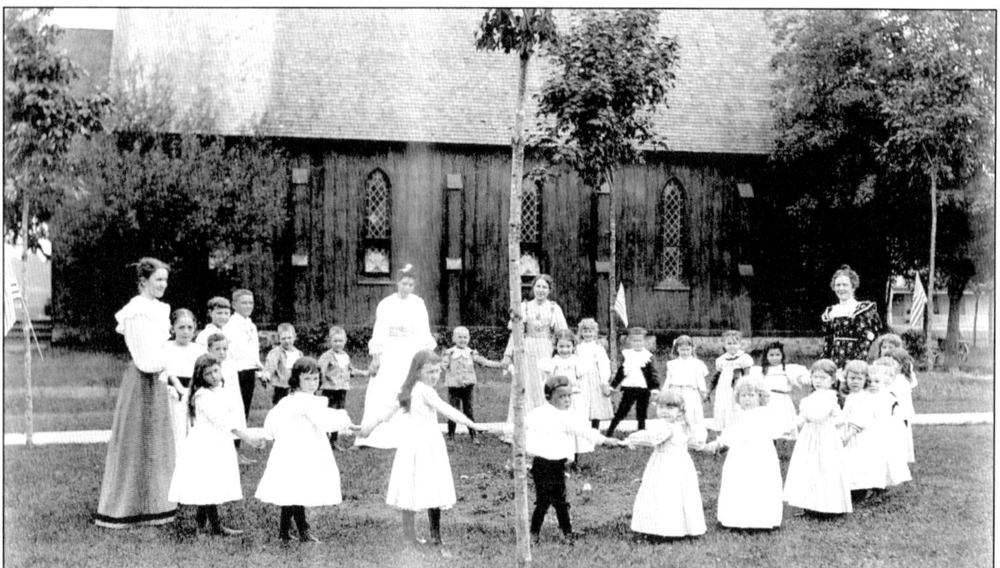

Dancing outside the Episcopal church in 1896 are, from the far left and around the circle, Jesse Thew, Gertrude Nichols, Clara Maentz, Peter Brander, John Shear, Harold Perkins, Howard Perkins, Helen Winchester, Verne Hanchett, Blanche Phillips, Anna Stratton, Mildred Stratton, Danny Ellinger, Hollis Baker, Vivian Jenner, Laura Stern, Blanche Martin, Grace Campbell, Mignon Sherwood, ? Jenner, Don Born, Guy Hanchett, Marjorie Baker, Vera DeLano, Ermanie VanOstrand, Margaret DeLano, Ethel Perkins, Georgette Fuller, and Pearl Koloff.

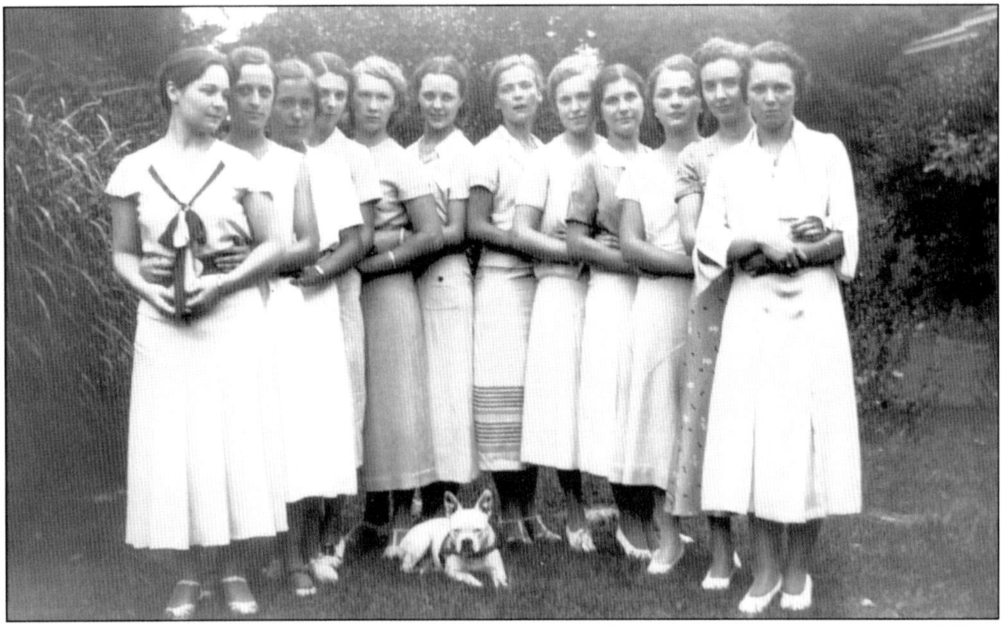

Posing together on a summer day in the 1930s are several young Allegan friends. From left to right are Connie Montague, Dorothy Brown, Katherine Winchester, Mary Armstrong, Dorothy Stratton, Jean Ellinger, Mary Helen Winchester, Nancy Cook, Miriam Wilcox, Barbara Lutz, Dorothy Miller, and Helen Herman. The lounging dog is unidentified.

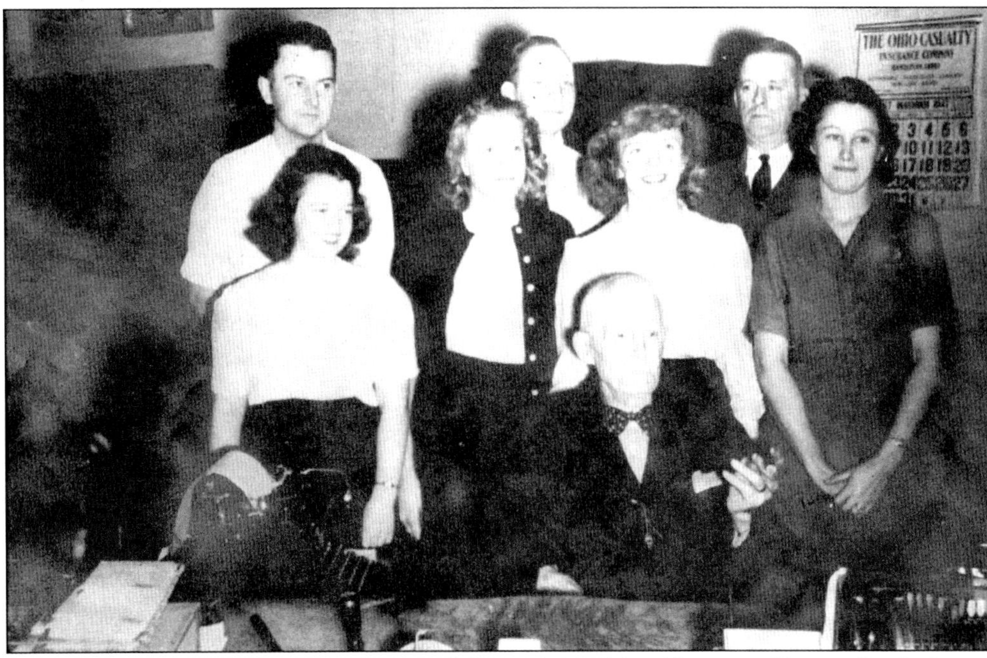

This 1947 photograph shows employees of the T. S. Updyke Abstract office on Brady Street. Theodore Updyke, seated in front, told many stories of his experiences as a U.S. marshal in the Wild West, an adventure made possible to him by his cousin, president of the United States Chester A. Arthur. Standing in the center of the back row is Allegan's beloved historian John Pahl.

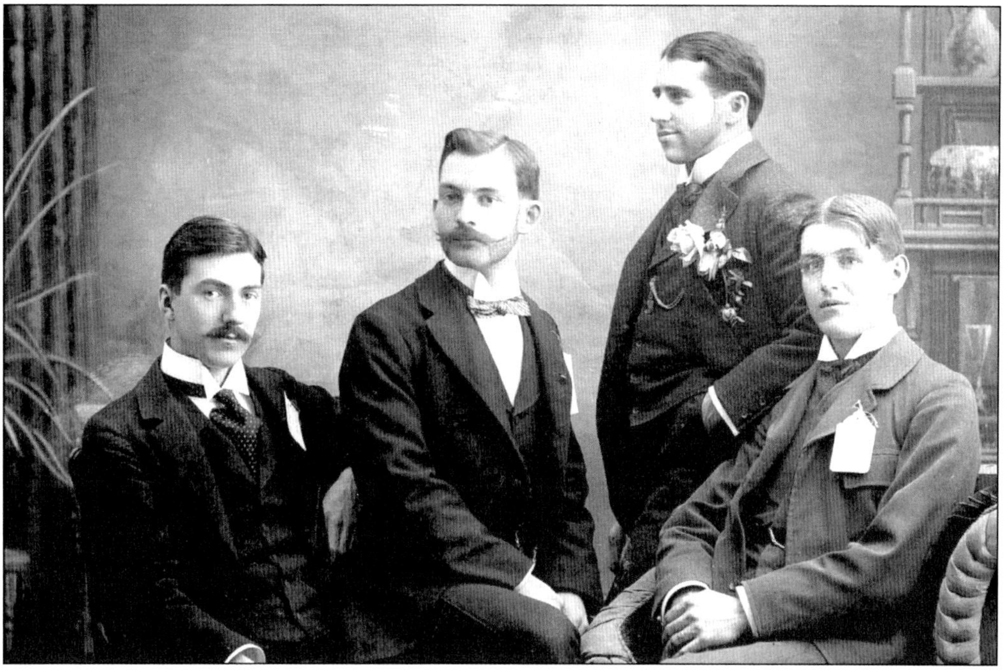

Posing like proper gentlemen are, from left to right, Harry Pritchard, Harry Porter, Keene Phillips, and Berneath Sherwood. This photograph was taken in Porter's photograph studio in Allegan. "Just Before the Battle" is the notation on the back of the photograph. Despite the contentious nature of the photograph below, these men remained lifelong friends.

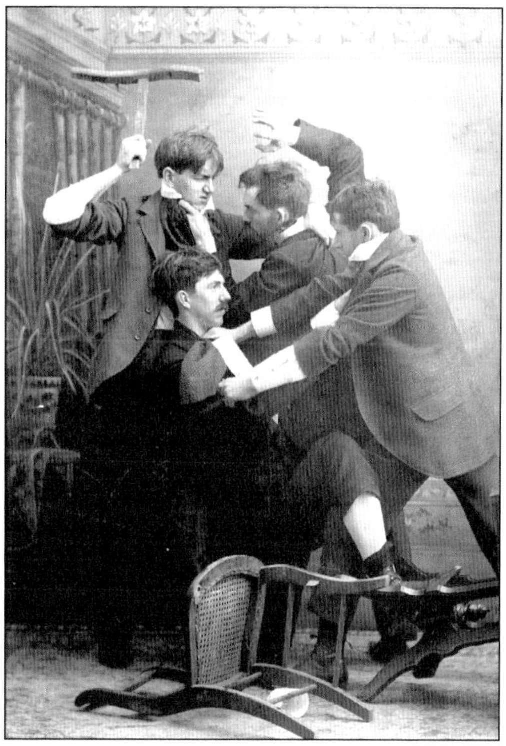

Evidently the four gentlemen, who are so formally posed above, decided it was time for some youthful hijinks. In this sequential photograph, titled on the back "In Combat," Keene Phillips wrestles with Harry Pritchard, while Berneath Sherwood tries to thump Harry Porter over the head with a broken chair leg.

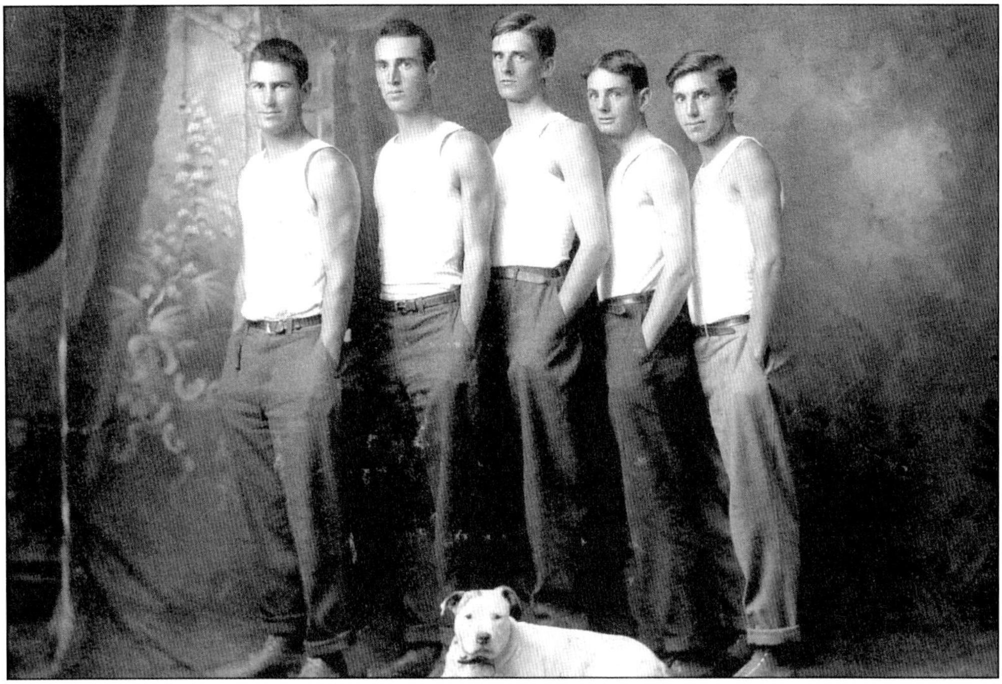

It is unclear why these young gentlemen are dressed in their "muscle shirts" for this studio photograph in the early 1900s. Posing with an unidentified dog, they are, from left to right, Charlie DeLano, Earl DeLano, George Updyke, Rasty Herman, and Ben Weeks. The dog appears to mimic their tough expressions with one of his own.

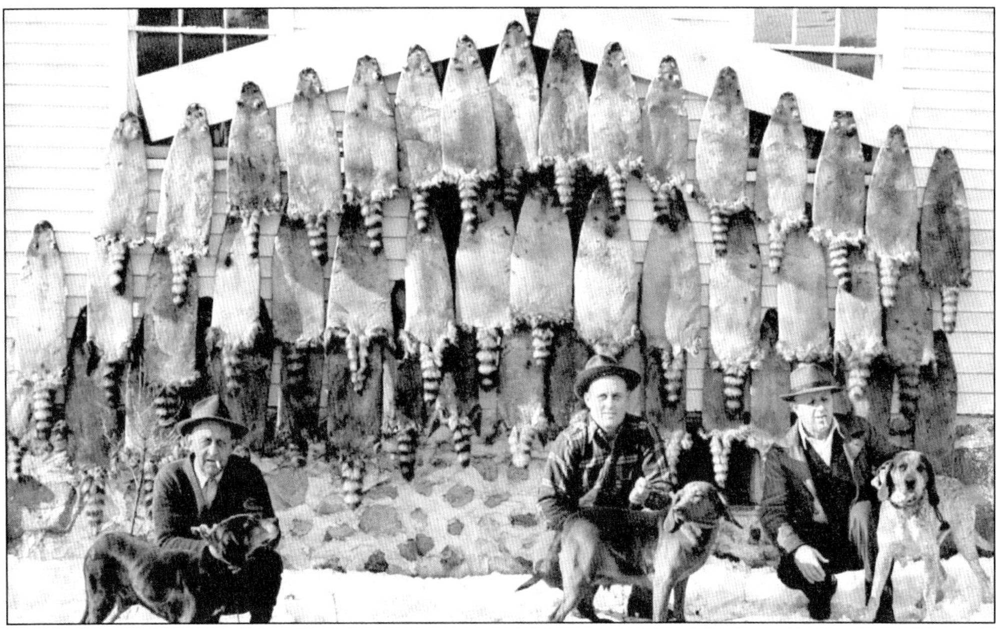

Pictured here, from left to right, Floyd Martin of Otsego, Willard "Bart" Miller, and his father, sheriff Fred Miller, pose with their hunting dogs in front of a large cache of raccoon pelts, around the 1930s. Bart was the husband of Marguerite Miller, the former director of Allegan's Old Jail Museum.

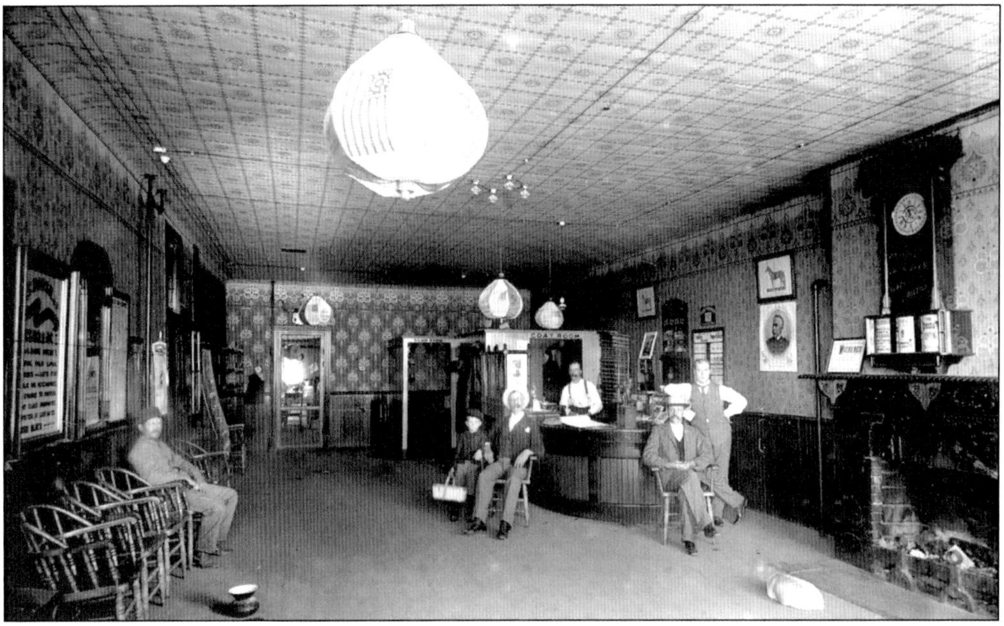

Citizens gather, around 1899, in the lobby of the City Hotel on Brady Street. Pictured are, from left to right, unidentified man in chair, Art Wheeler and unidentified boy, dentist Dr. Giles Piper, Chet McDuffee, and H. D. McDuffee. The dog sleeping in front of the fireplace is unidentified. Decorations honor Spanish-American War hero Adm. George Dewey and entreat the public to "Remember the *Maine*."

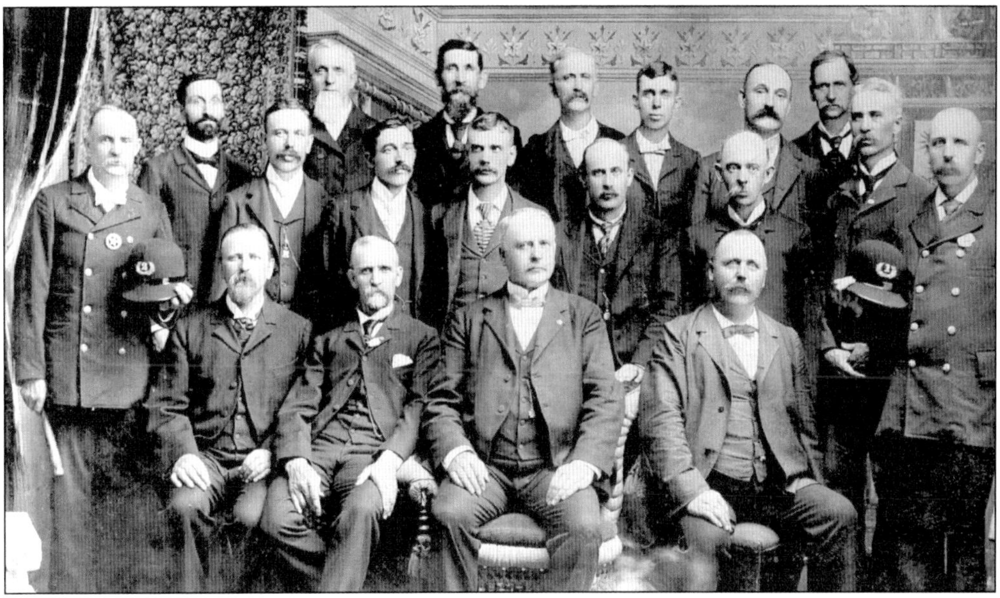

Allegan city fathers pose in this early-1900s photograph. From left to right are (first row) Jim Krumbien (monument works), ? Green, Dr. Thomas, and Chris Maentz (meat market); (second row) Jim Barney, Gus Stern (clothing store), Gus Butler, ? Bond (bicycle shop), unidentified, Orlin Priest (blacksmith), E. Reed (newspaper), and L. Chronister; (third row) ? Wirick (grocery store), Austin Sherwood (undertaker), C. Tubah (tinsmith), unidentified, sheriff George Smith, Jay Fenton (painter), and city marshal Clark Collins.

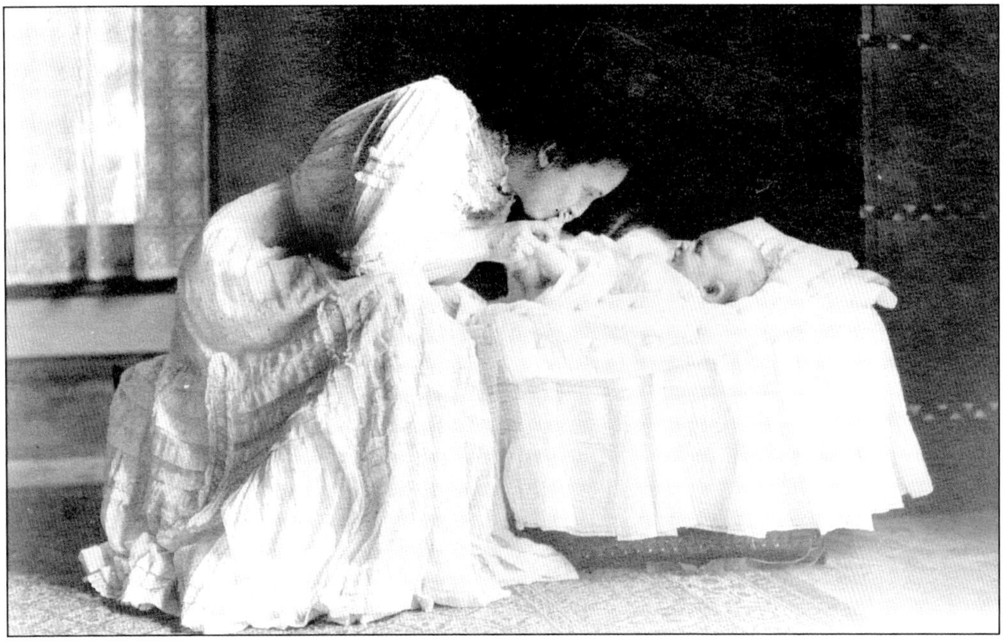

This charming photograph shows Hazel VanOstrand Stone and her baby William around 1900. Hazel's husband, Ethol Stone, was an active attorney in Allegan until a week before he died in 1969 at age 89. His modest lifestyle and shrewd stock market investments made possible a gift of $1.2 million in 1969 to the newly formed Allegan Community Foundation.

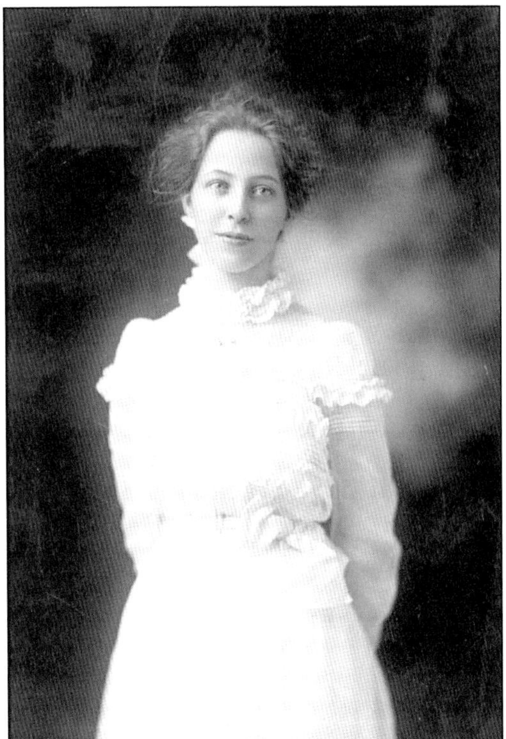

Louise Delano graduated from Allegan High School in 1901, along with her future husband, Frank Peck. A member of one of Allegan's most prominent families, in later years Louise would take on the project of furnishing the bedroom of the sheriff's residence of the Old Jail Museum with furniture of the 1860s.

Allegan attorney Leo Hoffman strikes a pose, around 1940, with downtown Allegan in the background. Like his father, Clare E. Hoffman, who represented Allegan in Congress from 1935 to 1963, Leo served his fellow citizens well for many years. He continued practicing law at his office in the Lawyers' Building well into his 80s and died in Naples, Florida, at the age of 87.

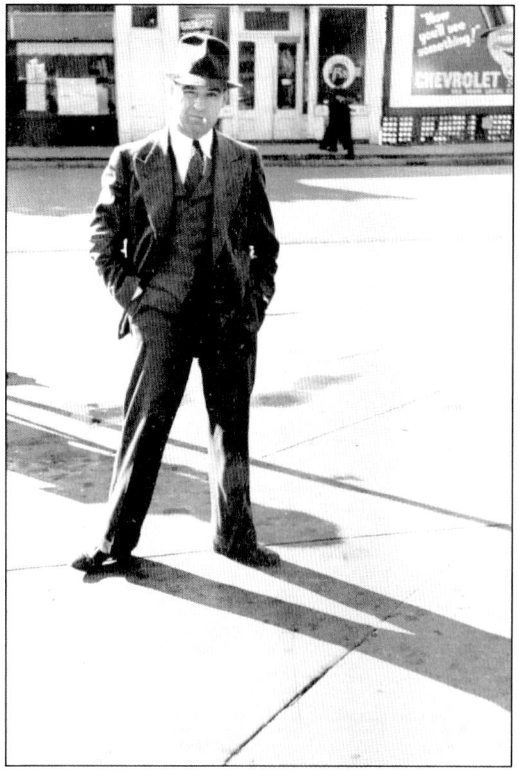

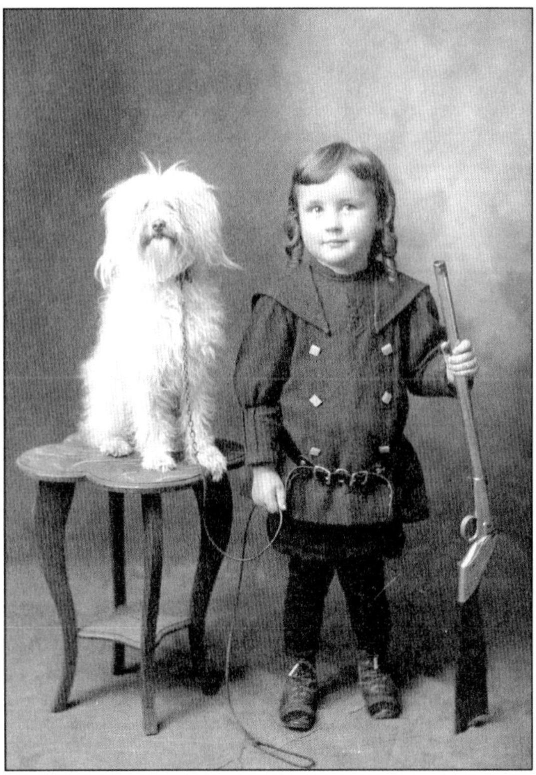

Most likely when this delightful photograph of Howard "Hod" Falk was taken, no one dreamed he would grow up to be Allegan's chief of police. The former co-owner of the City Bakery served as police chief from 1947 to 1970. It is safe to say that his shaggy companion did not grow up to be a police dog.

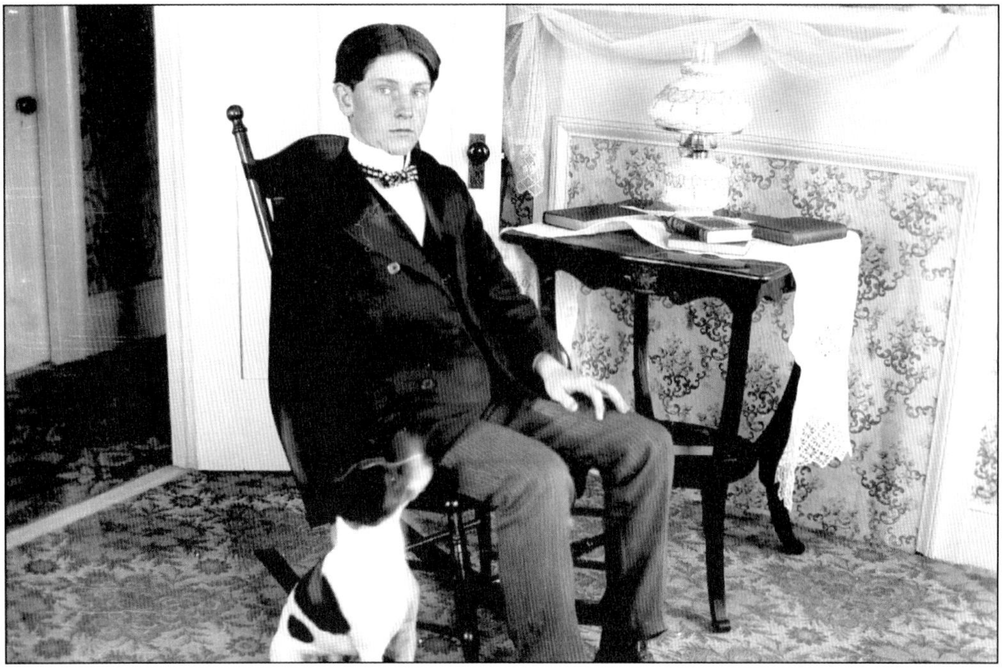

Frank Peck poses at his home on the corner of Cutler and Cedar Streets with the family dog Razzle. Later in life, as a graduate engineer, he would be involved in the design of Allegan's new Carnegie library. His marriage to Louise DeLano brought him into her family business as vice president of Allegan State Savings Bank.

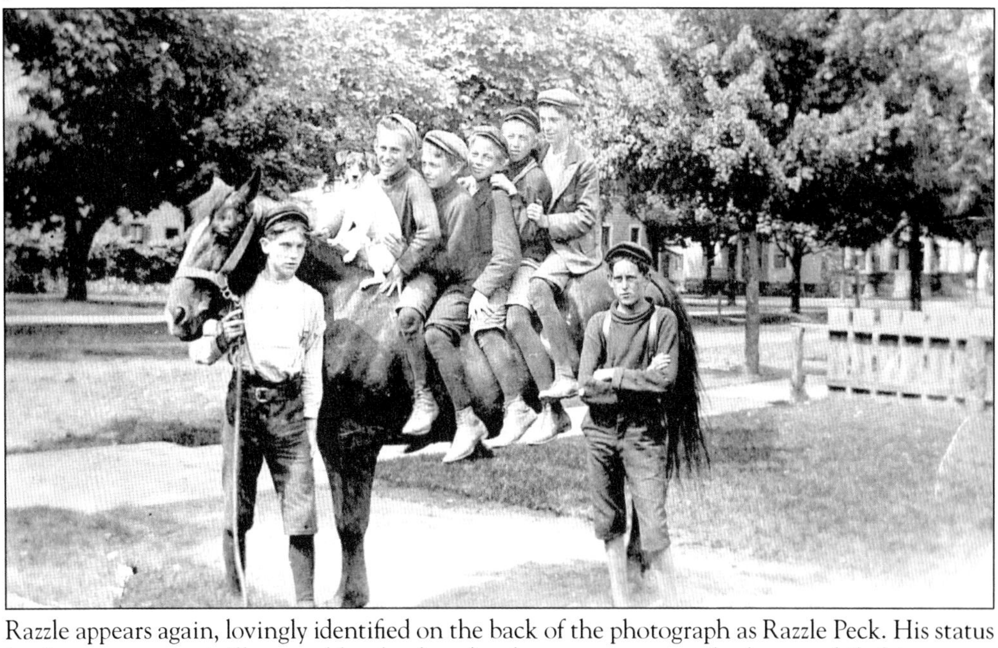

Razzle appears again, lovingly identified on the back of the photograph as Razzle Peck. His status in the community is illustrated by the fact that he rates space on the horse, while his master, Frank Peck (left), and Dennis McGinn (right) must stand. Seated with Razzle on Queenie's back are, from left to right, Eddie Horan, Cecil Hollinger, Grover Tripp, Arthur Perry, and Earl Delano.

Upon graduating from Allegan High School in 1888, Elizabeth Wetmore desired nothing more than to become a teacher. After receiving her degree in Ypsilanti, she eventually returned to Allegan. This daughter of pioneers grew up in Monterey Township, near the lake named for her ancestors. Many of her gifts grace the museum. She died in 1963 at the age of 91, remembered by many as a much-loved former teacher.

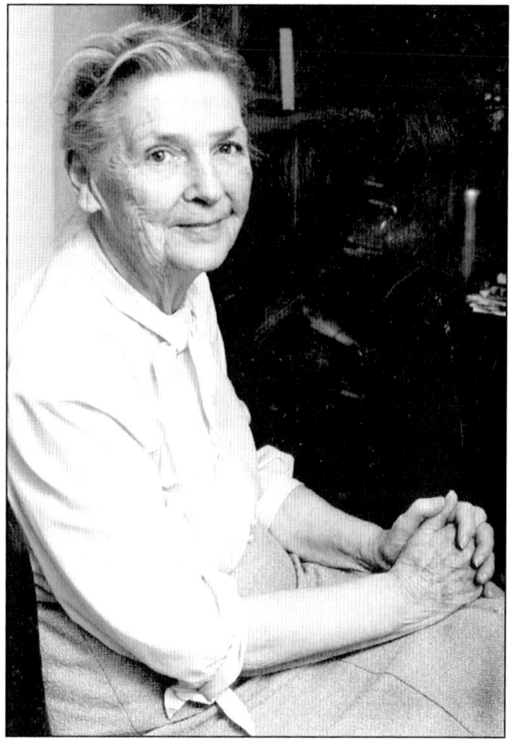

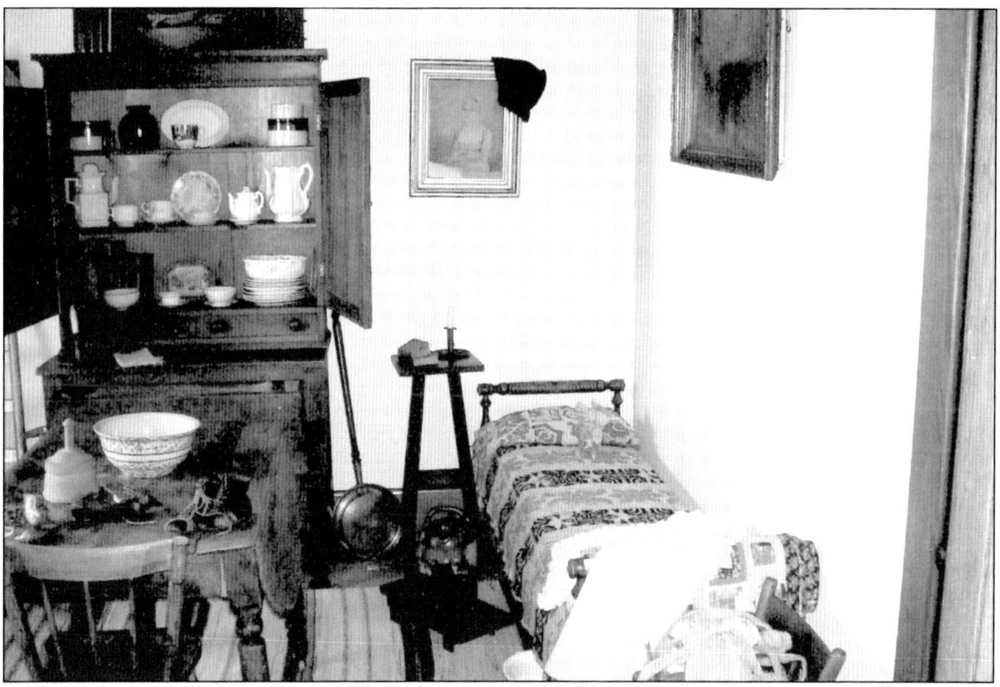

This photograph shows the pioneer room in the Old Jail Museum. This room is dedicated to Elizabeth Wetmore, who supplied many of the items that are showcased in the display. Elizabeth's family was one of the first pioneer families in Allegan County. Chester Wetmore, her grandfather, was the first settler outside the village of Allegan in Allegan Township.

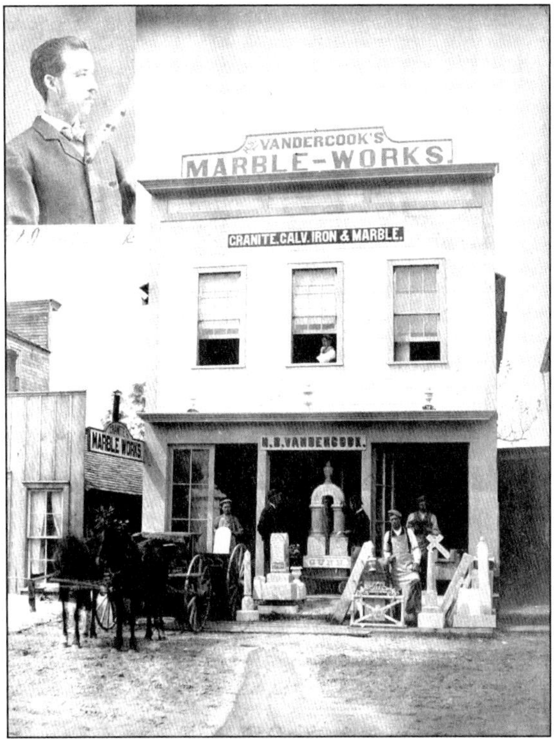

Shown here in this 1882 photograph is the Vandercook monument works. Inset on the left side is the photograph of the owner, H. B. Vandercook. These marble works were located on South Main Street in Allegan. The large monument in the middle of the picture was for the Gunn family, and it is in Allegan's Oakwood Cemetery today.

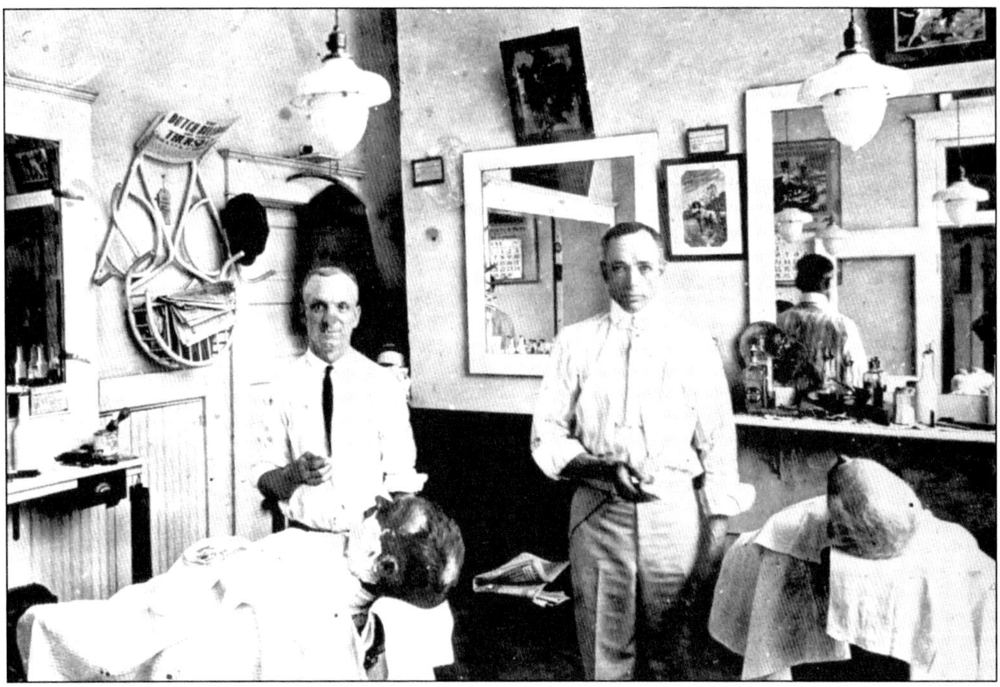

The photograph above is of a c. 1900 barbershop, which was located in the Sherman Hotel. Standing to the left is Kenny Gates, and to the right is Mack Ginzell. The two customers are unidentified. The Old Jail Museum has set up an early-1900 barbershop display in one of the cells with some of the items from the Sherman Hotel barbershop.

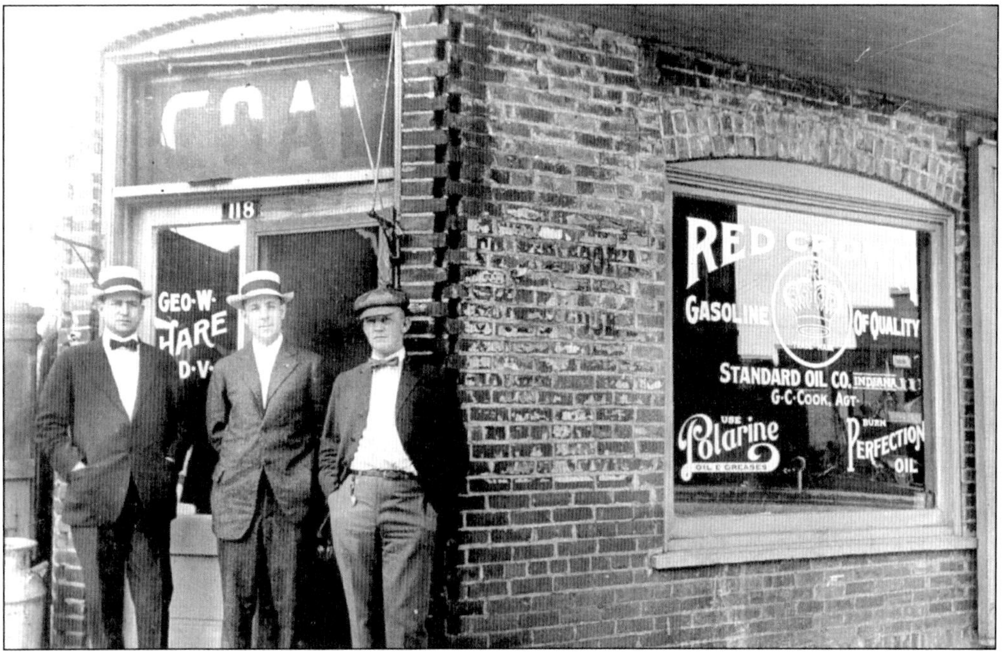

The gentlemen in the 1915 photograph shown here are, from left to right, Rene S. Walker, Dr. Harry A. Sprague, and Grover C. Cook. They are standing in front of Cook's gasoline station, which earlier had been a Schuler Coal Company building. The gasoline station later moved to the corner lot next door.

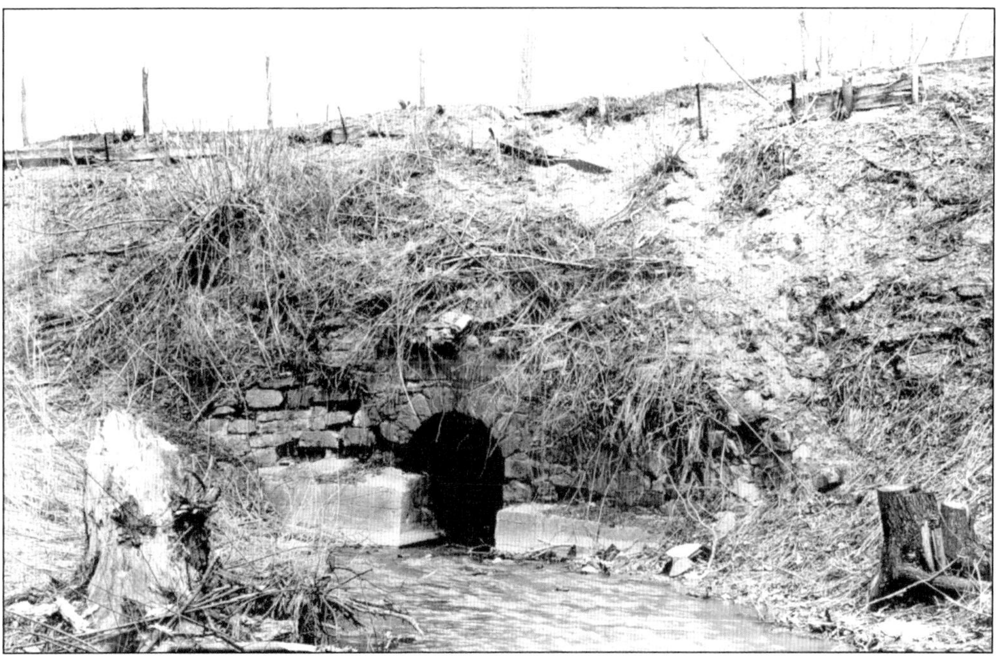

There is no date on this photograph of Tannery Creek, which flows under M40. A long ravine stretches on both sides of this highway overpass. Allegan has many other creeks and ravines located over much of the town. For the children of Allegan, they represented a wonderful place for summer fun, adventure, and exploration.

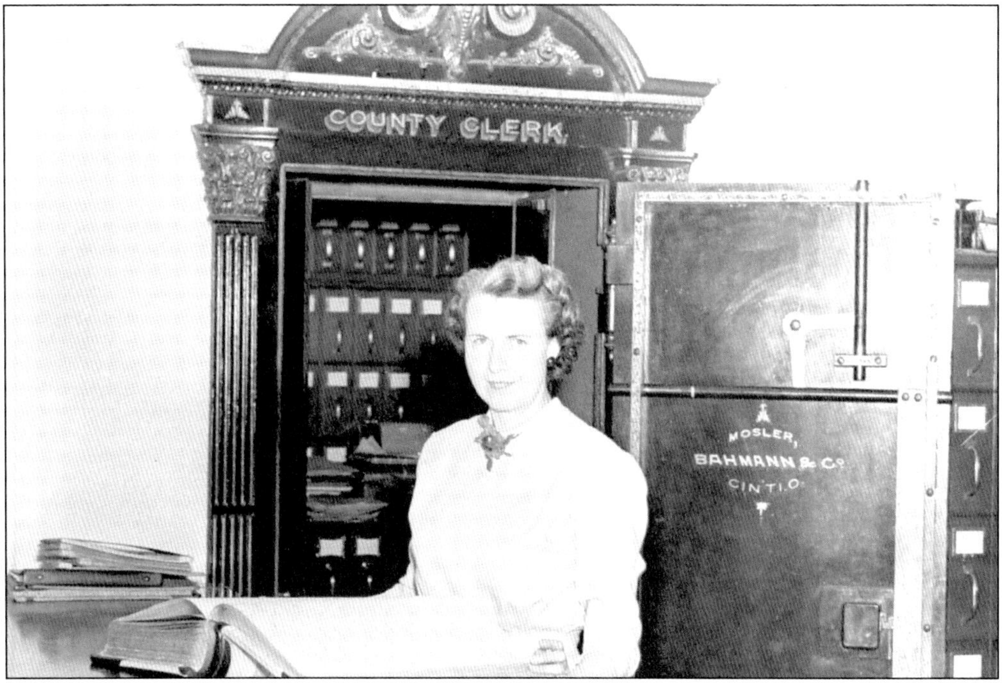

This undated photograph is of Esther Warner Hettinger, the Allegan County clerk for many years. She is standing in front of the safe where important county documents were stored. Warner began working for the county as deputy county clerk, later becoming county clerk. Warner served the county for 32 years, retiring in 1972.

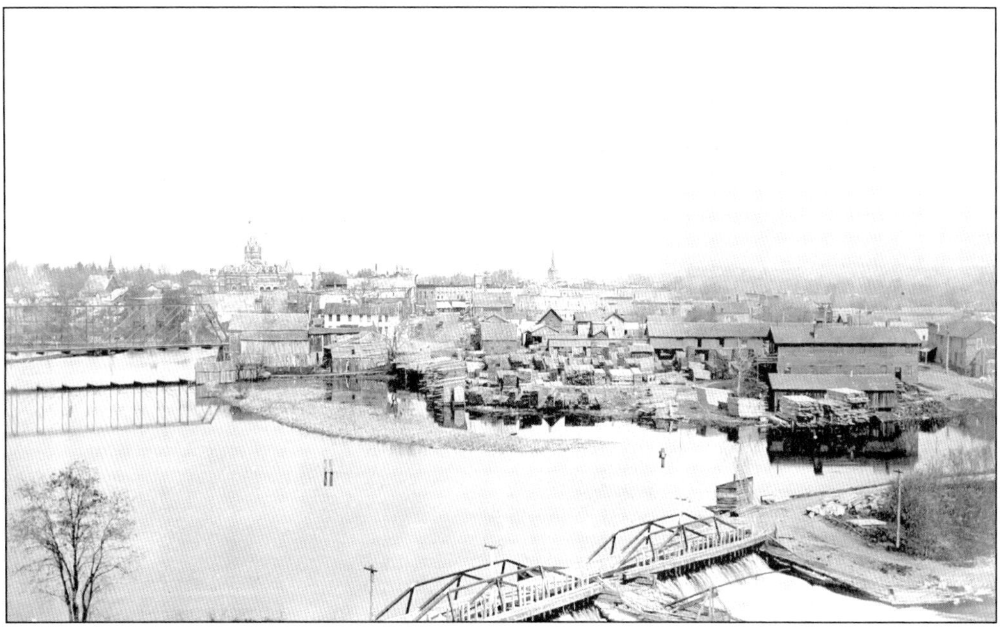

This c. 1900 photograph shows the dam that is located next to the mill district. This is where it all began for the town of Allegan. When the earliest developers arrived here in 1835, they sited the town in this location because the drop in the river was perfect for a dam to produce the power needed for the early sawmills. By 1837, the dam was built and working.

Two

FROM THE ASHES

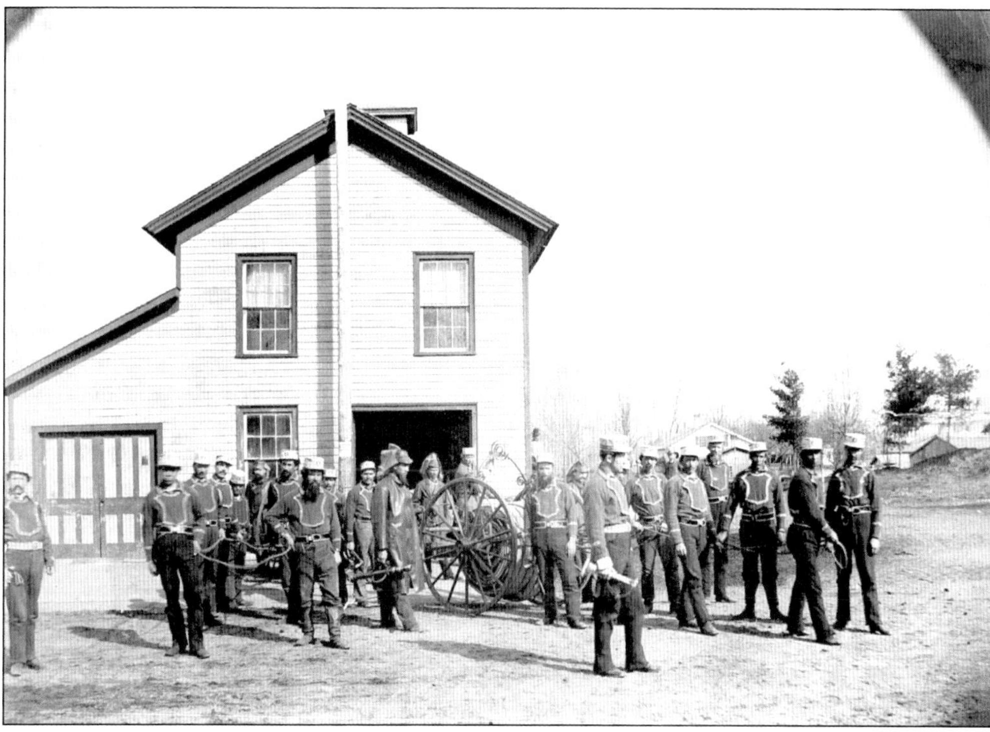

Pictured in 1880 in front of the old firehouse are fire marshal L. Y. Cady, nozzle and leather hose in hand, and fellow volunteers. In four years this group will face the challenge of their lives as Allegan's "great fire" will spread rapidly through the downtown. Even later, Cady, injured falling under a hose cart, was deemed dying. Although he read his newspaper obituary the next day, he lived another 50 years.

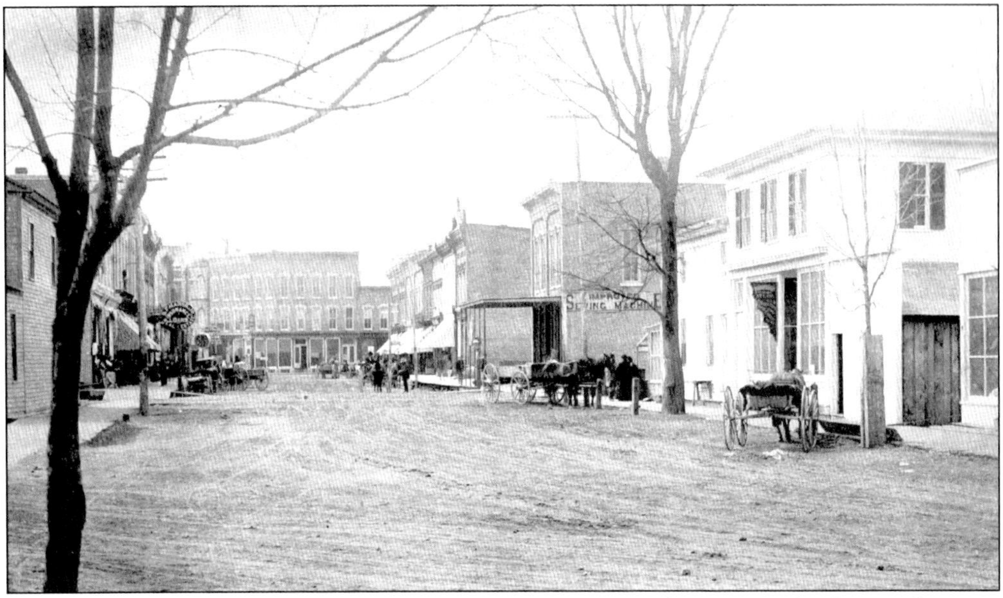

This photograph shows the beginnings of Locust Street as the center of Allegan's business district. The three-story buildings of Brady Street are in the background. Fortunately the mill district, with its diverse factories and mills, was untouched by the 1884 fire. This allowed for a certain level of commerce to continue in the devastated town.

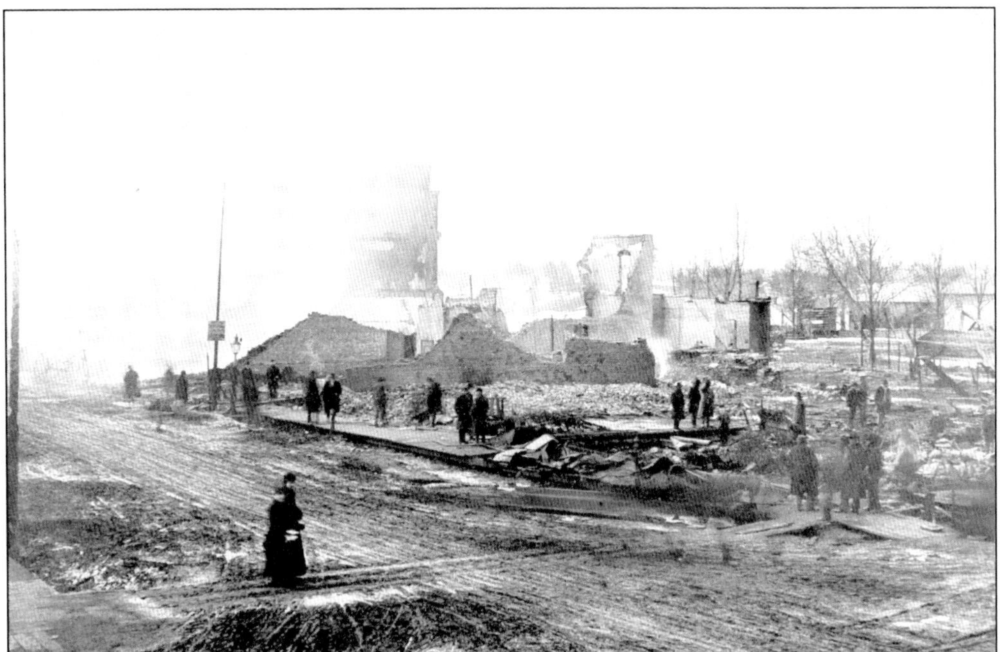

People stand in stunned silence the morning after the fire, surveying the destruction of March 12, 1884. When the fire began, store merchandise and personal belongings were moved to the sidewalks and alley surrounding Locust Street, supposedly out of harm's way. To everyone's horror, the fire changed course and Locust Street was also reduced to rubble.

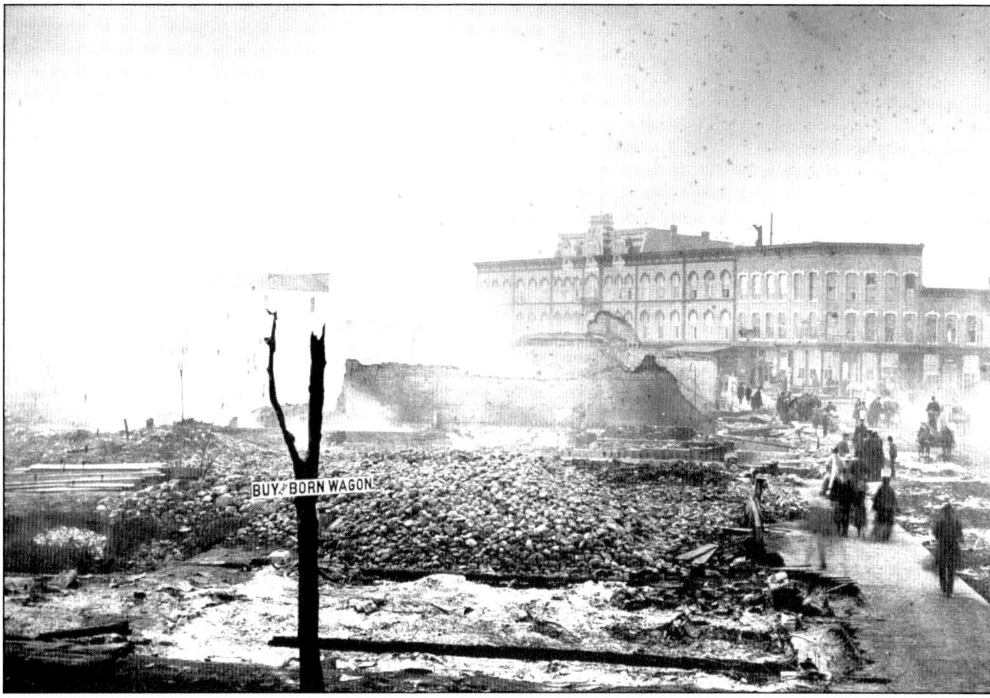

In the ruins of Locust Street all that remains is a small sign on a scorched tree advertising Born Wagon Works. The fire began on Hubbard Street, and upon approaching the intersection at Brady Street, turned left onto Locust Street. It continued all the way down Locust to Water Street and did not stop until it reached the Kalamazoo River.

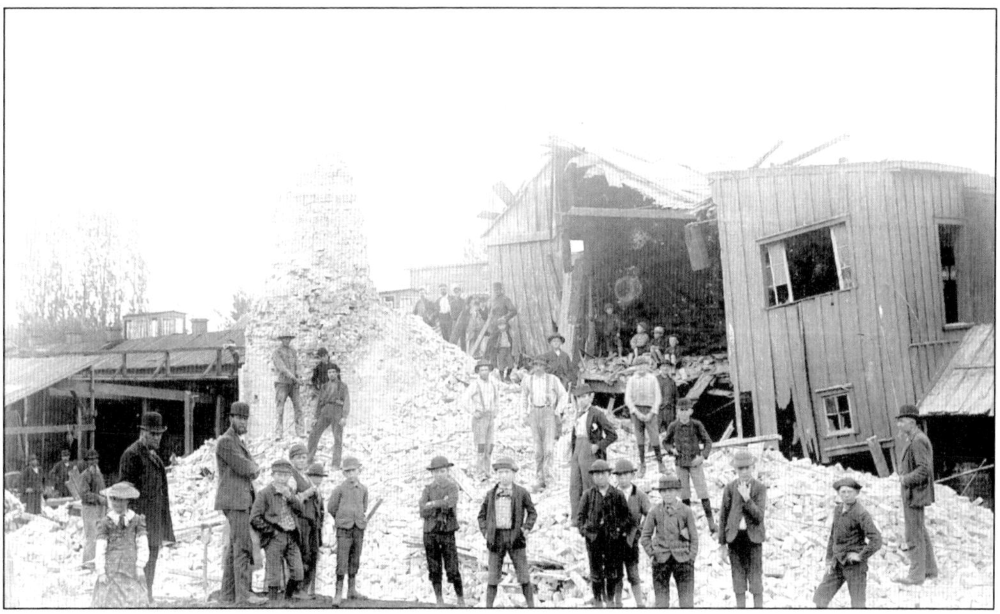

Born Wagon Works was the oldest manufacturer in Allegan. German immigrant Englebert Born first established his wagon and carriage factory in 1854. On three separate occasions, the last being in 1884, he paid out of pocket to have his factory rebuilt after being destroyed by fire. Born did not believe in insurance but was financially able to rebuild after each fire.

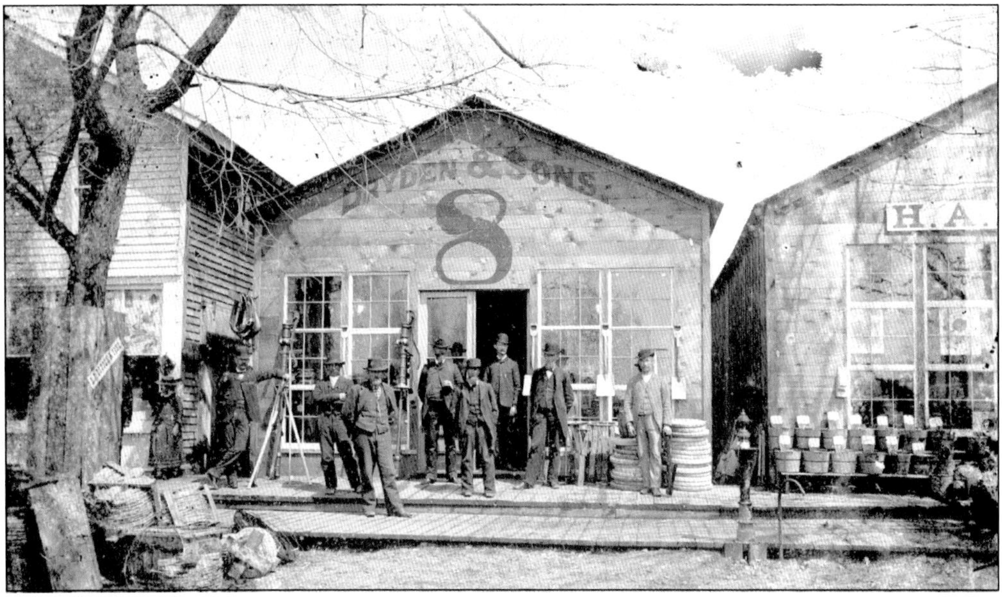

After the fire, Allegan merchants did not spend any time feeling sorry for themselves. They immediately began construction in the destroyed downtown area. Flimsy "slab" buildings were hastily erected to continue commerce while more permanent structures were built. Dryden and Sons, shown here, was open for business in a very short time.

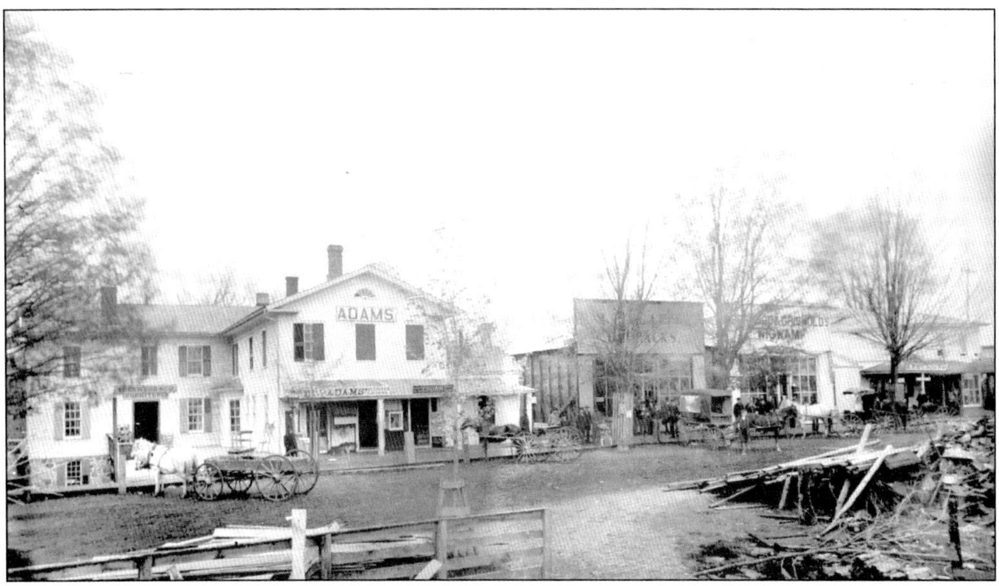

This view of Trowbridge Street in the late 1800s shows the area where the Grange Store was eventually located. The streets are dirt, and the sidewalks are wood. Through the tree branches (right) the sign on the white building proclaims it to be Sherwood and Griswold's Wigwam. This indicates, in the jargon of the day, that this was their temporary store.

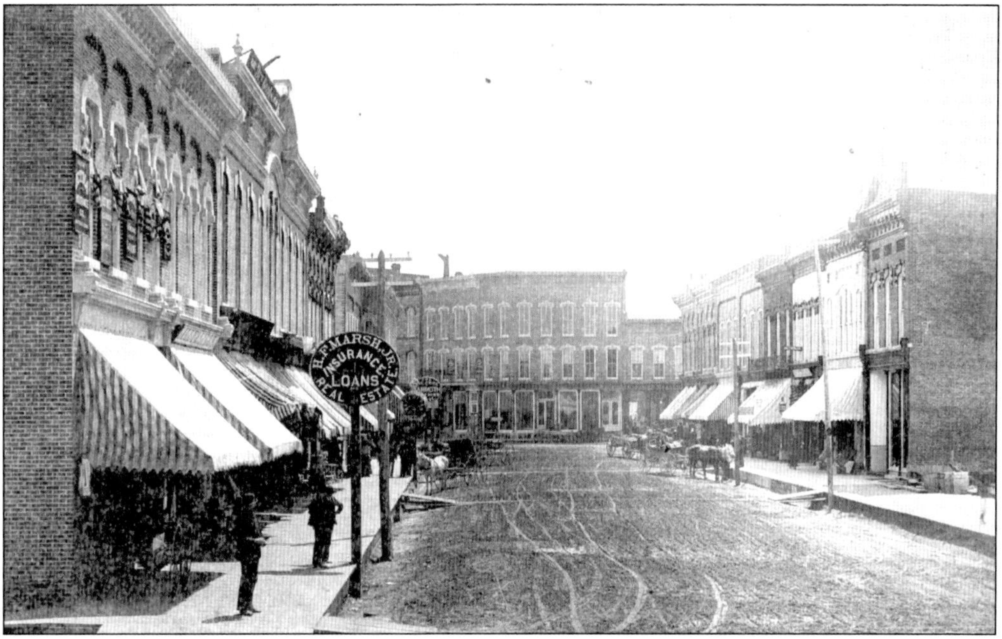

Two years after the fire of 1884, Allegan's business district was once again a bustling center of commerce. Pictured here is a view of Locust Street looking south from the intersection of Trowbridge and Locust Streets. The new brick edifices on both sides of the street were all rebuilt as two-story buildings, in contrast to the pre-fire three-story buildings on Brady Street.

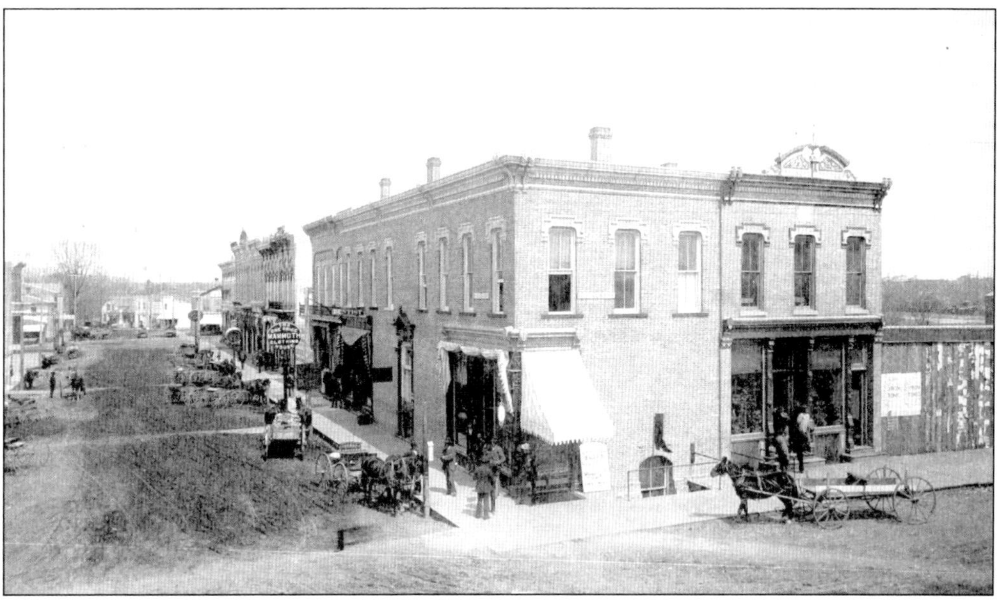

Following the fire, the rubble from the streets was graded in a manner that raised the level of the streets. Today many of the underground levels of Hubbard and Brady Street buildings are still accessible. Basement windows, built to add light, are still visible, although they are boarded and bricked.

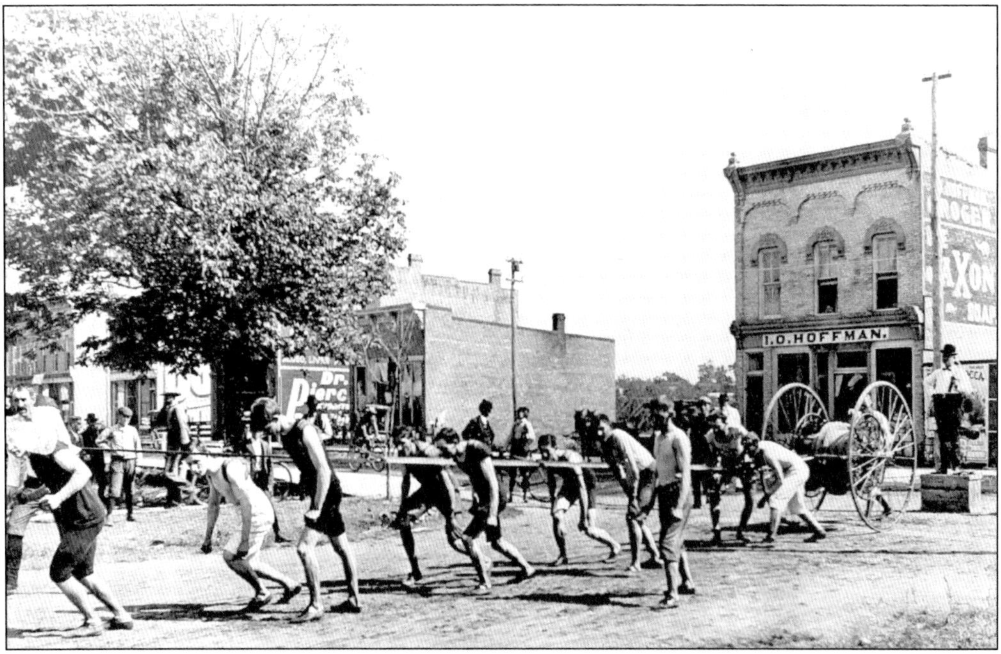

Allegan's fire hose running team is shown practicing for competition. Standing tall and slim, third from left, is Clare E. Hoffman. In future years, Hoffman would represent Allegan in the U.S. House of Representatives from 1935 to 1962. In the background is the I. O. Hoffman Building, where the fire of 1884 began its destructive path through downtown Allegan.

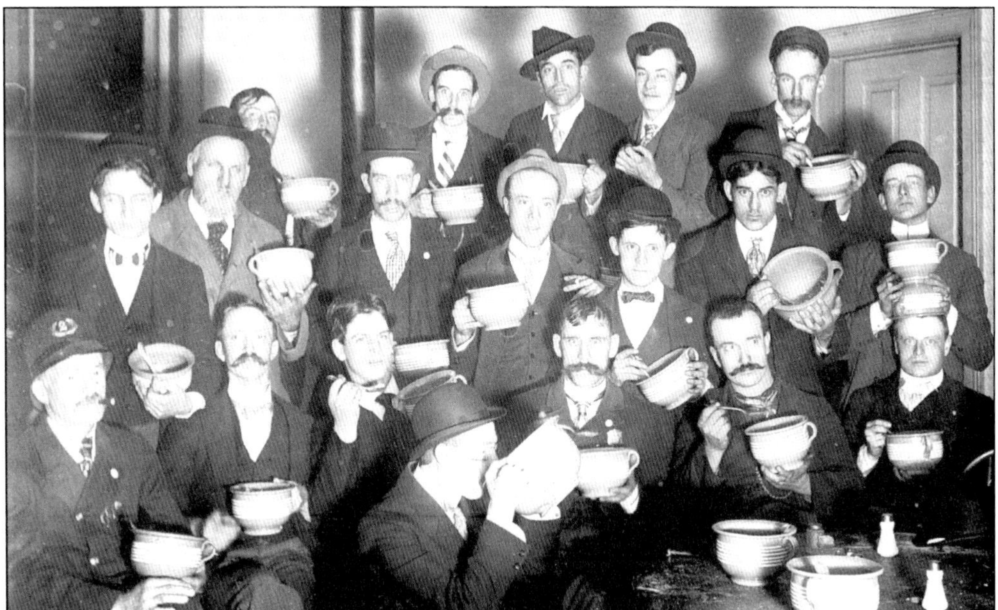

Early unidentified firemen enjoy an oyster soup dinner on the second floor of the fire hall. With pots borrowed from the hardware store, they clowned for the camera. Note the gentleman (first row, right) being crowned with two soup pots by his friend behind him. Information on the back of the photograph states that later the same evening the fire hall burned down, presumably through no fault of the firemen.

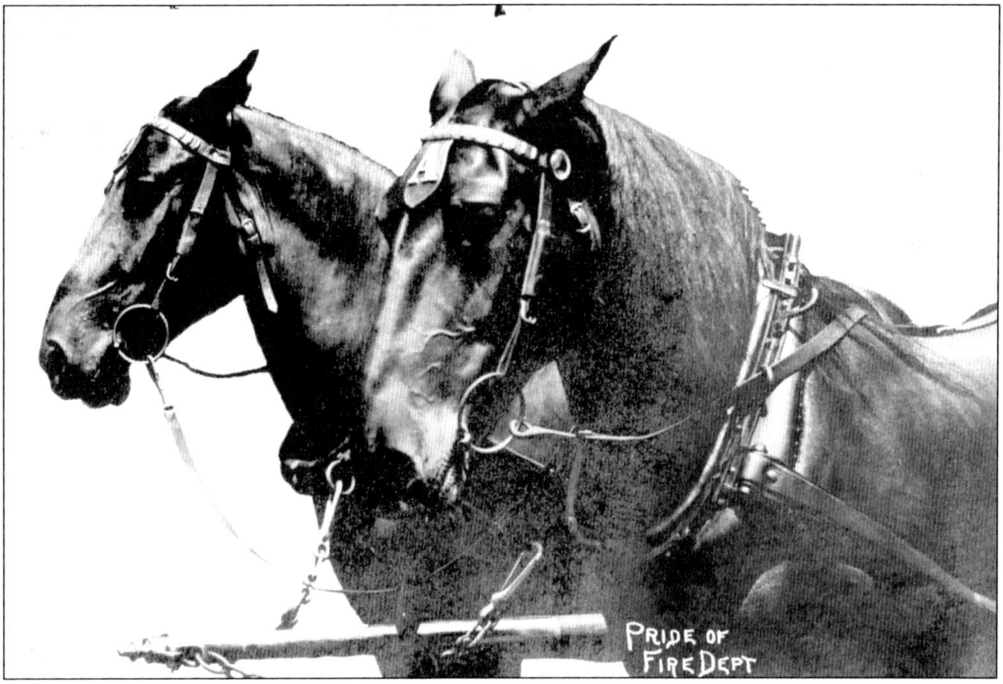

Fire wagon team Mick and Mack served the city for many years before their retirement in 1924. One of historian John Pahl's earliest memories is of being downtown with his father, hearing the fire bell peal, and seeing Mick and Mack galloping out of the firehouse with sparks flying as their hooves hit the street.

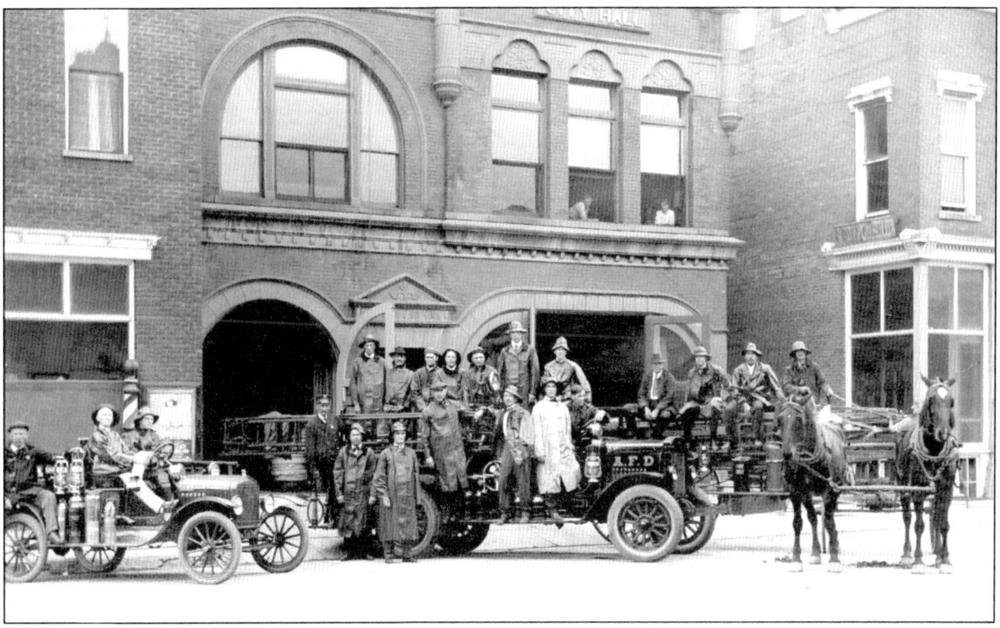

The outgoing Mick and Mack team, along with their driver William Barham at the reins, poses with replacement horseless vehicles and other unidentified men in 1924. They are posing on what may have been Mick and Mack's last day in service in front of the 1888 fire hall on Trowbridge Street.

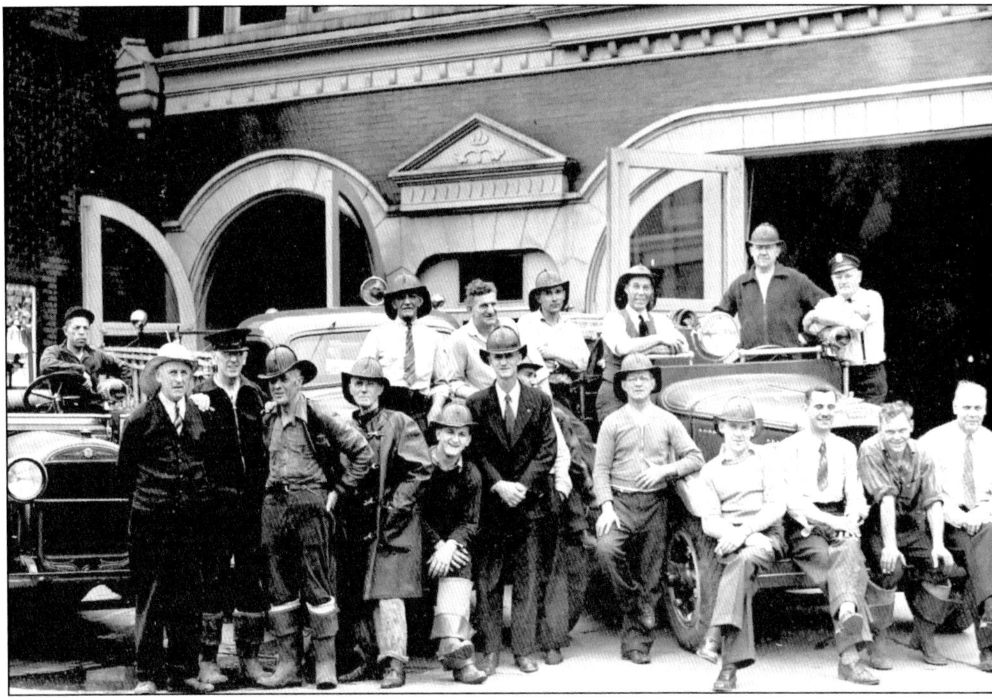

Posing in the 1930s in front of an assortment of fire department vehicles are, from left to right, (first row) Chief Henry Maentz, Floyd Harter, Glenn Knapp, Orson Coburn, Gilbert McKinnon, Oscar Lemon, Walt Hitchcock, Merle Hare, Harold Falk, Mel Truax, Sonny Hettinger, and Walter Ellinger; (second row) driver Bert Terry, John McKinnon, Loren Baker, unidentified, Alec Clark, Billy Falk, and Corlan Wood.

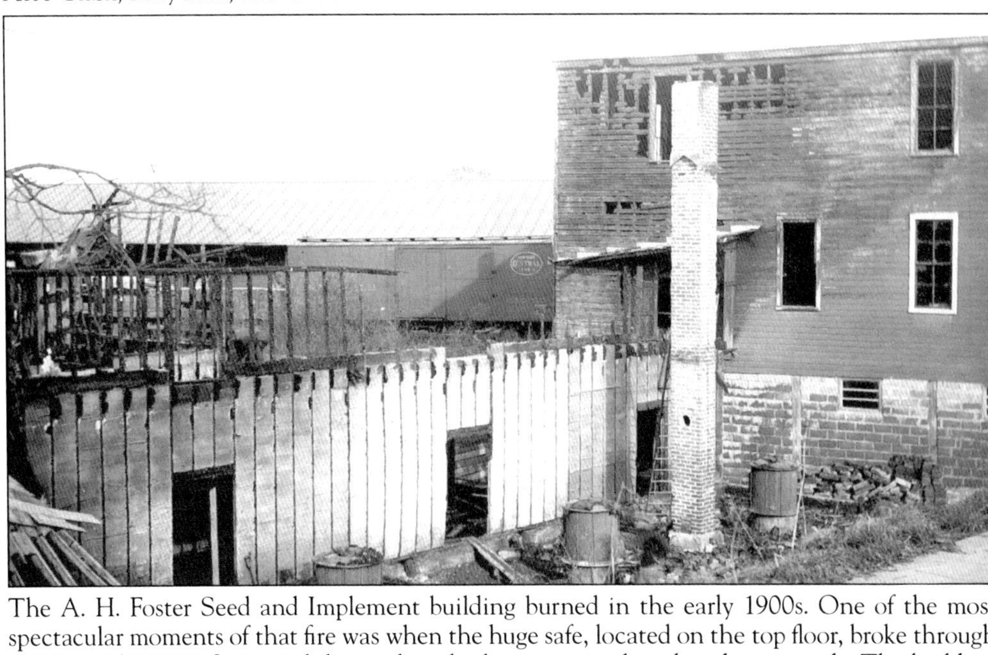

The A. H. Foster Seed and Implement building burned in the early 1900s. One of the most spectacular moments of that fire was when the huge safe, located on the top floor, broke through the lower, burning floors and dropped to the basement with a thundering crash. The building was never rebuilt, and Alton Foster returned to farming in the Monterey area.

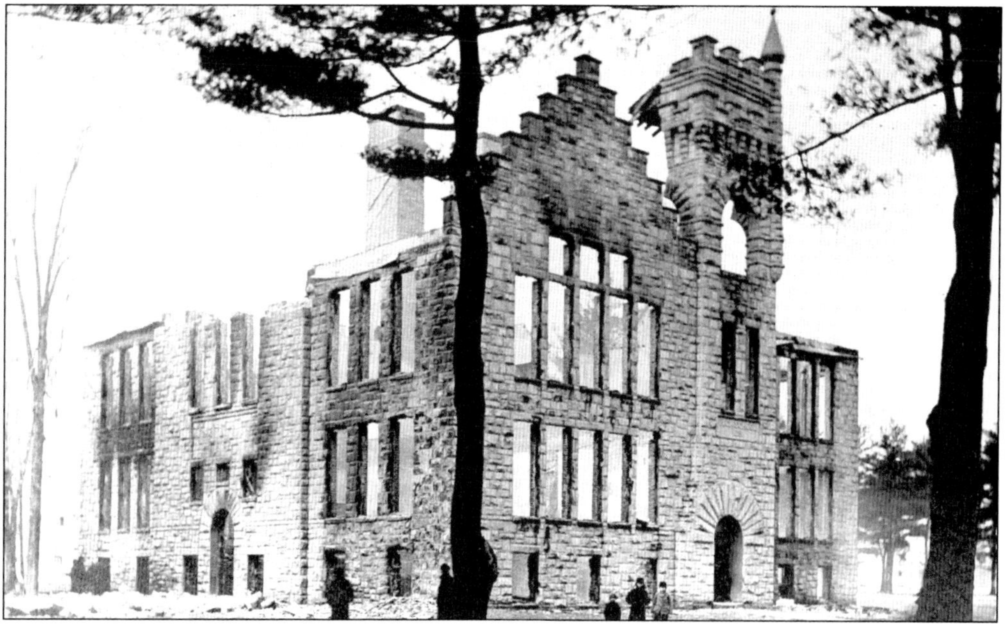

This c. 1899 photograph shows Allegan's first high school after it was destroyed by fire on March 19, 1899. Prior to its construction, Allegan residents attended Pine Grove Seminary. A private school, Pine Grove was purchased by the school board in 1857 and the building moved north of its then location. The new high school was built where Pine Grove had stood previously.

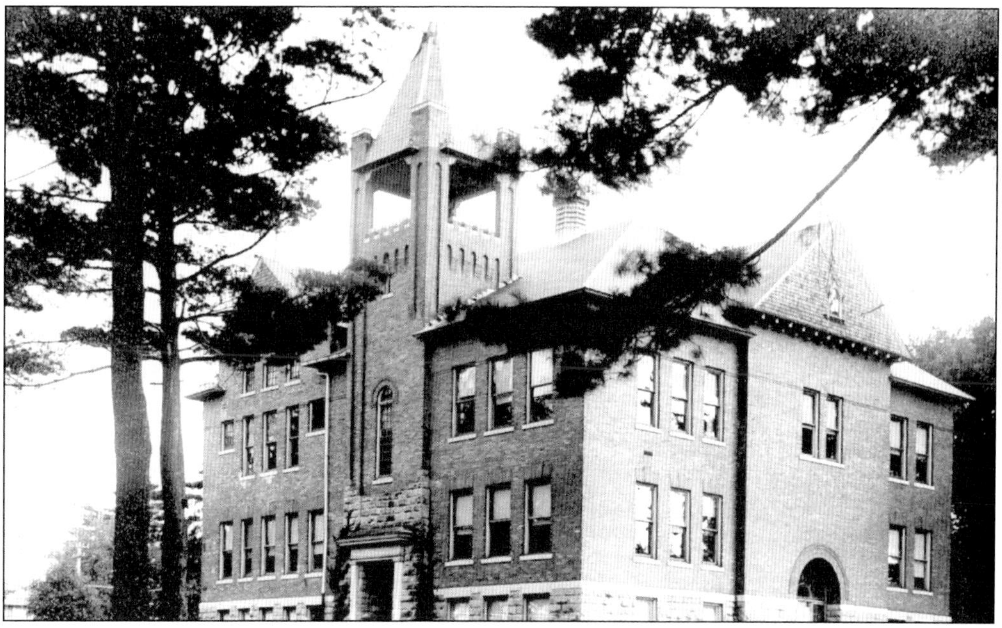

This c. 1900 photograph is the high school built in 1899, immediately after the previous building burned. It was built using the stone foundation of the 1890 building. In 1922, a new high school was again constructed, and the old high school then became the junior high school. The building was finally torn down in 1958 when the new junior high and high schools were built north of town.

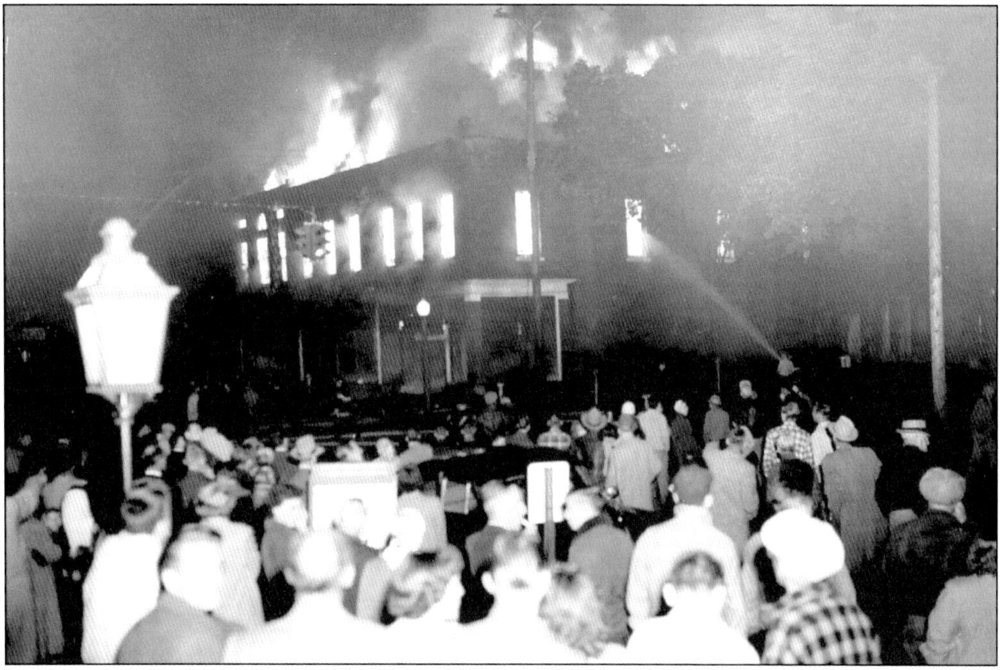

On the evening of September 23, 1952, people came from miles around to watch another spectacular fire. Despite the best efforts of Allegan firemen, and assistance from Otsego and Plainwell, the Burgess Furniture building was a total loss. Billed as "the largest furniture store in the world in any city less than 20,000," the store, with its 33,750 feet of floor space on Trowbridge Street, was never rebuilt.

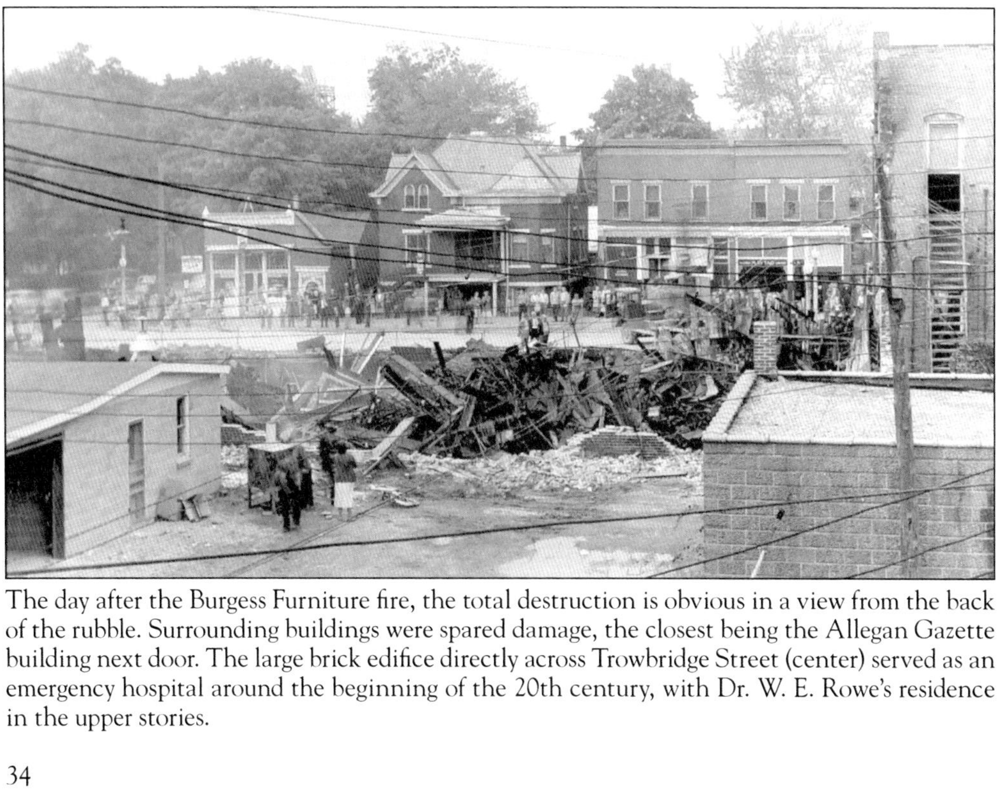

The day after the Burgess Furniture fire, the total destruction is obvious in a view from the back of the rubble. Surrounding buildings were spared damage, the closest being the Allegan Gazette building next door. The large brick edifice directly across Trowbridge Street (center) served as an emergency hospital around the beginning of the 20th century, with Dr. W. E. Rowe's residence in the upper stories.

This 1870 photograph shows the bank that Gen. Benjamin Pritchard started in 1870. It was located on Locust Street and burned down in the 1884 fire; however, it was rebuilt and remained in business until 1905. This was one of the first banks to install safety deposit boxes. The bank grew under Pritchard's direction to be a large and important financial institution.

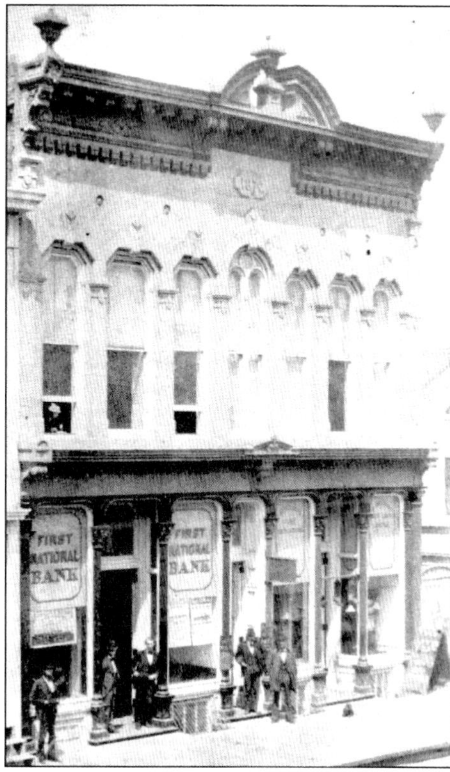

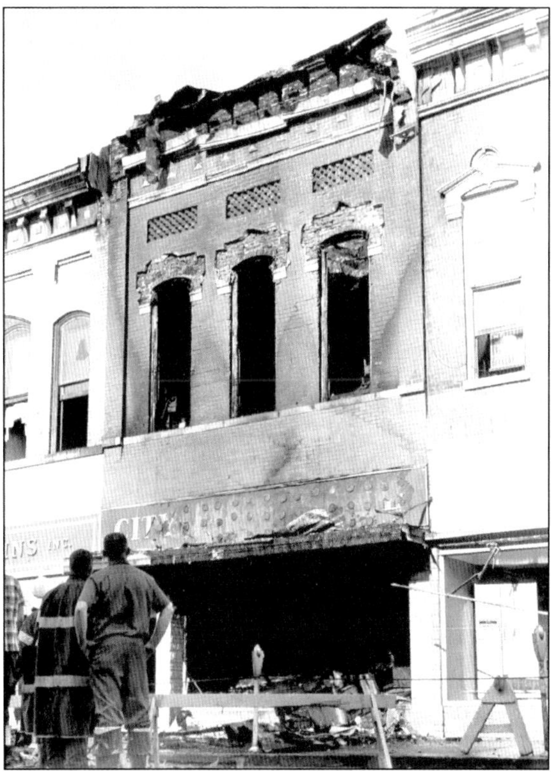

This August 12, 1969, photograph shows the morning after the City News Stand went up in flames. This is the building where Pritchard's First National Bank was located from 1870 to 1905. When Pritchard rebuilt the bank after the 1884 fire, he wanted to make it fireproof so he put up heavy fire walls and constructed it to be as fire safe as possible.

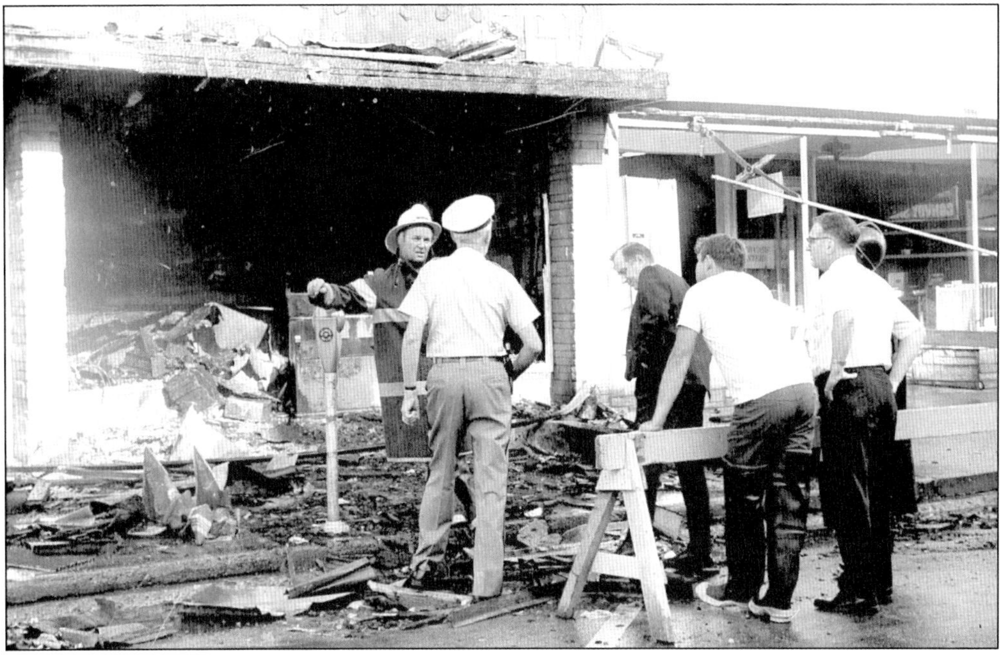

This photograph, also taken on August 12, 1969, shows unidentified firemen and townspeople standing in front of the City News Stand's burned building. Looking closely at the photograph it can be seen that the damage was confined to the interior of the building due to the construction methods that were used by Gen. Benjamin Pritchard in 1884.

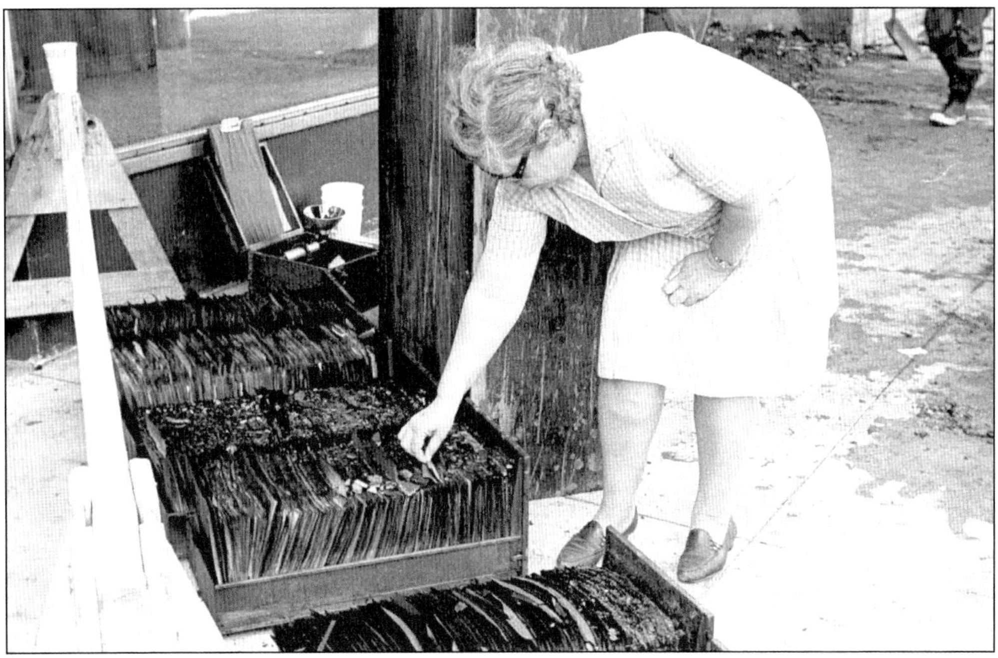

The City News was not the only operation that was affected in the August 12 fire. In this photograph, draft board secretary Mildred Bennett is looking at the fire damaged draft board files. In 1969, the selection service office was located at 119½ Locust Street on the second floor of the City News building.

Three

Churches and Schools

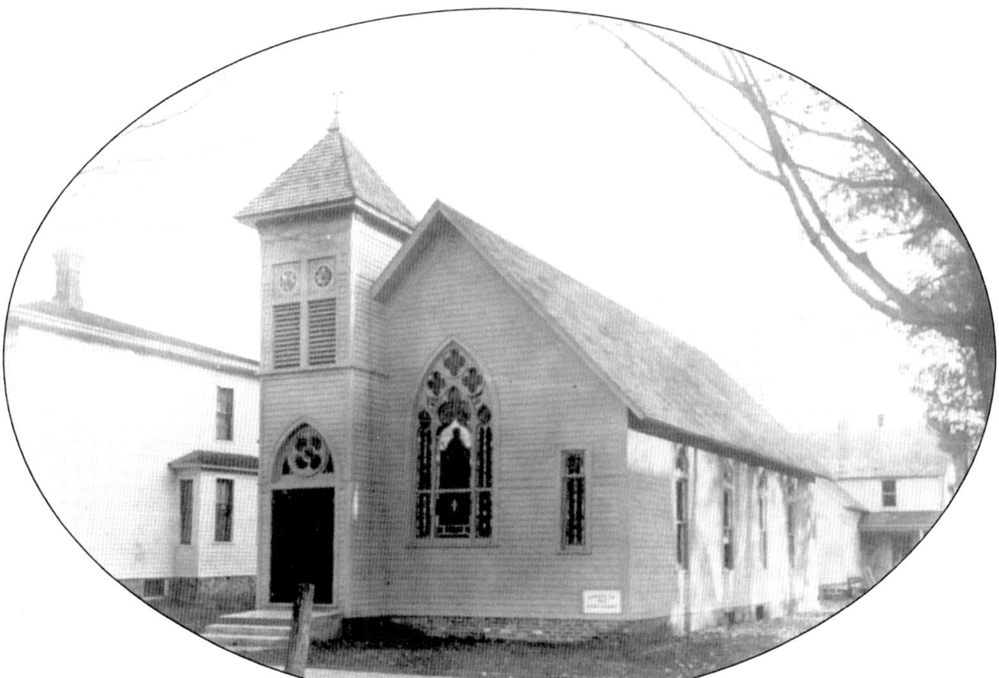

This 1926 photograph shows the original wooden church of the Catholic mission established in Allegan in 1907. Before this building was erected, the small congregation had been meeting in a home on the corner of Cedar and Trowbridge Streets. The first mass celebrated in the present brick-and-stone building of the Blessed Sacrament Church was in August 1935.

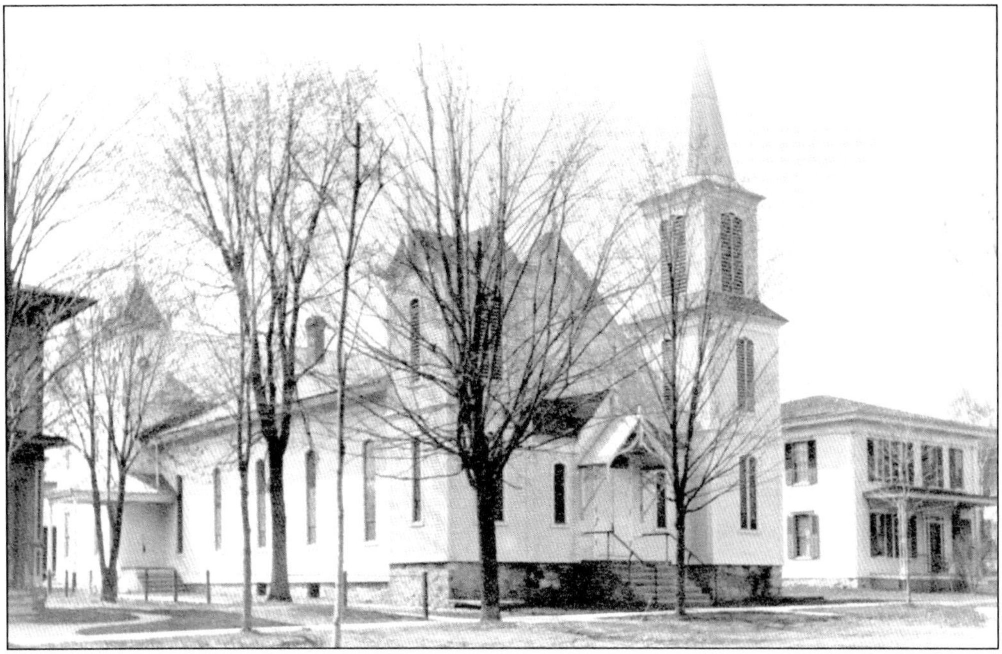

The First Congregational Church of Allegan was established in 1858. The present building on Cutler Street was dedicated in 1865 and has benefited from many construction projects over the years. Marilla Griswold was one of the first major benefactors with her gift of a large fellowship hall and kitchen.

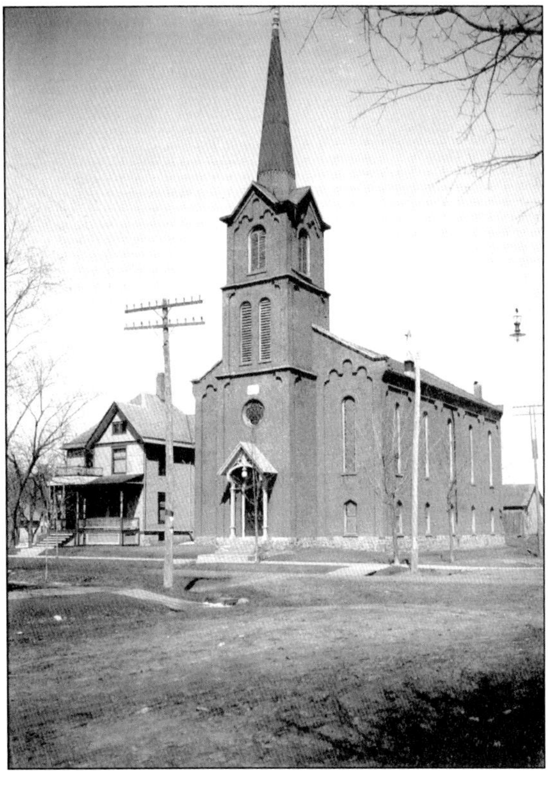

The First Presbyterian Church was established in 1838 on property deeded to the society by the Allegan Company. The new, small building burned in just a few weeks. In 1842, another church was built on the site and later was burned down by a pro-saloon group in protest to a temperance meeting held that evening. The present building was erected in 1875 with "donations" from apologetic saloon keepers.

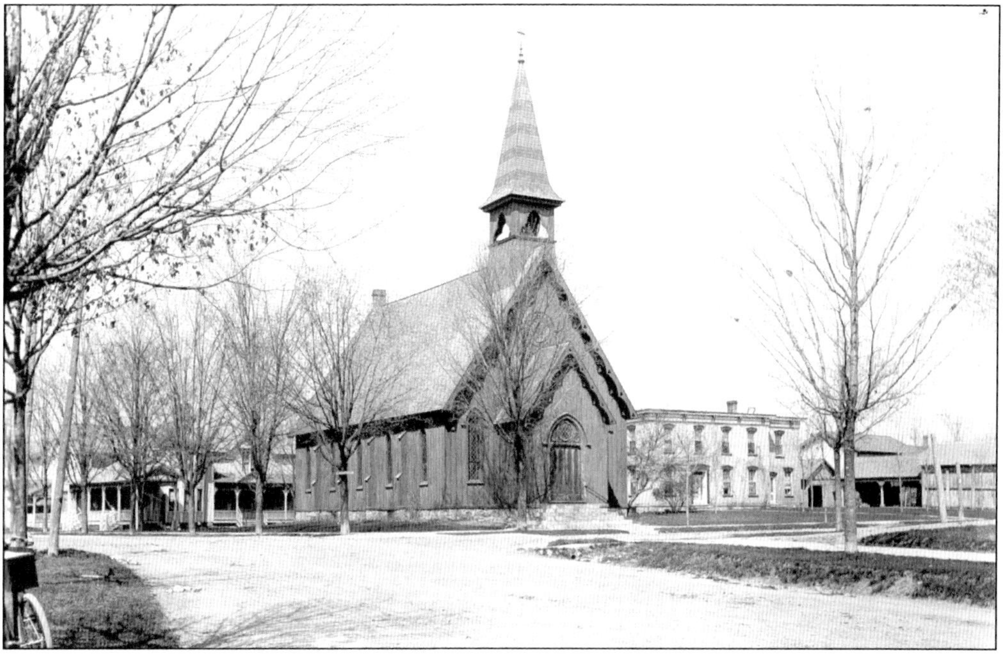

The Episcopal Church of the Good Shepherd was built in 1868 and is a fine example of Gothic Revival style. It was designed by Gordon W. Lloyd of Detroit, a noted architect of churches, who also designed the Episcopal church buildings in Holland and Saugatuck. In this *c.* 1890 photograph, the brick building to the right of the church is the old 1862 Allegan County jail.

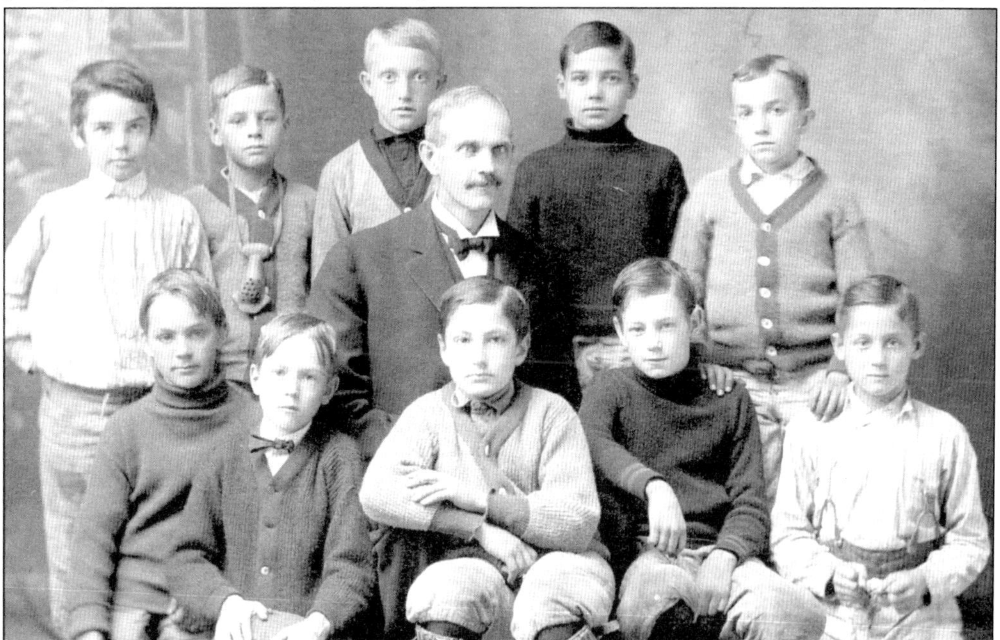

Pictured here is the Episcopal Church of the Good Shepherd Sunday school football team of 1906 with their coach C. R. Wilkes. Holding the ball (first row, second from left) is Dudley Pritchard. Others identified with only surnames are (first row) Vickers, Herman, and Green; (second row) Gulphin, Ferris, Blenn, and Hoisington.

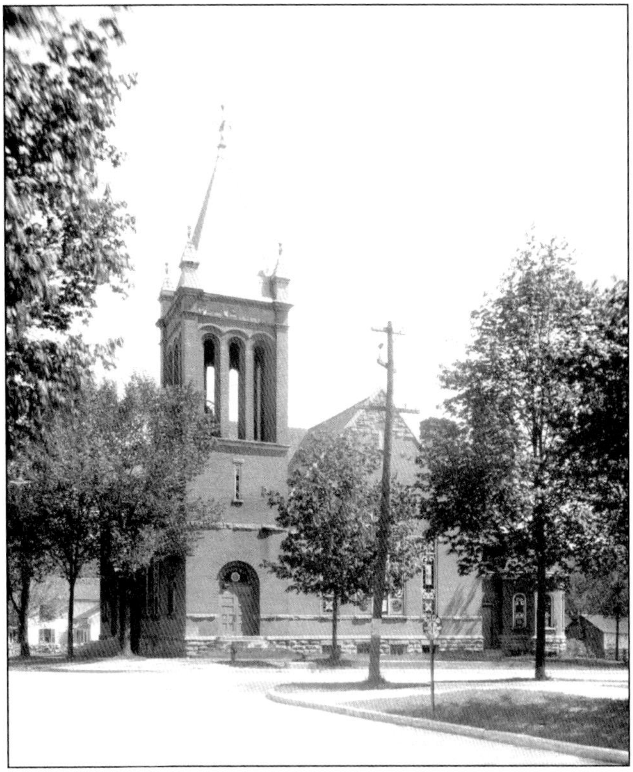

In January 1841, a branch of the Otsego Baptist Church was formed in Allegan. In 1877, Hannah Davis, widow of David Doane Davis, died and bequeathed her estate of $60,000 to the church. The present building on the corner of Walnut and Trowbridge Streets was vacated by the Baptists in 2001 when they moved to their new church on M40 South. The community center now occupies the building.

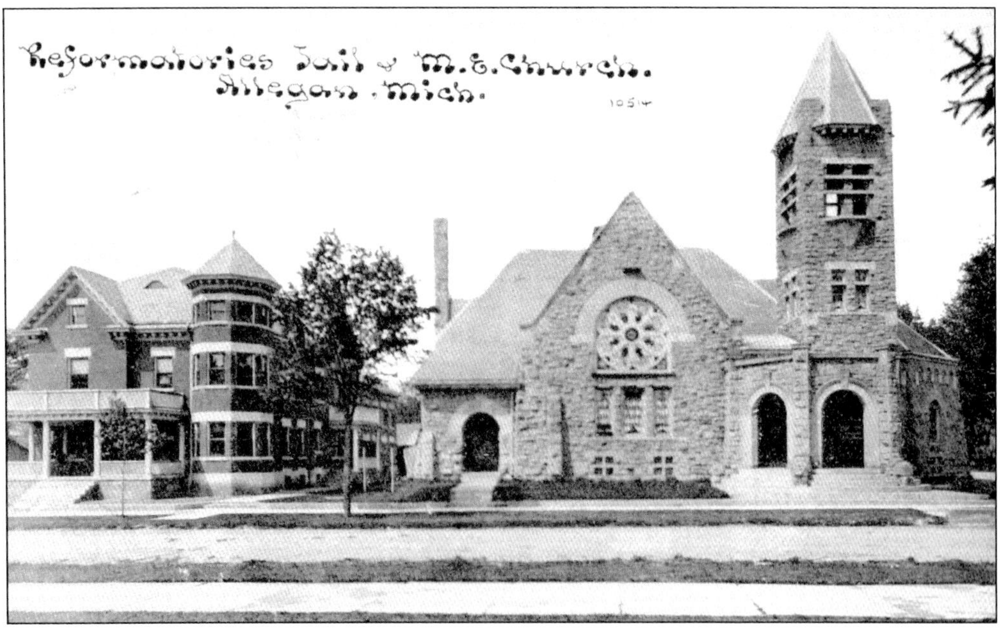

In 1836, the Methodist Society consisted of eight souls. By 1839, they built a church at the corner of Walnut and Trowbridge Streets, which was destroyed by fire 14 years later. They soon rebuilt, but by the dawn of the 20th century, the building was sold and moved. The present building was built and dedicated in 1905. The church still stands on the same property, adjacent to the Old Jail Museum.

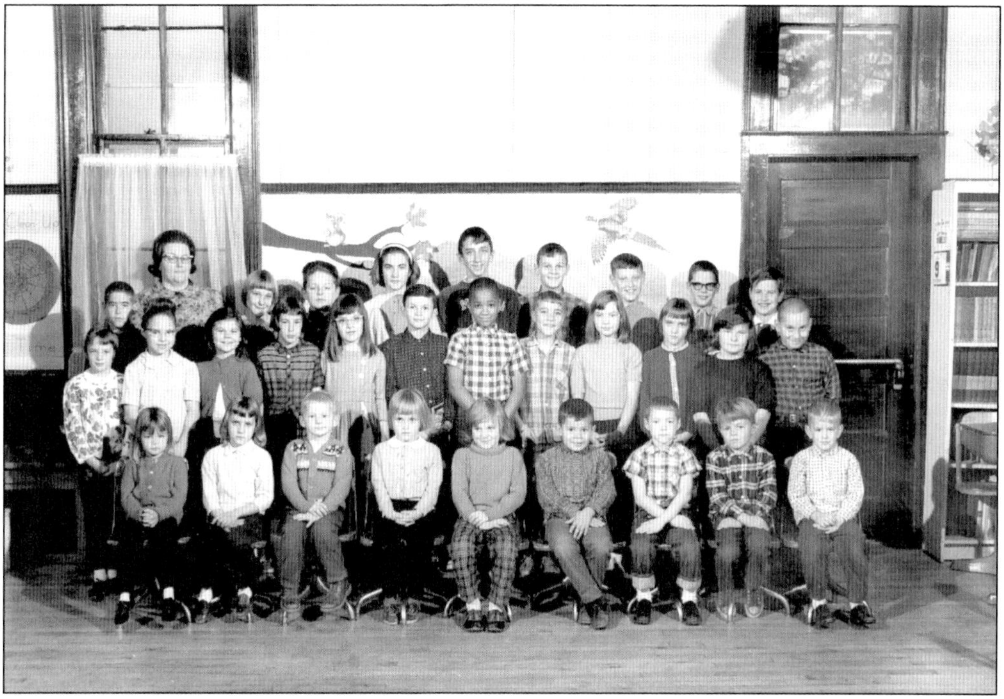

This photograph shows the last class of the Jewett School in 1965 with their teacher Marge Guptil. In its rebirth as a popular fixture at the county fair, the building once again resounds to the voices and laughter of children. Classes from all over Allegan County are invited to attend, and spelling bees are held, with prizes for the winning children.

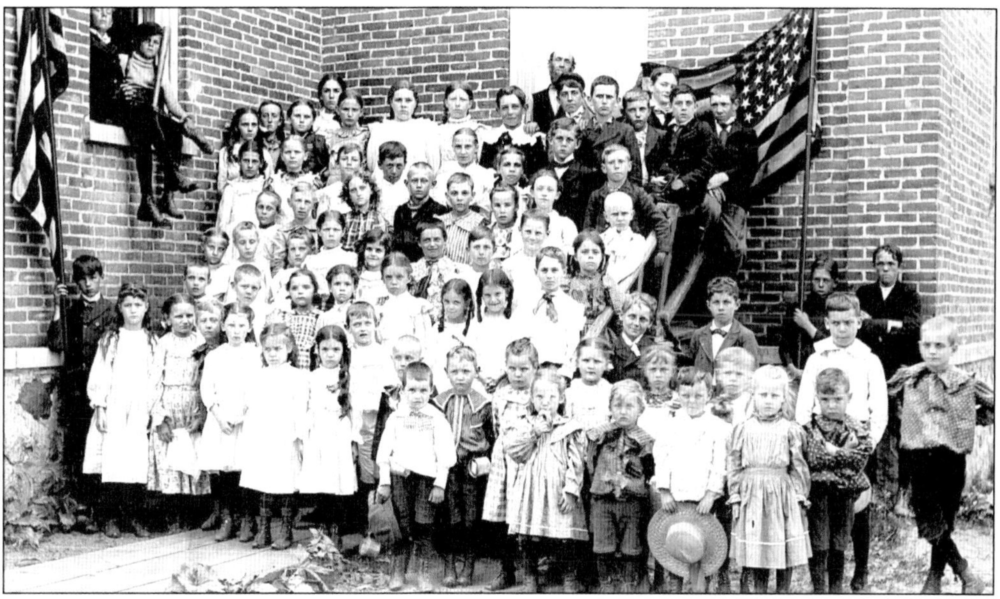

The above photograph, taken in 1899 at the old North Ward School, shows a more lax attitude toward school photographs than would be exhibited today. Most likely today no children would be allowed to sit precariously on the window sills of the school. The lovely old brick building stood on North Street.

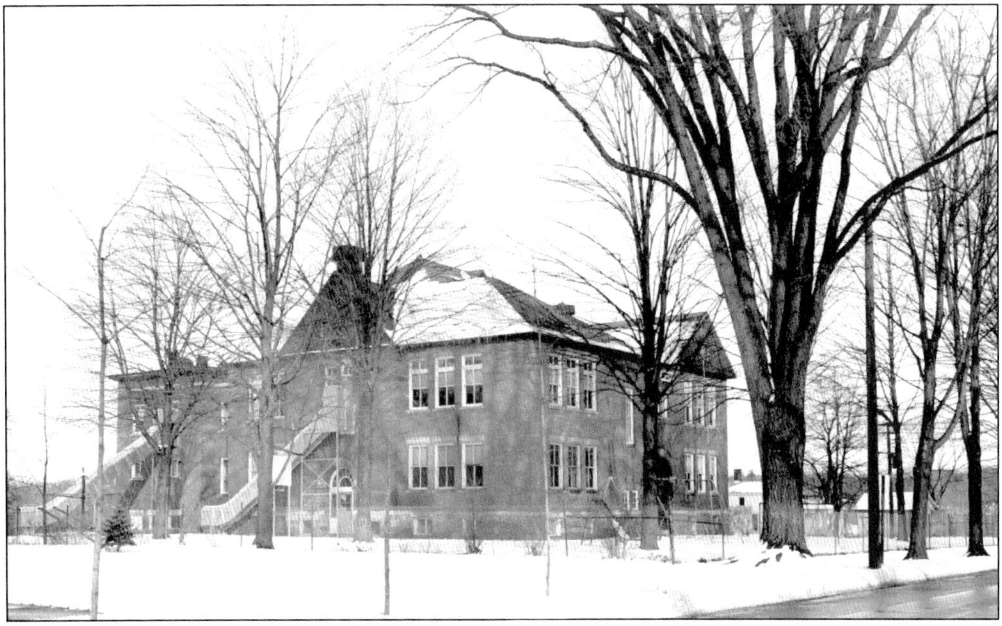

Pictured above is Dawson School on Monroe Street where the fire station stands today. Past students fondly remember flying down through the metal tube fire escape in weekly fire drills and exploring the forbidden river flats behind the school. Many returned on weekends to climb the fire escape from below for an exciting slide back down. Dawson was also the site of county normal teacher training and women's history class programs.

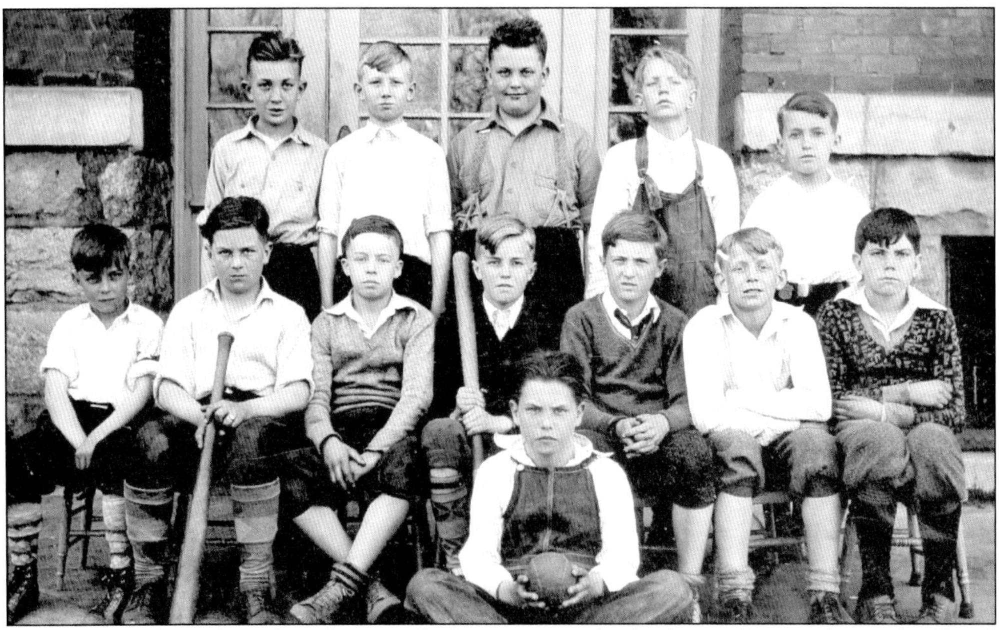

No date is indicated on this photograph, however, on the back it indicates this is the "best" Dawson baseball team. Identified here from left to right are (first row) Bill "Shine" Miller; (second row) Bud Tripp, Byard Baker, Milton Hunter, Norm Goodwin, Roy Nyberg, Harry Classon, and Don Watson; (third row) Don Wood, Jimmy White, Dale Johnson, Harold Hoagland, and Buster Stuck.

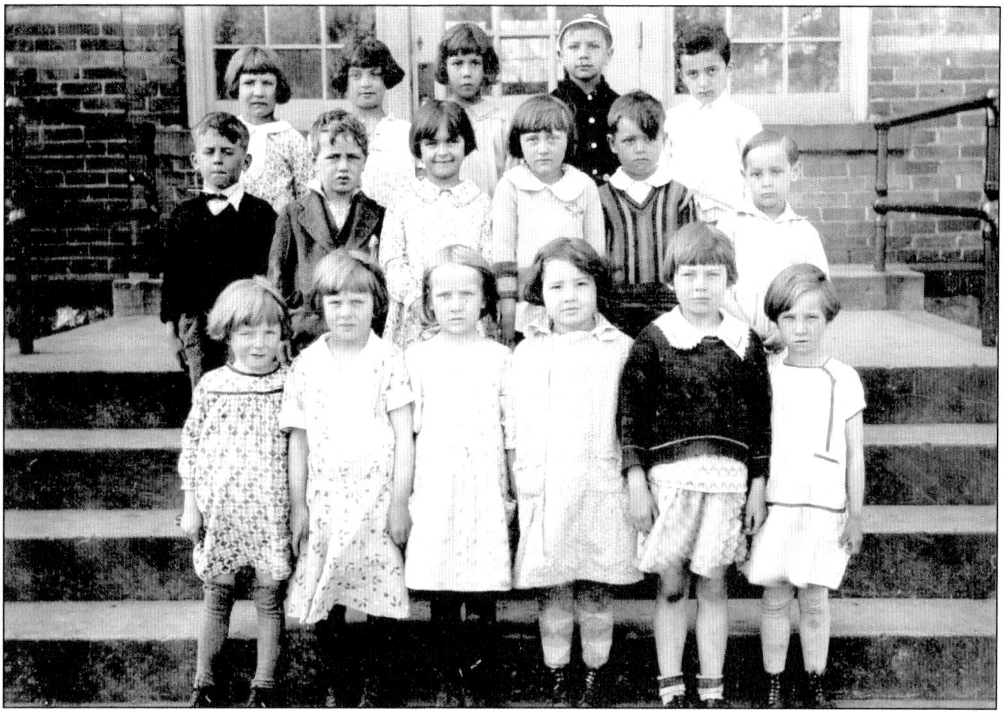

Pictured here is a 1930 class from North Ward School. From left to right are (first row) Lorna Cooley, Betty Foster, Dorothy Brinklow, Beatrice Stuck, Lois Wray, and Margaret Walter; (second row) Bobby Lenardson, unidentified, Betty ?, Jean Bazan, Carl Bills, and Frank Sturgis; (third row) Barbara Hare, unidentified, unidentified, Lawrence Brinnegar, and Bill Nahikian. Their teacher was Harriet Adams.

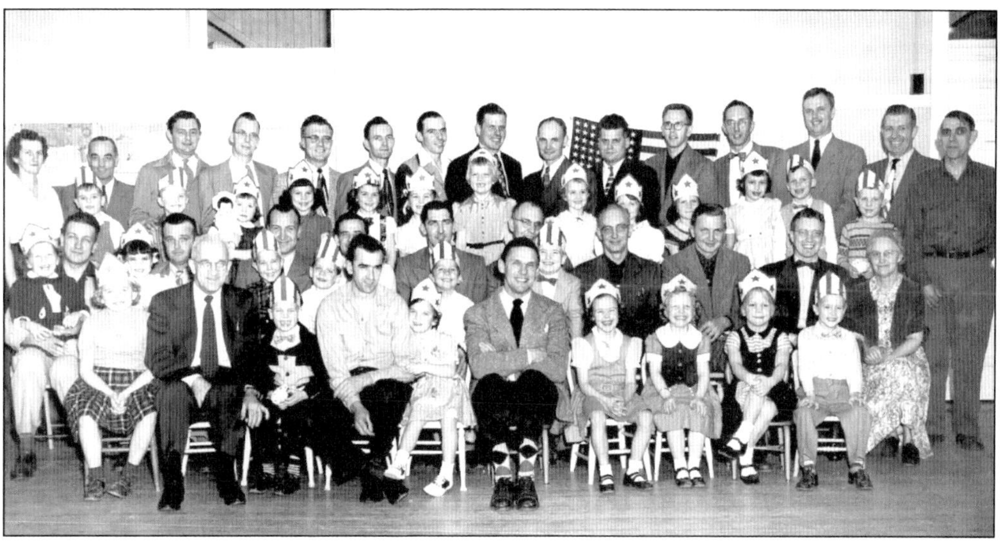

Dawson kindergarten fathers attend a luncheon with their children and teacher Harriet Adams in 1954. In the first row, with his classy argyle socks, is Ted Hunter, a much-loved figure in Allegan. Many children received their first bicycle from Hunter. When he recently passed away, the *Allegan County News* received letters from around the country relating wonderful memories of him. His son Tom now runs the same bike store.

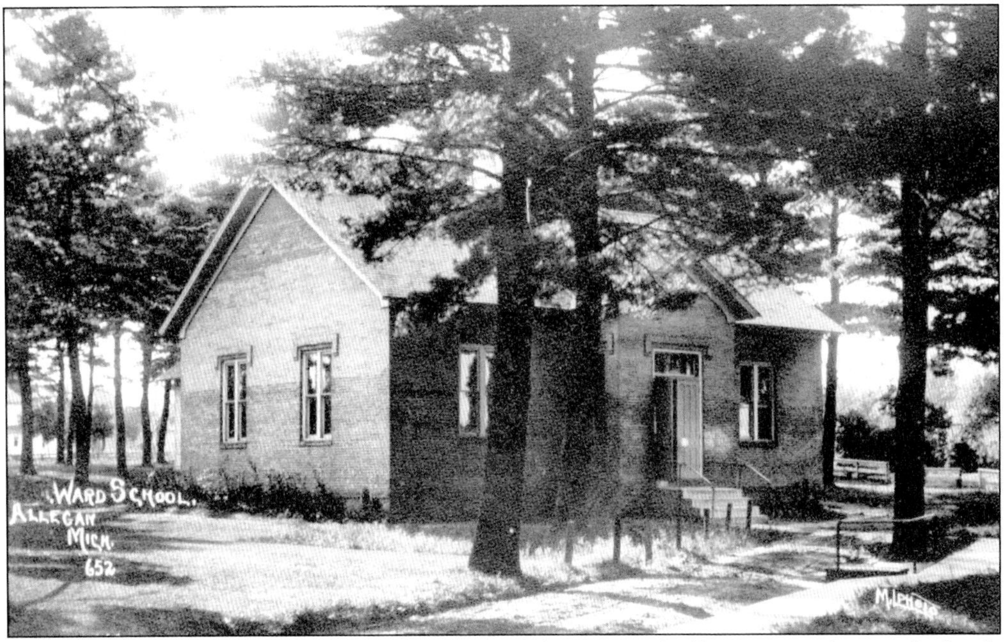

Named for an early teacher, Nina Carter, this school was one of Allegan's very first ward schools and housed first and second grades. It was created from an overflow from District No. 1, which was the West Ward. In the late 1800s, it stood on the hill where the development center now stands.

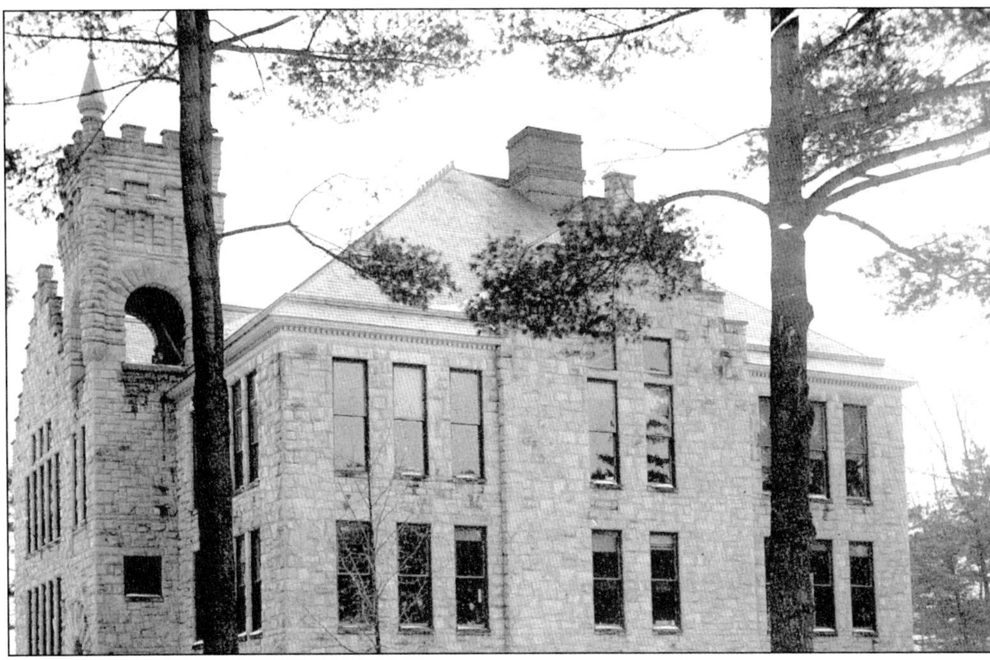

This is the original Allegan High School, built in the late 1890s and showing its bell tower. Each morning the janitor would pull the rope to ring the bell and announce the beginning of the school day. The school was also built on the hill where the development center stands. It burned down in 1899.

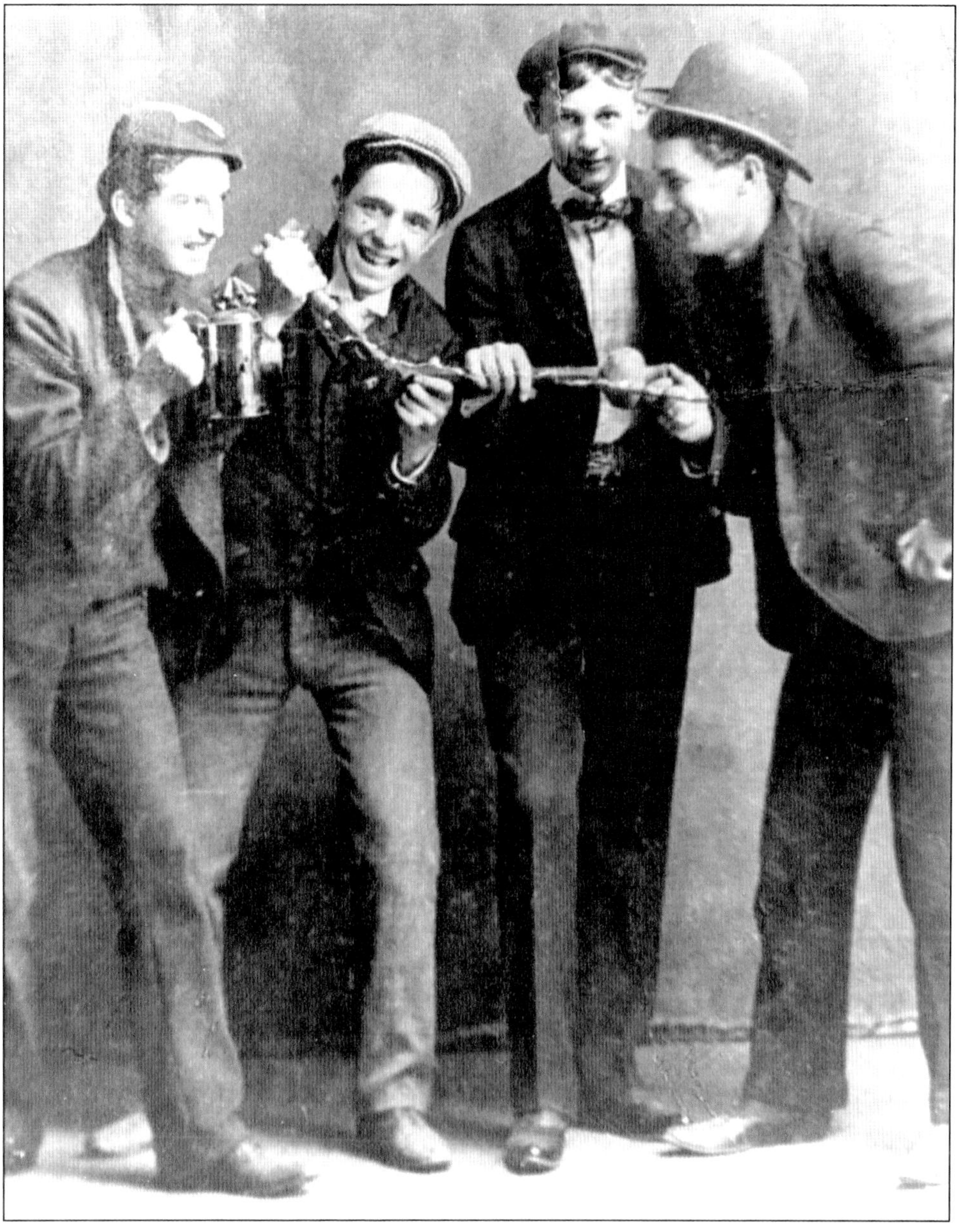

The above young members of the 1899 Allegan High School graduating class were perpetrators of one of Allegan's most legendary heists. One night, in a fit of youthful exuberance, they climbed to the top of the old high school's bell tower and removed the clapper from the bell. The following school day, when the bell rang silent, the principal threatened that the parties found guilty of this thievery would not graduate in the spring. No one came forward, and the entire class of 24 received their diplomas. With the threat of spending another year in high school behind them, Roy Adams, Jim Butrick, Fred Hanchett, and Paul Lidner finally confessed to the "clapper caper." By then their misguided prank was taken in good humor and they received a bit of local celebrity. This splinter of Allegan history, still in their possession after a trip to California and back, was donated to the Old Jail Museum in 1996, along with this photograph of the four young men with the pilfered clapper.

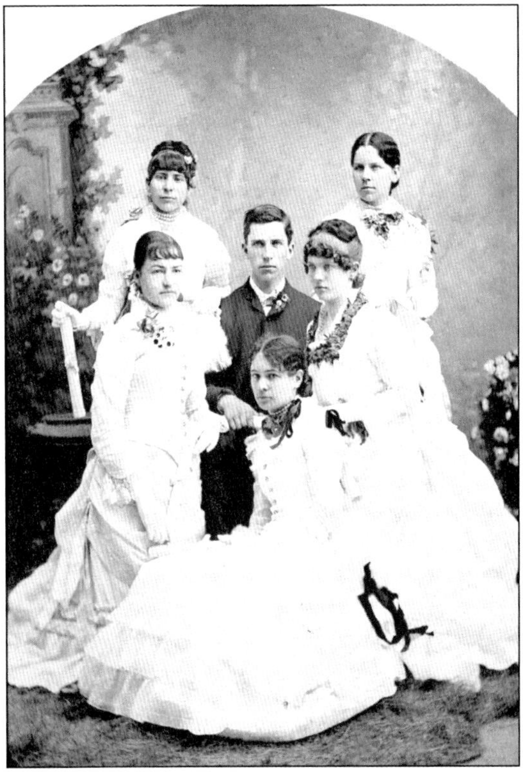

The Allegan High School class of 1883 had but one male graduate, Chester Wetmore. He was the older brother of beloved Allegan teacher and museum benefactor Elizabeth Wetmore. The females in the class are, in no particular order, Zella Leighton, Ella Colburn, Minnie Eisenberg, Anna Young, and Ellen Hudson. Wetmore does not seem to be bothered by the fact that he is surrounded by females in this photograph.

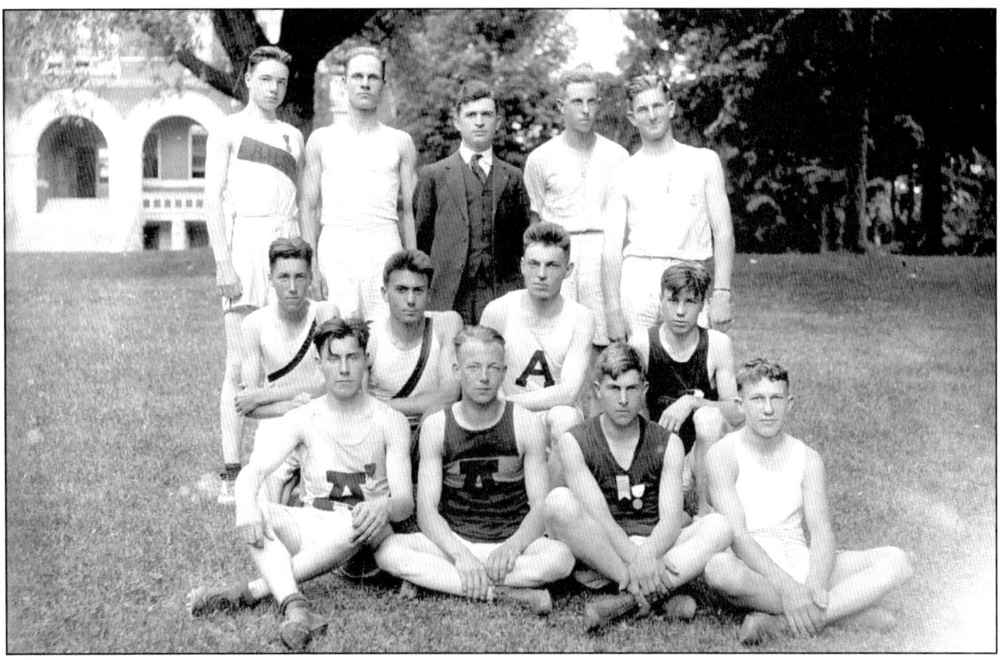

Posing on the grounds of the old courthouse is the 1922 Allegan High School track team. From left to right are (first row) ? Whistler, ? Reynolds, Gerald Ritchie, and Emil Schmitz; (second row) ? Smith, Floyd Noren, Eugene Osmun, and Charles McAlpine; (third row) Kent Pritchard, Wayne Edgerton, coach John Damoth, ? Volker, and Loren Baker.

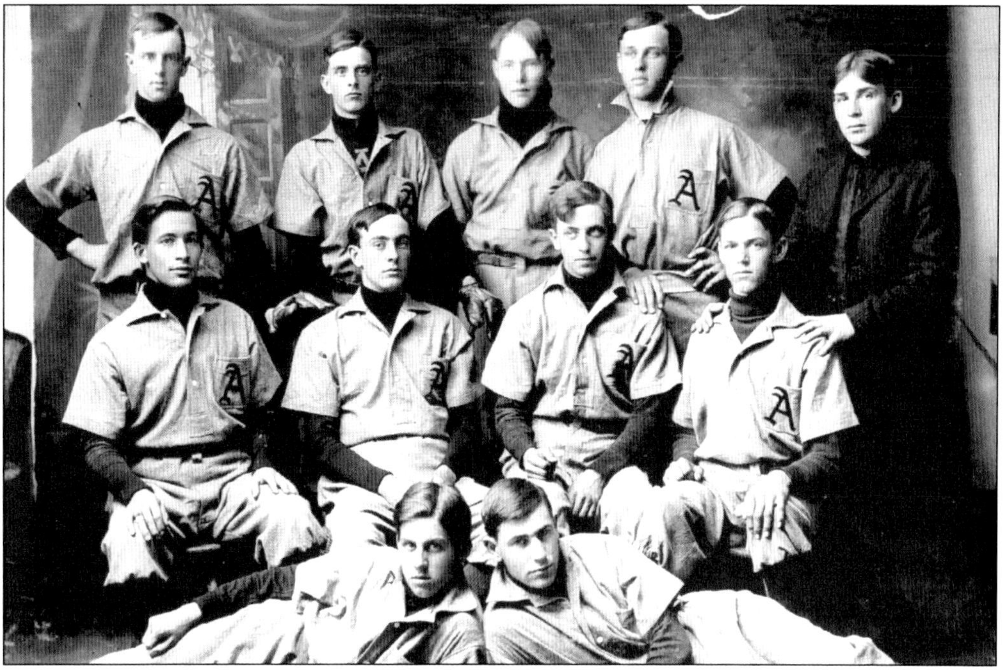

The uniformed members of the 1904 Allegan High School baseball team are pictured here. From left to right are (first row) Clarence Messinger and Charles DeLano; (second row) Clare Bliss, Claude Firestone, Ray Perrigo, and Danna Post; (third row) Fred LaDue, George Updyke, unidentified, Floyd Holland, and Otto Armstrong.

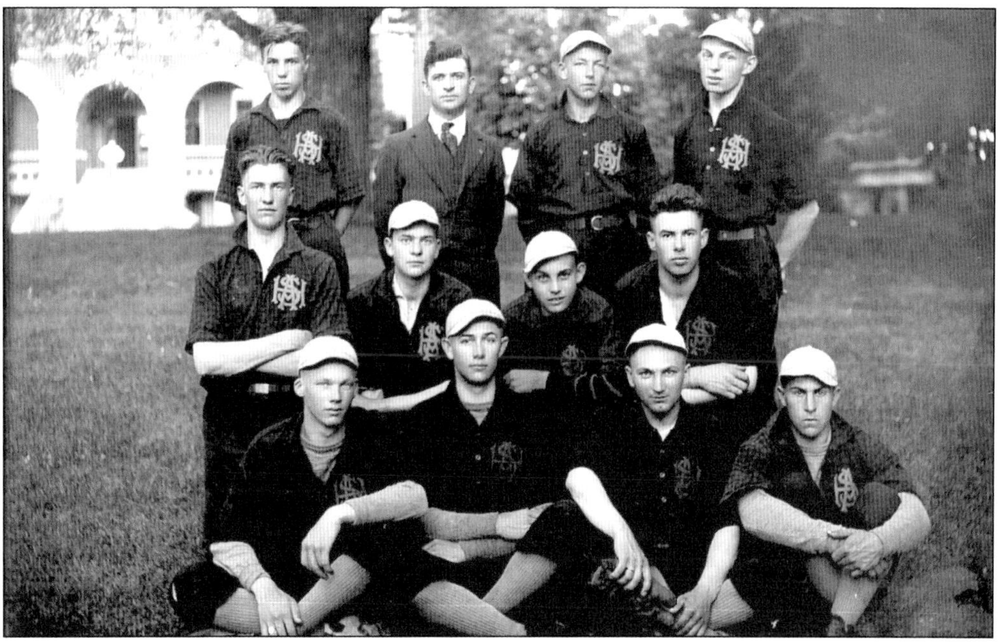

This 1919 photograph shows the Allegan High School baseball team in their uniforms on the lawn of the high school. Identified from left to right are (first row) ? Coburn, ? Edmire, ? Sweet, and Gerald Ritchey; (second row) Orrin Foster, Harold Foster, Franklin Grannis, and ? Thayor; (third row) Charles McAlpine, coach John Damoth, ? Reynolds, and Eugene Osmun.

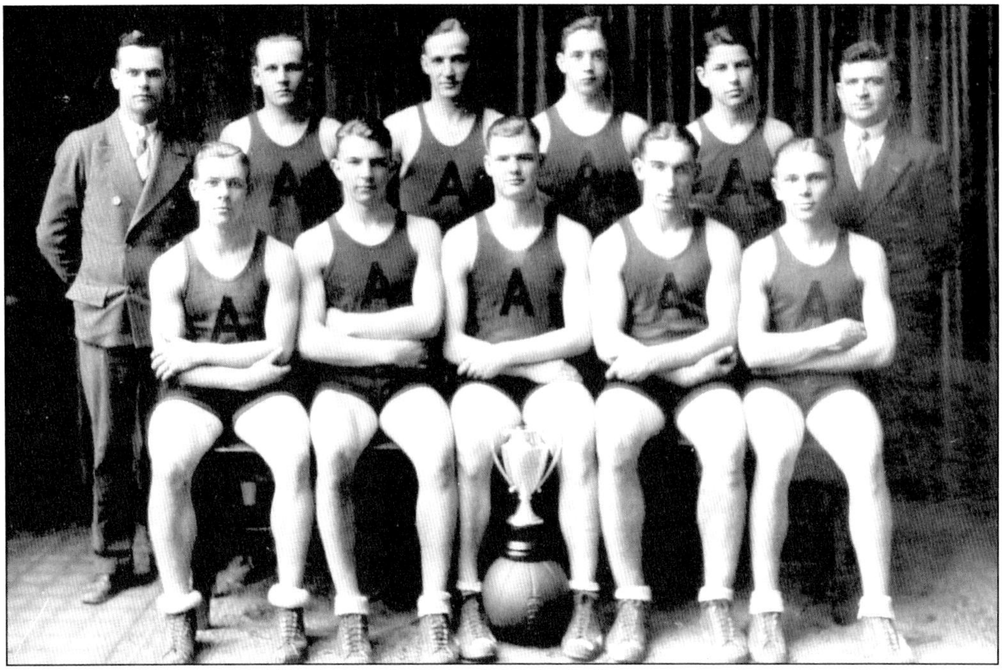

Members of this 1927 Allegan High School basketball team are pictured with their state quarter-final trophy. From left to right they are (first row) Henry Sisson, John Boyer, Verl Gulick, George "Stub" Myers, and Ernie Kronberg; (second row) assistant coach Scottie Ramsdal, Mahlon Davidsmeyer, Gerald "Hoot" Gibson, Harry Stanley, Robert Maentz, and coach John Damoth.

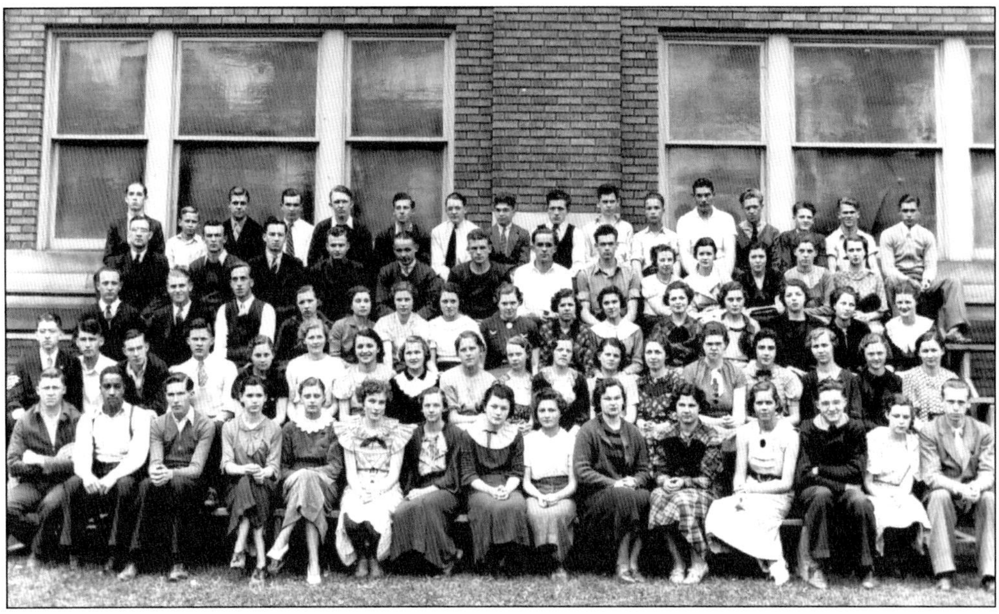

This photograph of the 1935 Allegan High School graduating class contains many names from old Allegan families. Edgerton, Haas, Peck, Morgan, Emmons, Cook, Blanz, Hiscock, Stone, Rumery, and Tripp are but a few names familiar to the area. In the fourth row, tenth from left, is Ruth Miller Berkin, who remains active in community projects and as a volunteer at the Old Jail Museum. (Courtesy of Ruth Berkin.)

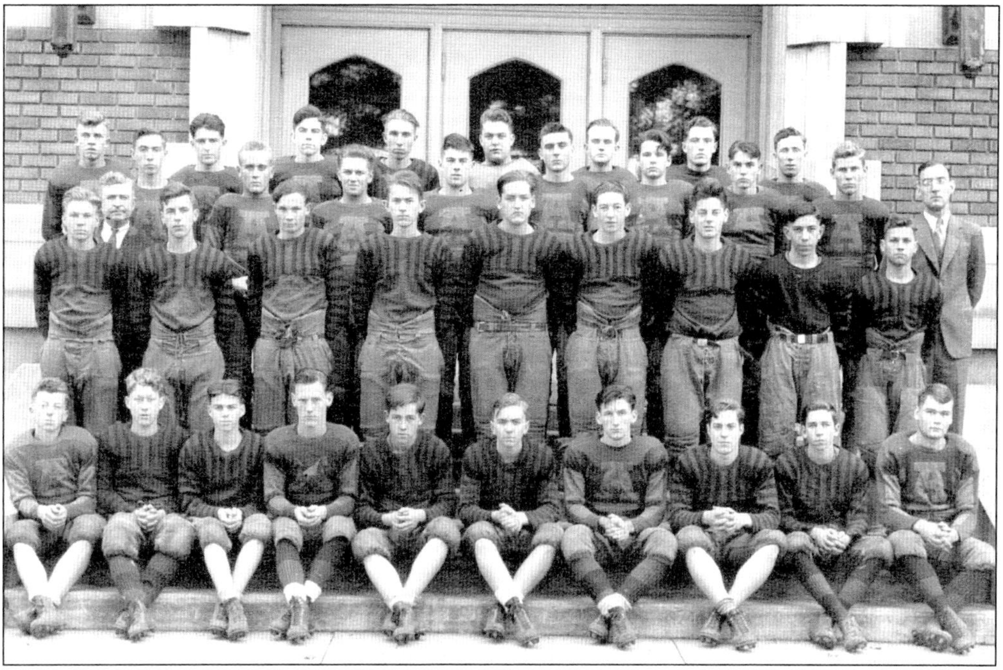

The Allegan High School football team poses on the steps of the old high school, around 1935, with their coach John Damoth. Small shoulder pads are barely visible under their uniforms. Bart Miller, son of sheriff Fred Miller, stands next to future fire chief Bud Blanz (third row, third and fourth from left).

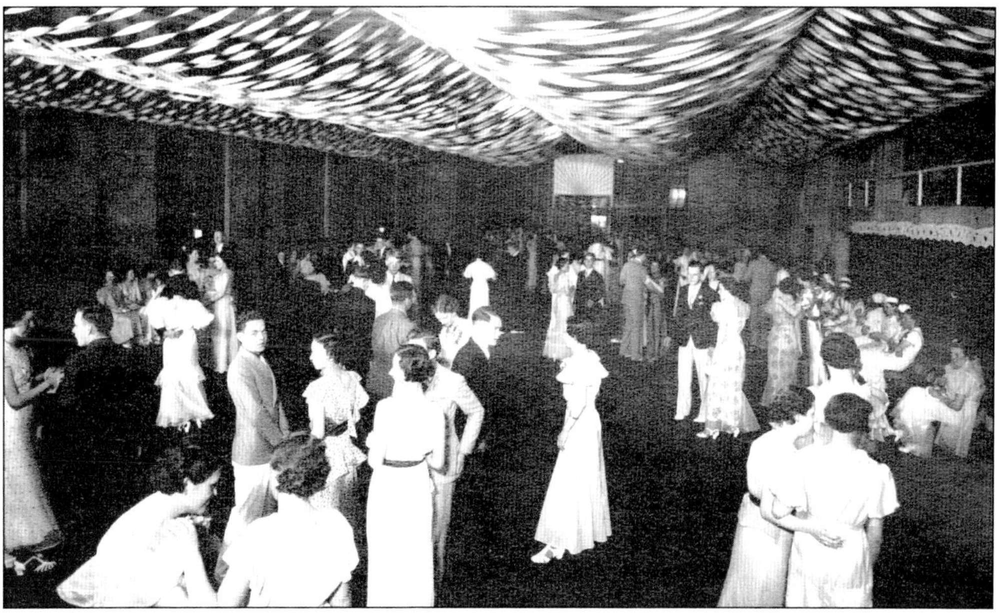

The Griswold auditorium was beautifully decorated for the Allegan High School junior and senior banquet and dance on May 8, 1936. Some of the identified couples are, from left to right, Marie Petill and John Born, Carl Isaacs and Helen Slate, Olivia Robinson and Raymond Weber, Bill Miller and Winifred Hodge, and Bob Pullen and ? Clark. John Pahl, Charles Peck, and Woodrow Gibson are listed, but not identified.

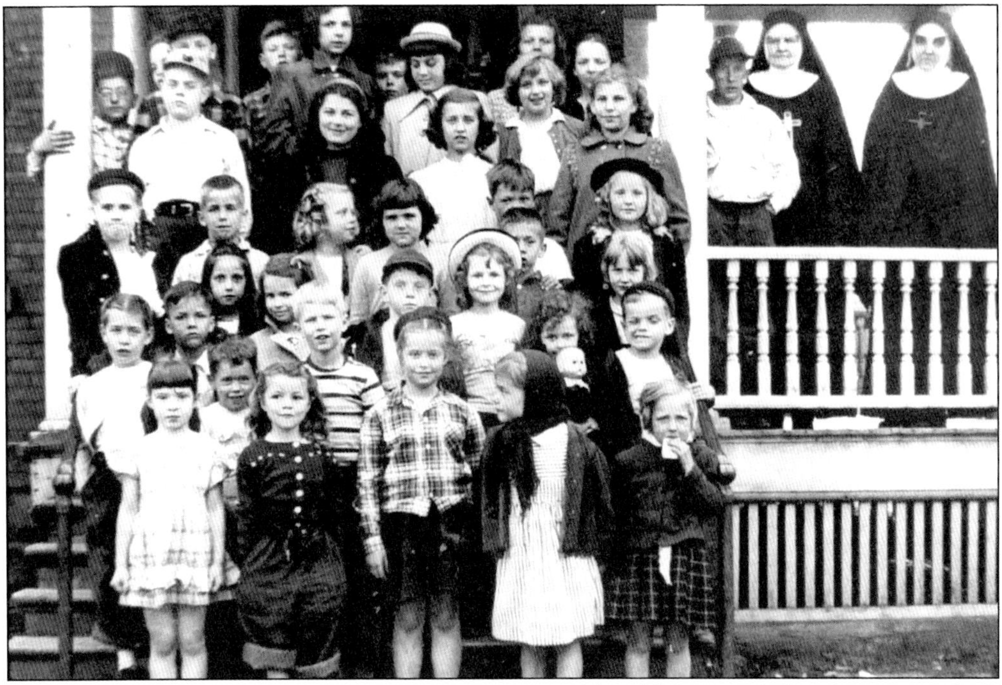

In this c. 1950 photograph, students pose on the steps of the old Episcopal church rectory, which was located on Walnut Street adjacent to the church. The students attended a week of religious training classes taught by the nuns. Identified, in no particular order, are Marilyn Boyce, Bucky Andrews, Gretchen Wedge, and Nan Hunter. (Courtesy of Nan Hunter.)

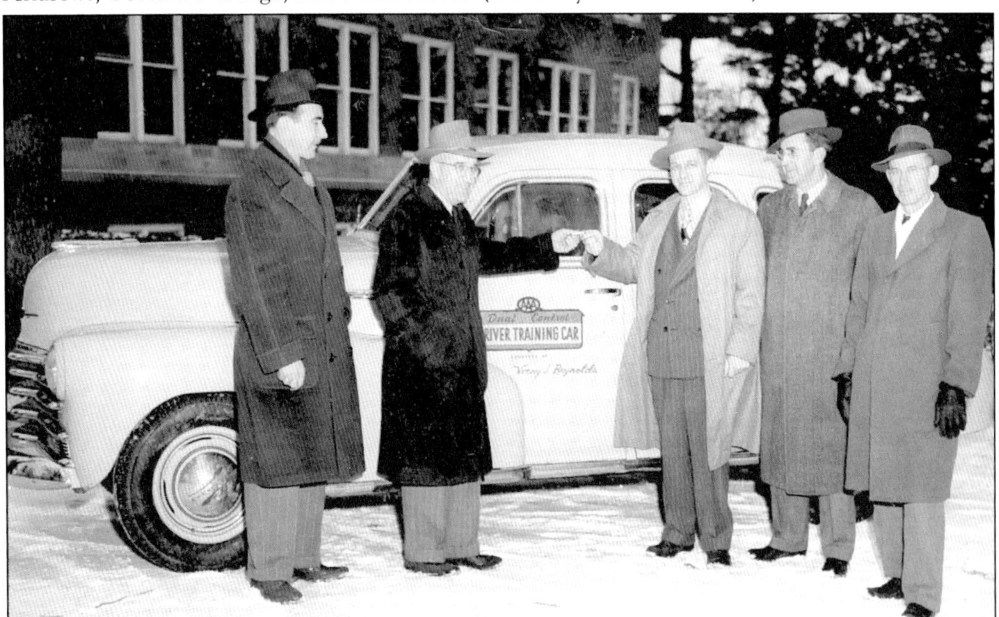

In this c. 1948 photograph, the keys to a new Chevrolet driver's training class car are being presented to Allegan High School. The car was donated by Verny J. Reynolds. From left to right are an unidentified man, school superintendent Arthur Kaechele, Jack McGeath, high school principal Ken Litsinger, and Elmer Rewalt, driver education teacher.

Four

A Stroll Downtown

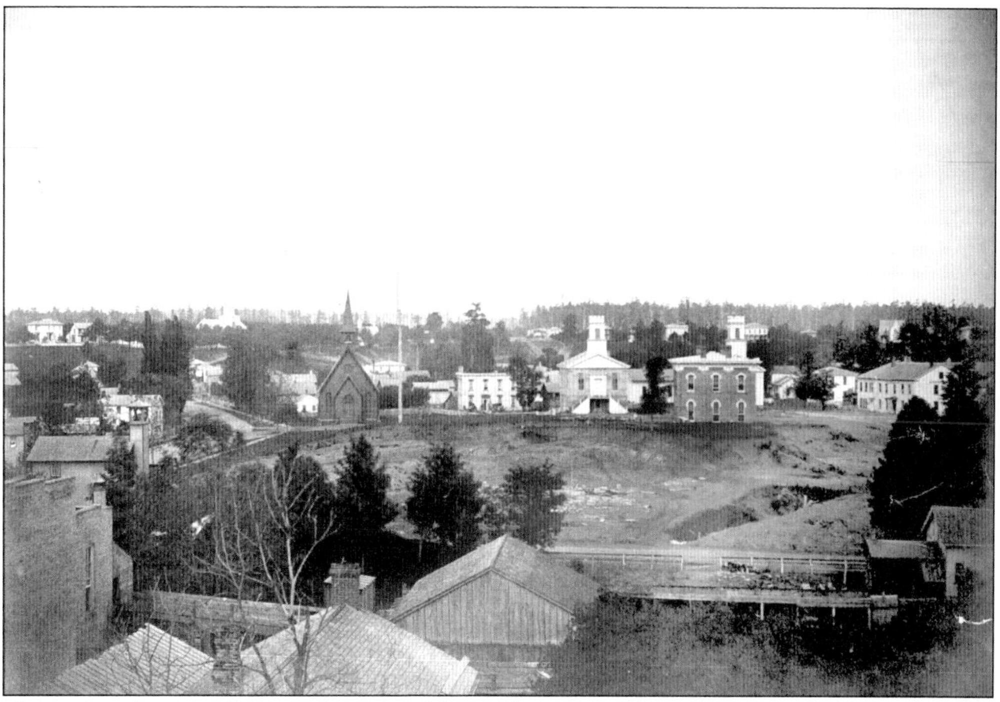

This 1800s photograph shows the area of the public square, then used as a gravel pit. On the far left is the fire station with its bell tower. A cannon on site was used to announce the attack on Fort Sumter in 1861, and citizens gathered to heed Pres. Abraham Lincoln's call for volunteers for the "insurrection."

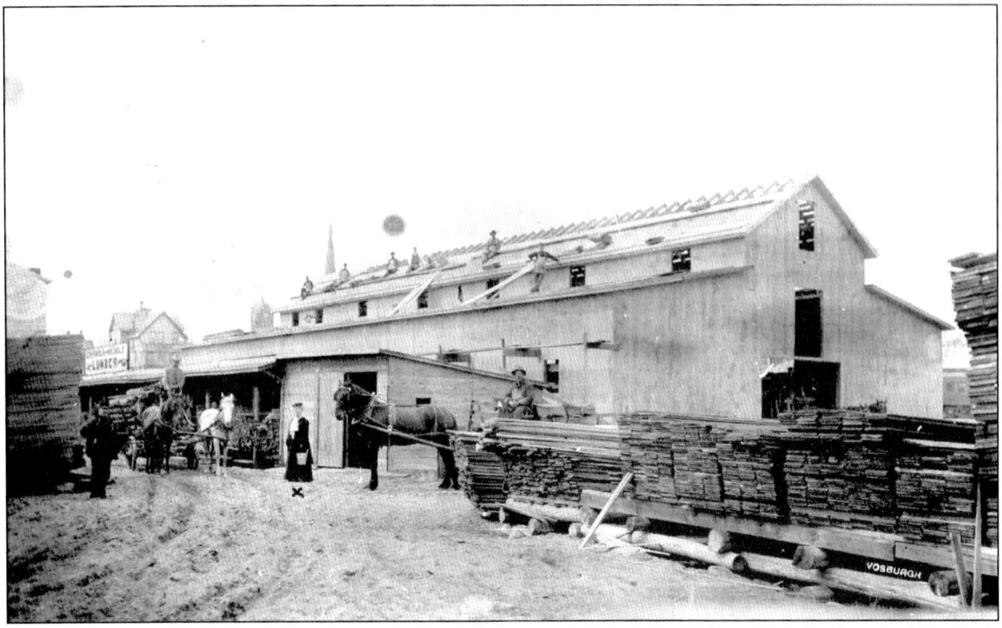

Allegan philanthropist Marilla Griswold is shown in the Griswold and Nichols Lumber yard. When her husband, Isaac Pardee Griswold, died in 1907, Marilla took over management of the company at a time when it was unusual for women to be involved in business. The business flourished under her management, and she became one of Allegan's preeminent philanthropists while living modestly above the Sherwood and Griswold store in downtown.

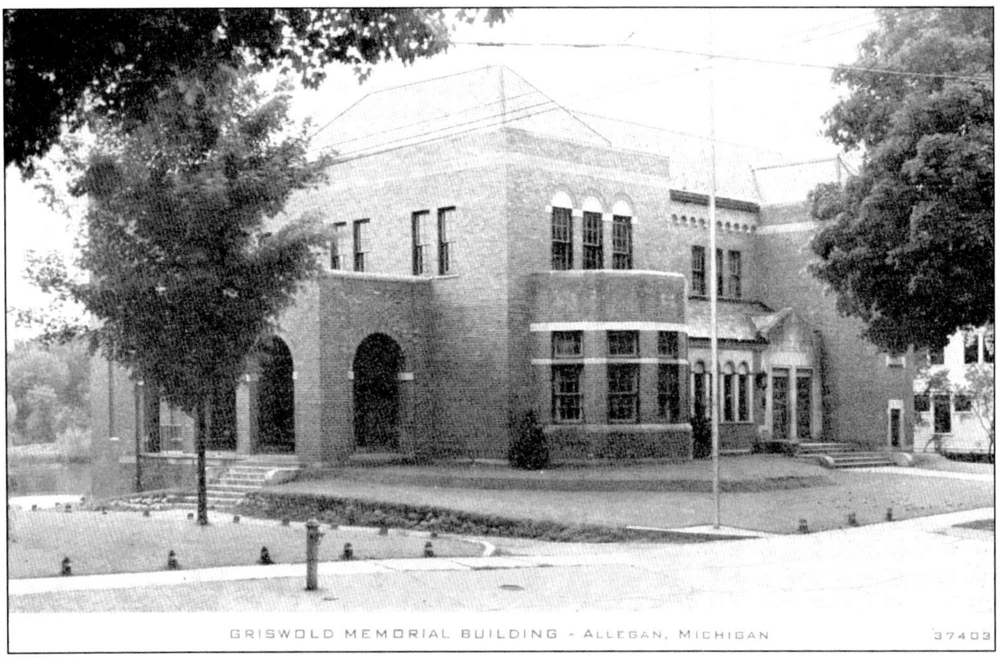

When Marilla died in 1918, her gift of $100,000 to Allegan bespoke her desire that there would always be a place in town for community theater. Although the 1929 stock market crash put a dent in her invested bequest, the Griswold Auditorium stands on Hubbard Street as a monument to her love for her city.

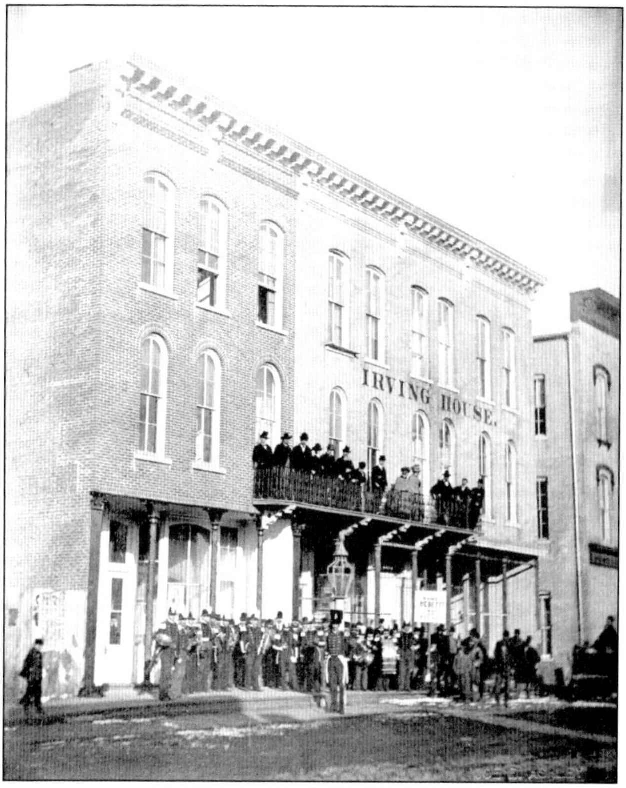

The Irving House hotel, one of the three-story buildings at the corner of Locust and Hubbard Streets in the pre-fire days, is shown in this 1870s photograph hosting a benefit for the Allegan City Band. Leader L. Y. Cady stands front and center while unidentified benefactors line the balcony.

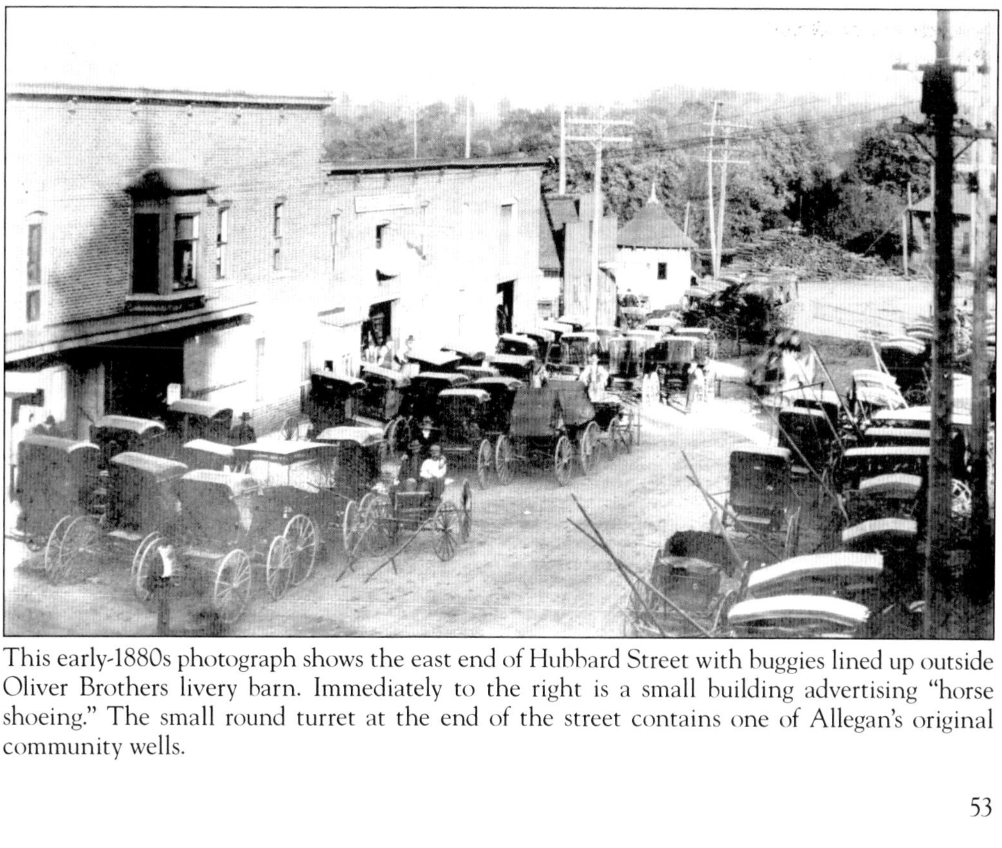

This early-1880s photograph shows the east end of Hubbard Street with buggies lined up outside Oliver Brothers livery barn. Immediately to the right is a small building advertising "horse shoeing." The small round turret at the end of the street contains one of Allegan's original community wells.

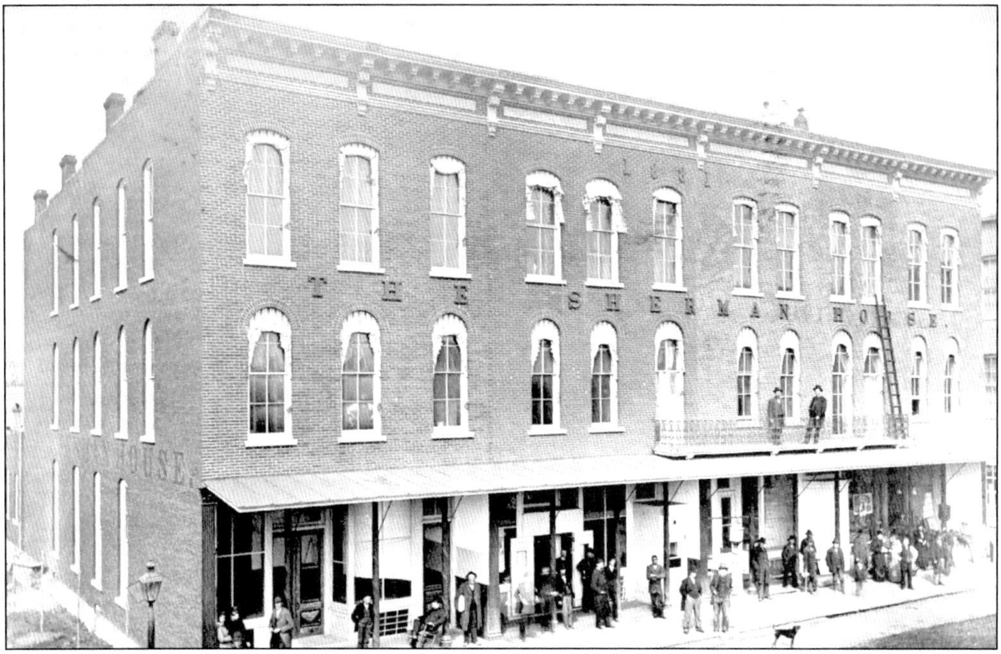

The block-long three-story Sherman House was built in 1881 but destroyed in the fire three years later. In 1900, so the story goes, Thomas Edison paid a visit to Allegan. He rented a large room in the Sherman House from which he would be able to delight Allegan residents with a demonstration of his newly invented phonograph.

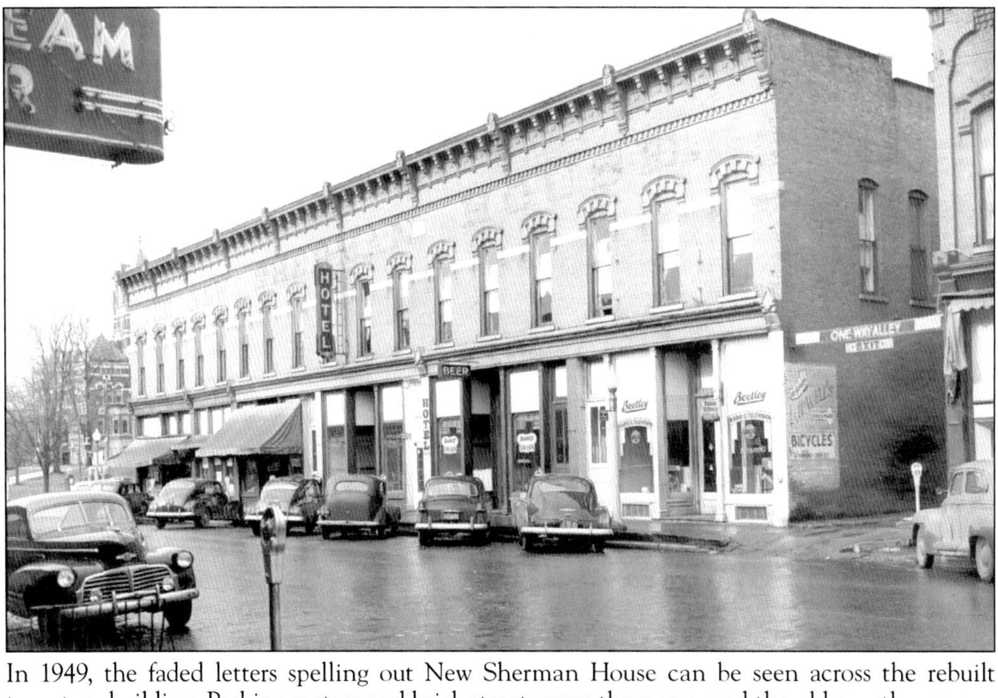

In 1949, the faded letters spelling out New Sherman House can be seen across the rebuilt two-story building. Parking meters and brick streets were the norm, and the old courthouse can be seen in the background. In the left foreground is part of the sign for the Ice Cream Dairy Bar, which was a favorite hangout of Allegan teens into the late 1950s.

After the original Locust Street Grange Store was destroyed in the 1884 fire, Albert Stegeman rebuilt his busy cooperative two years later on Trowbridge Street. Grange organizations were a focus of rural life throughout America. In 1896, the Horan family began a four-generation continuum of ownership. From Ed Horan to his great-grandsons Ed and Yori, Horans operated the Grange store until it closed in 1987.

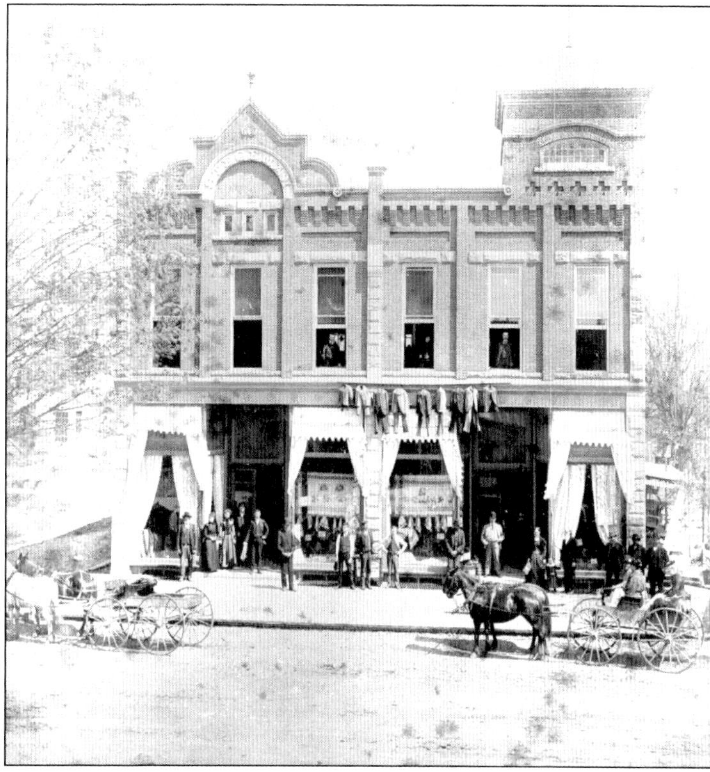

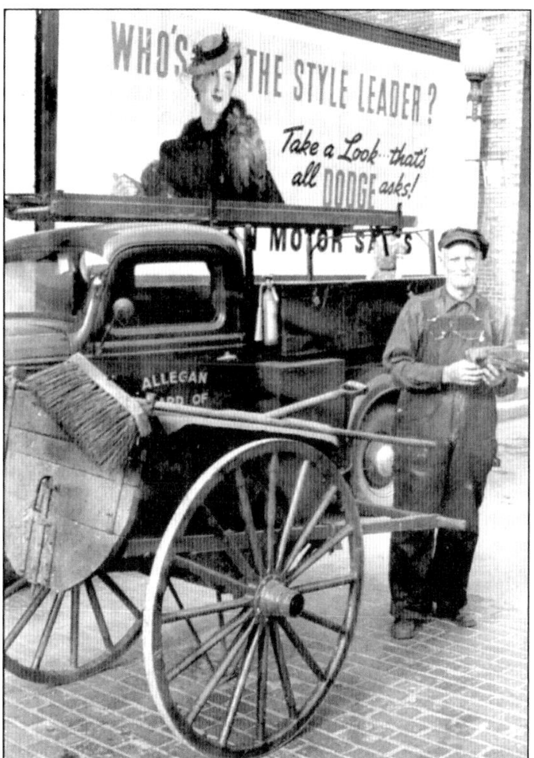

This 1938 photograph shows William Barham, an employee of the city sanitation department. Beside Barham is a two-wheel cart that was used to hold street-cleaning supplies as Barham went about the task of keeping the streets of Allegan clean and tidy. Parked behind the cart is the Allegan Board of Public Works truck.

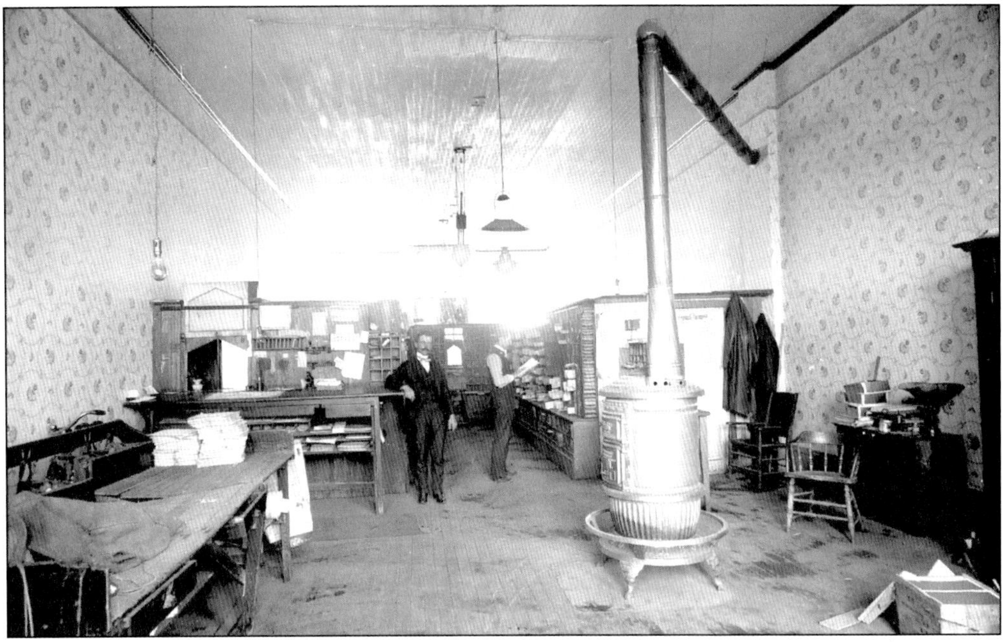

This 1890s photograph shows Allegan's post office in a Locust Street storefront. In later years, this would become a J. C. Penney department store and the post office would move to its new building now occupied by Minnie Sophrona's restaurant. In 1935, the federal government gifted Allegan with the new building on Trowbridge Street, which is still in use today.

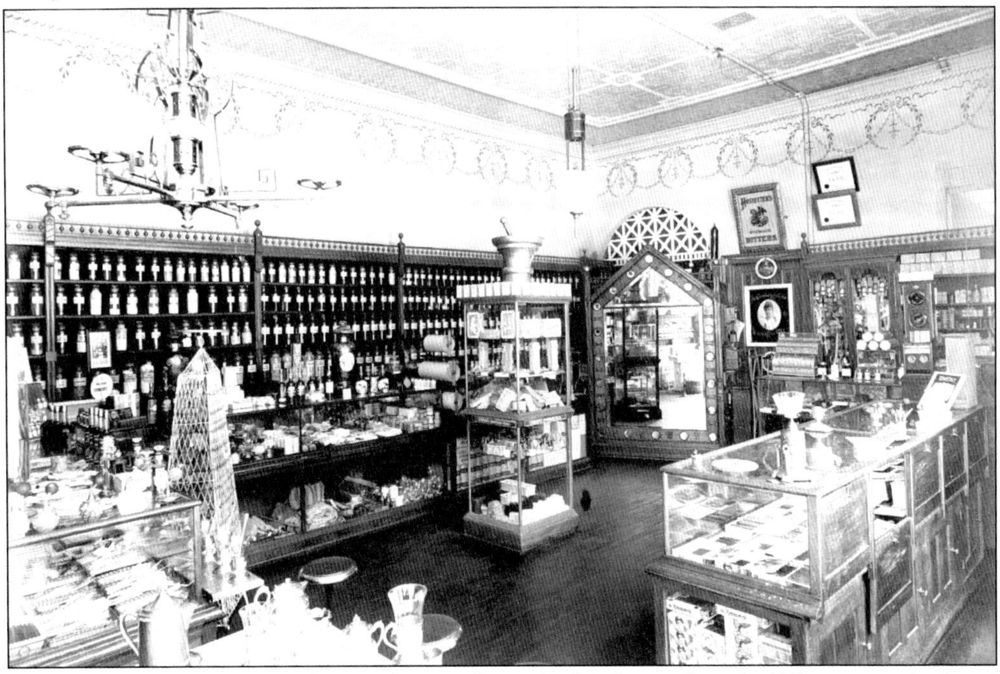

Druggist Edward VanOstrand's certification from the Michigan Board of Pharmacy, displayed on the wall, is dated 1898. His well-stocked early-1900s drugstore contains cigars, perfumes, home remedies, and pharmacy bottles filled with compounds from Acacia to Zincate, which he would mix with mortar and pestle into remedies. A small coffee bar is in the forefront.

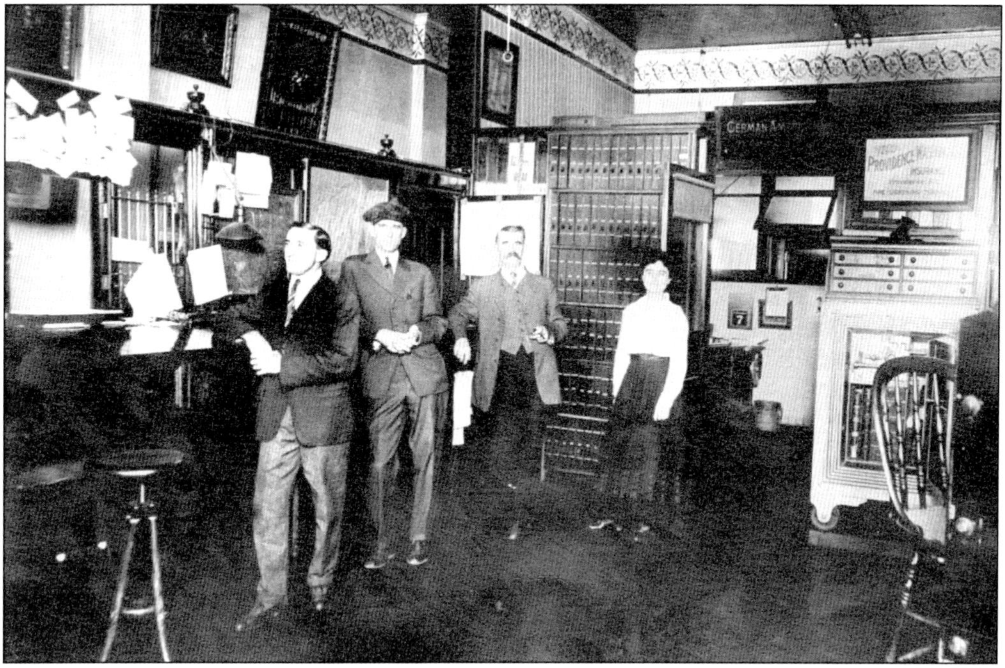

This 1912 photograph shows, from left to right, George Wise, George W. Updyke, Theodore S. Updyke, and Nora Fox in the Allegan County abstract office and Updyke Agency on Brady Street. The notation on this early photograph, showing the colorful T. S. Updyke, mentions only that Fox was known to carry an umbrella rain or shine.

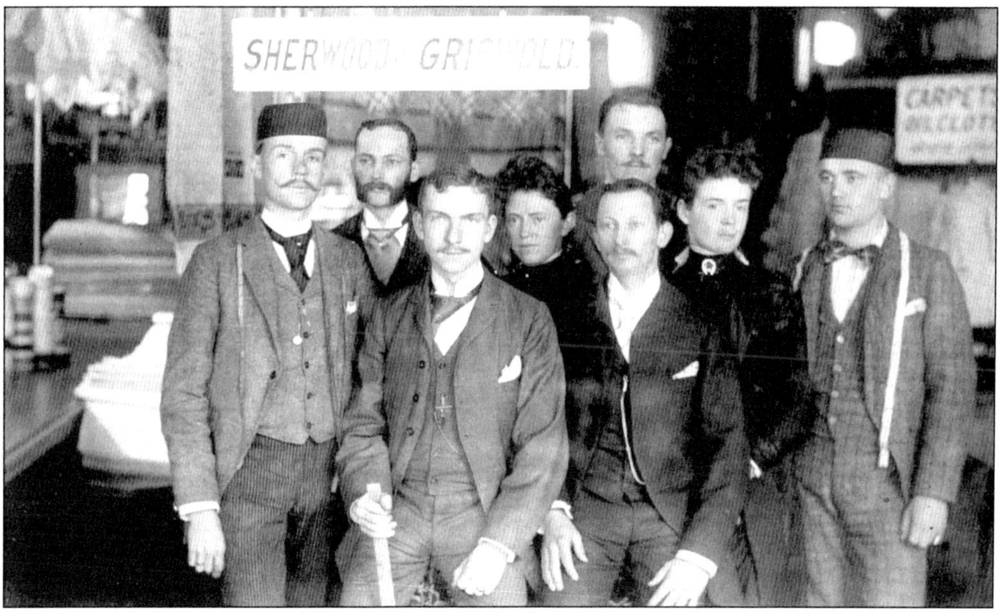

Workers at Sherwood and Griswold Department Store stand ready to serve their customers in June 1899. Dan Webster, Leonard Stein, Abe Stein, and Vina Webster are named in no particular order. Marilla Griswold was the sole proprietor of the entire block and lived upstairs in an apartment. Upon her death in 1918, the Stein family would purchase the business and it would be known as Stein and Griswold until it closed.

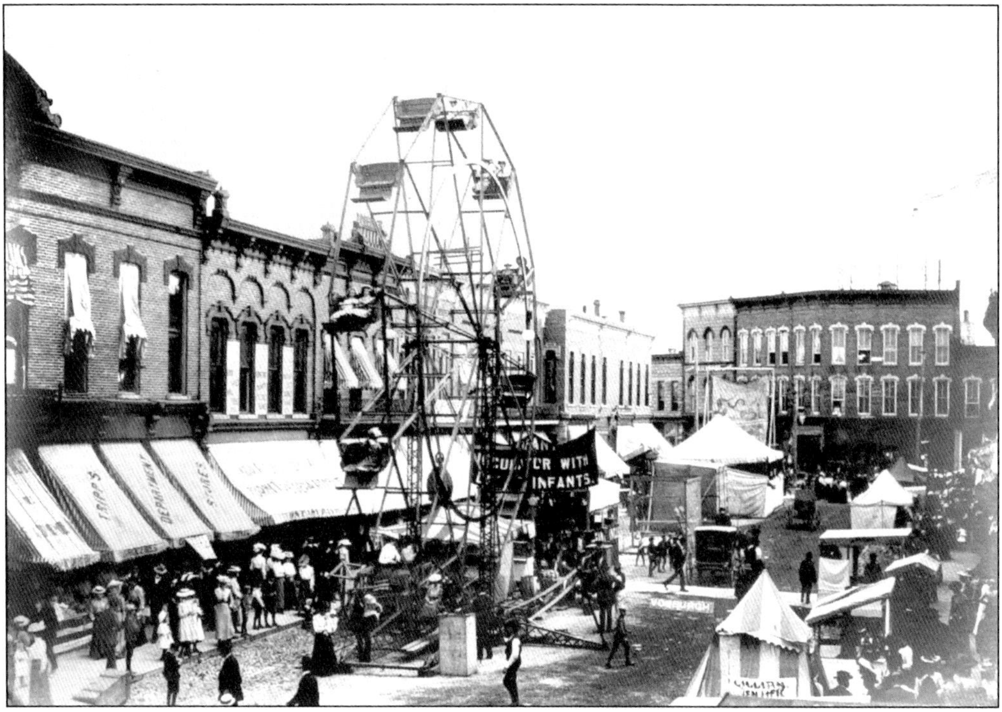

Locust Street in the early 1900s became the temporary site of a street carnival, complete with tents and a Ferris wheel. A novelty attraction at the time, having first been shown at the 1893 Columbian Exposition in Chicago, it was a chance for citizens to get a bird's-eye view of their town.

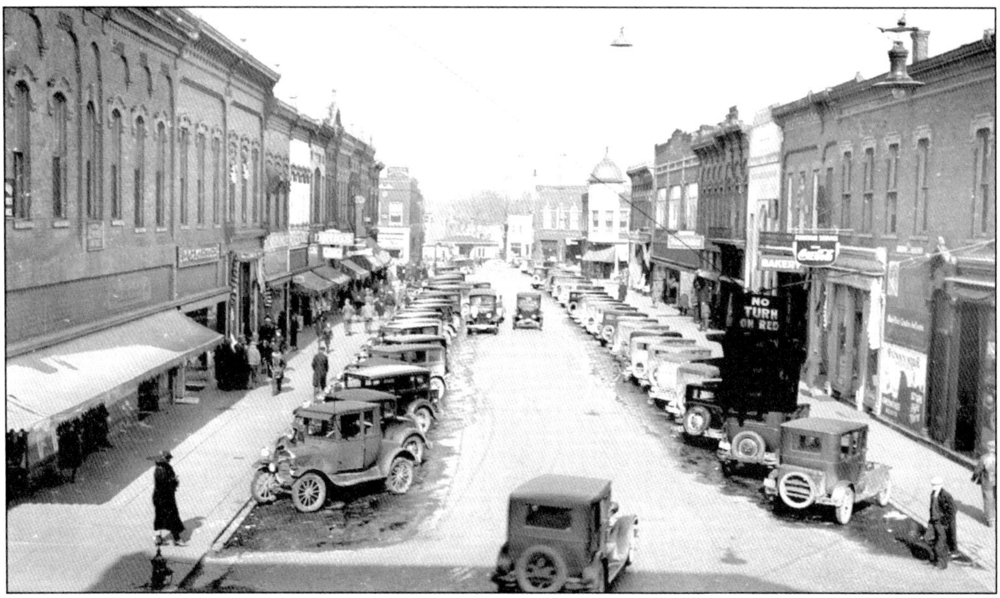

This 1932 photograph shows Locust Street as a two-way street, with a traffic light on the corner where Locust, Brady, and Hubbard Streets meet. At the far end of Locust, the building with the turret, which once housed the post office and the Grill restaurant, is now Minnie Sophrona's restaurant. The Allegan City Hall is located in the middle of the block on Locust Street.

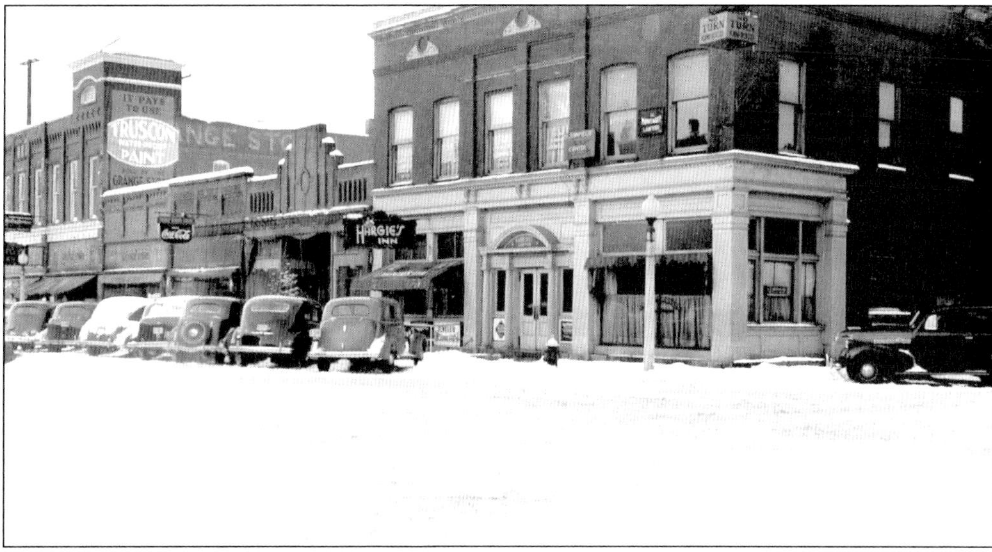

This winter view of Trowbridge Street, around 1940, shows Hargie's Inn, a popular restaurant and meeting place of the day. The old Grange store building is visible down the block. Hargie's occupied the old First National Bank building on the northwest corner of Trowbridge and Locust Streets and was owned by James A. and Elnora Hargie.

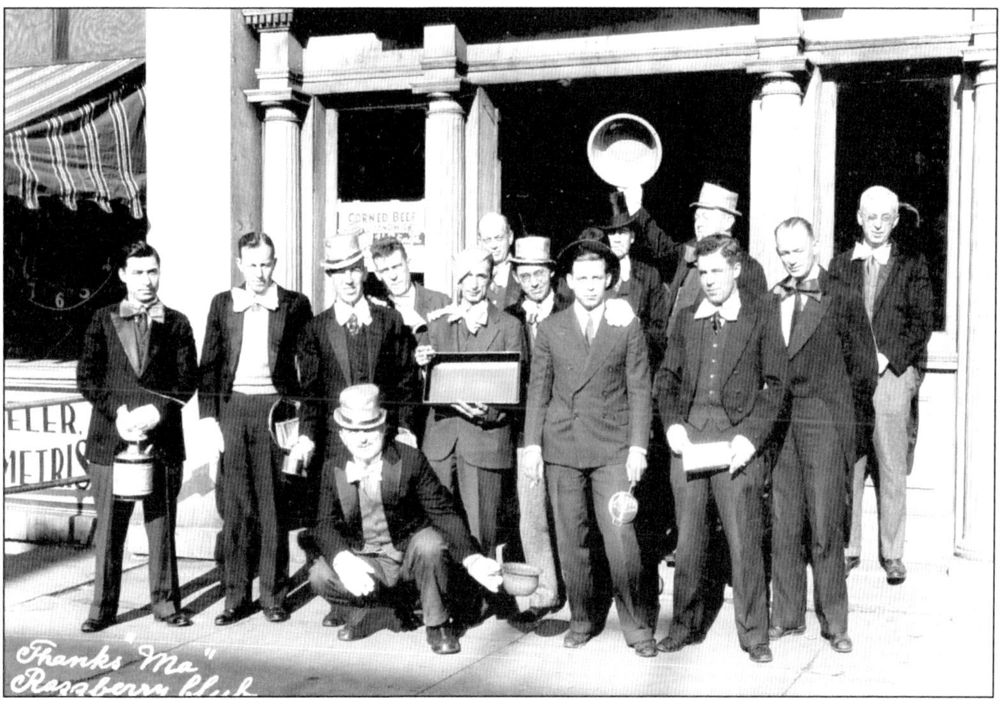

A group of regulars who met at Hargie's for coffee called themselves the "Razzberry Club." Pictured on the left, standing, is Dan Conroy, manager of J. C. Penney, and the others, in no particular order, are John Axe, Bud Tripp, Grover Tripp, Ray Perrigo, Doug Nash, Bing Perrigo, Bill Tripp, and Paul Perrigo. This photograph was given as a gift to owner "Ma" Hargie.

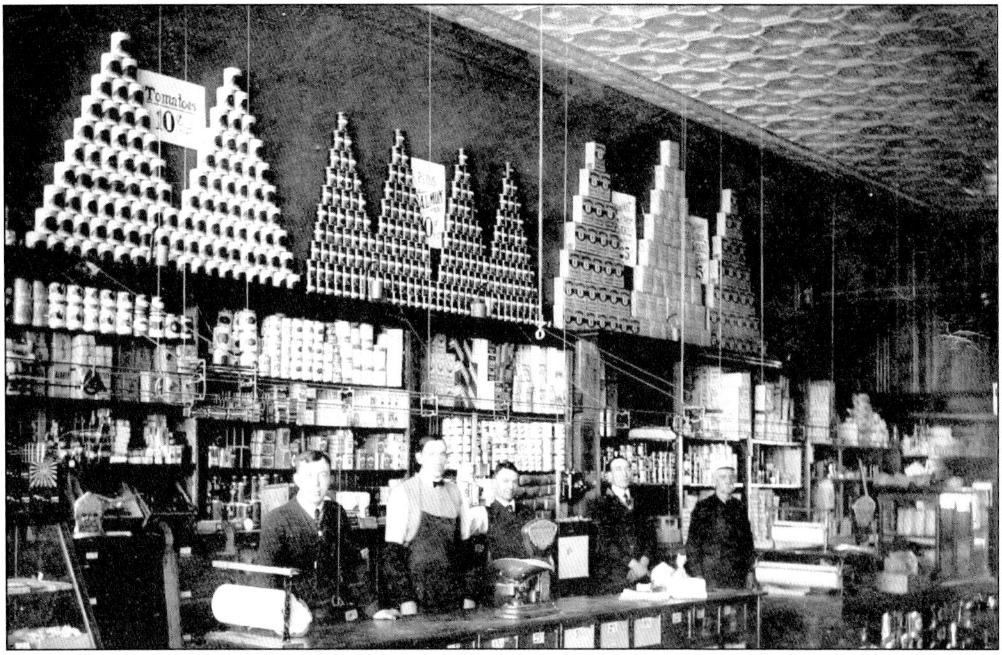

During World War I the Surprise and McLaughlin grocery store was located on the street level of the New Sherman House on Hubbard Street. Philip McLaughlin (third from left) and Clarence Surprise (fourth from left) pose behind the counter with three of their workers. Here 10¢ cans of tomatoes and pink salmon are artfully displayed with 25¢ boxes of corn flakes.

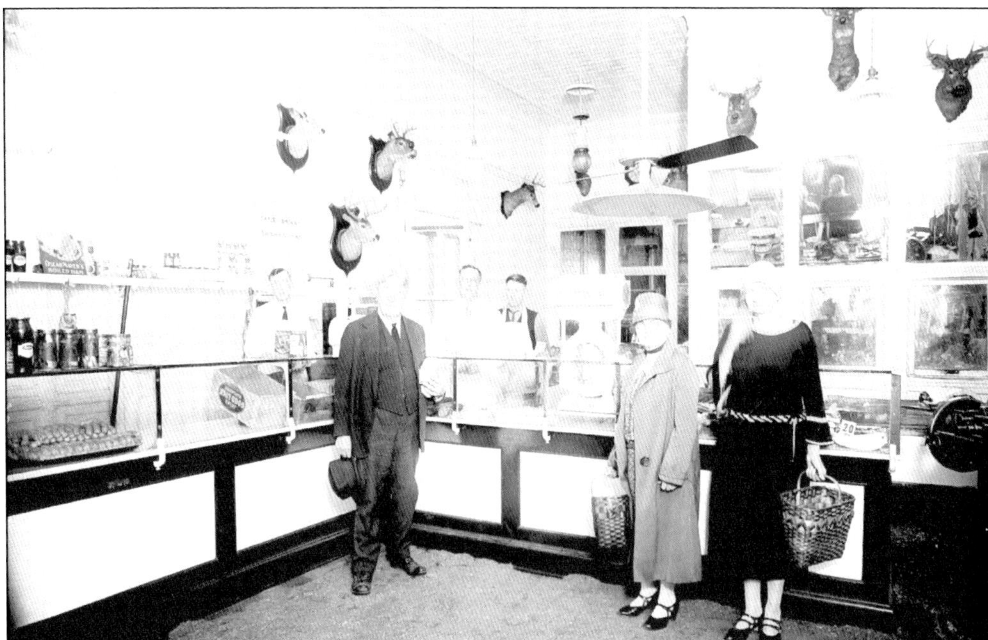

Behind the counter, around 1920, of the Maentz Meat market are, from left to right, Dirk Wesseldyke Sr., Pete Roon, and Henry Smith. Customers Rev. H. L. Potter of the Methodist Episcopal Church, Cora Rando, and Lena Barlow are standing on the sawdust-covered floor in front of the counter, which was well stocked with sausages made by Maentz himself.

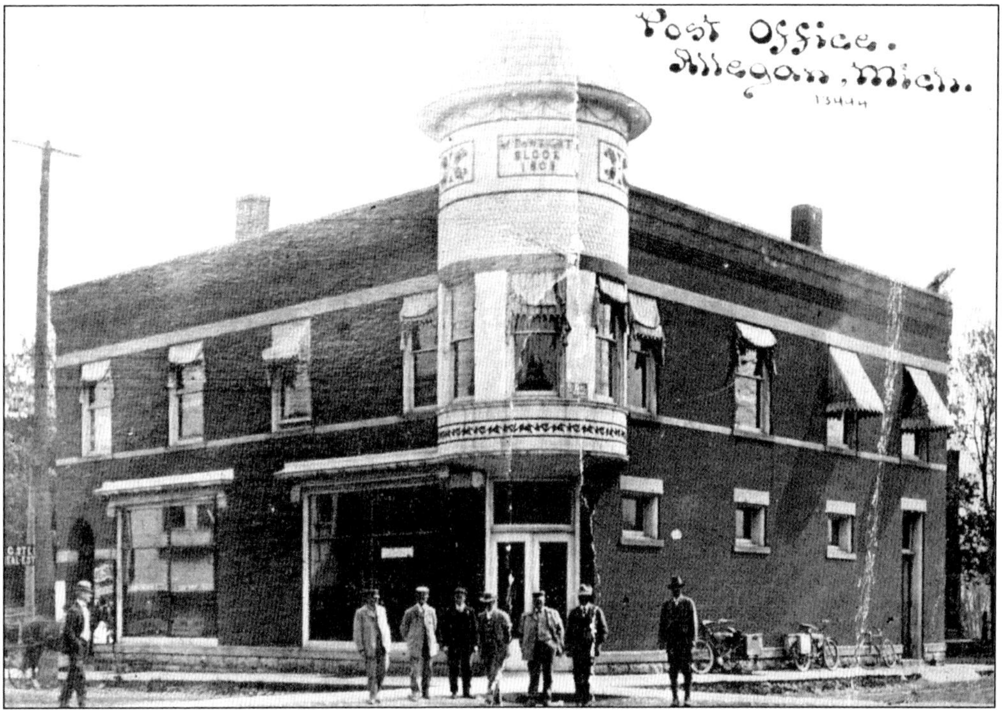

The ever-expanding post office moved in 1903 to the new flat-iron building on the corner of Trowbridge and Locust Streets. The new building was needed because the post office was now offering rural mail delivery, and space was needed for the increase in the amount of mail processed. Bicycles with panniers to hold the mail are shown leaning against the building.

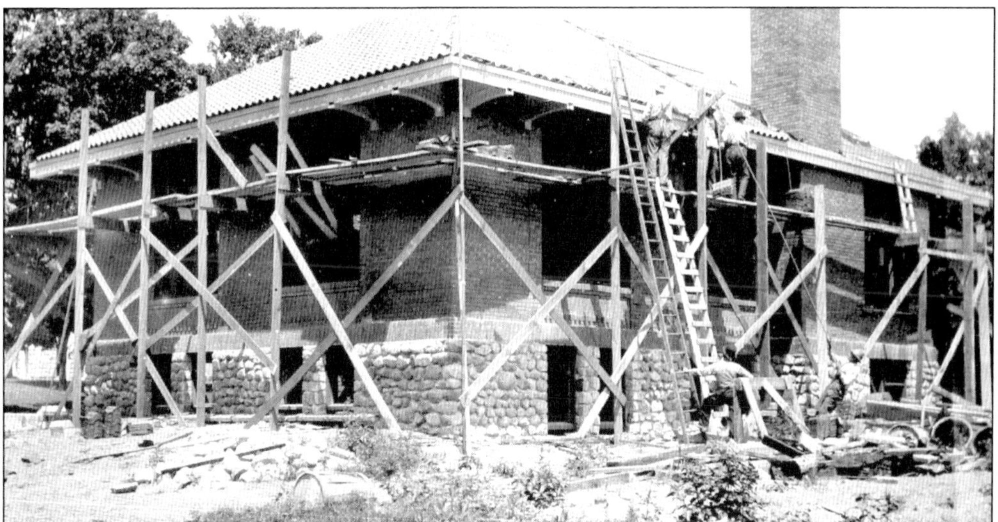

This 1914 photograph shows the Allegan Public Library under construction. In 1912, Allegan had a small public library. People in the community heard that Andrew Carnegie was engaged in funding libraries for small towns all over the United States to honor the importance books played in his life, and they urged the city fathers to quickly apply. Funding was approved and construction began in 1914.

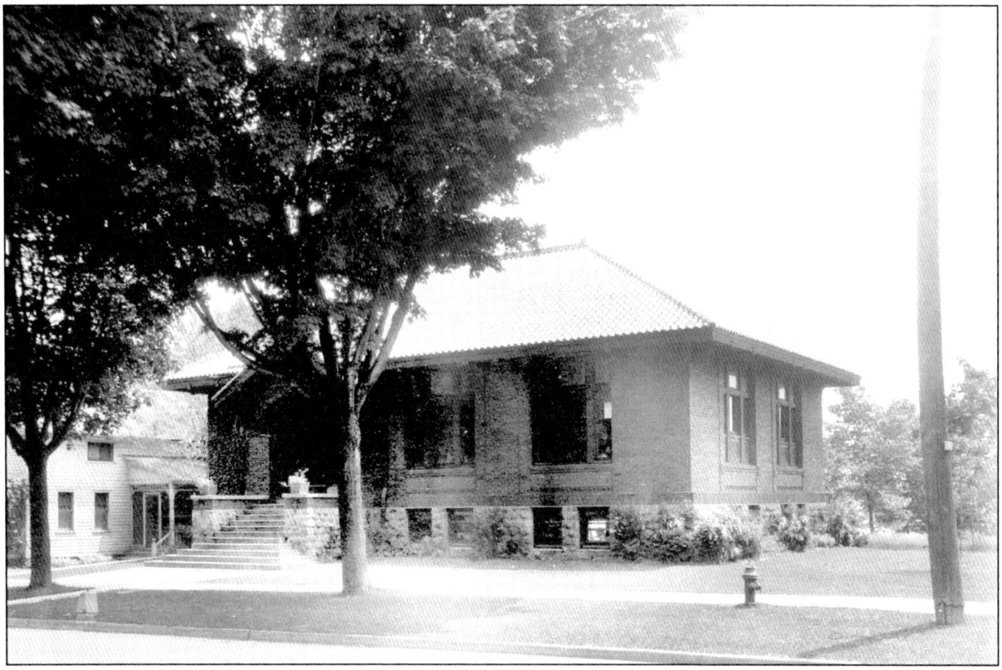

This photograph, taken in 1915, shows the completed Allegan Public Library on Hubbard Street. The original building is still being used; however, a major construction project in 1976 added on a new wing in the back that now functions as the main library. The old building has a second floor Carnegie Meeting Room that the library board of trustees, assisted by the library friends committee, renovated to its former period splendor in 2006.

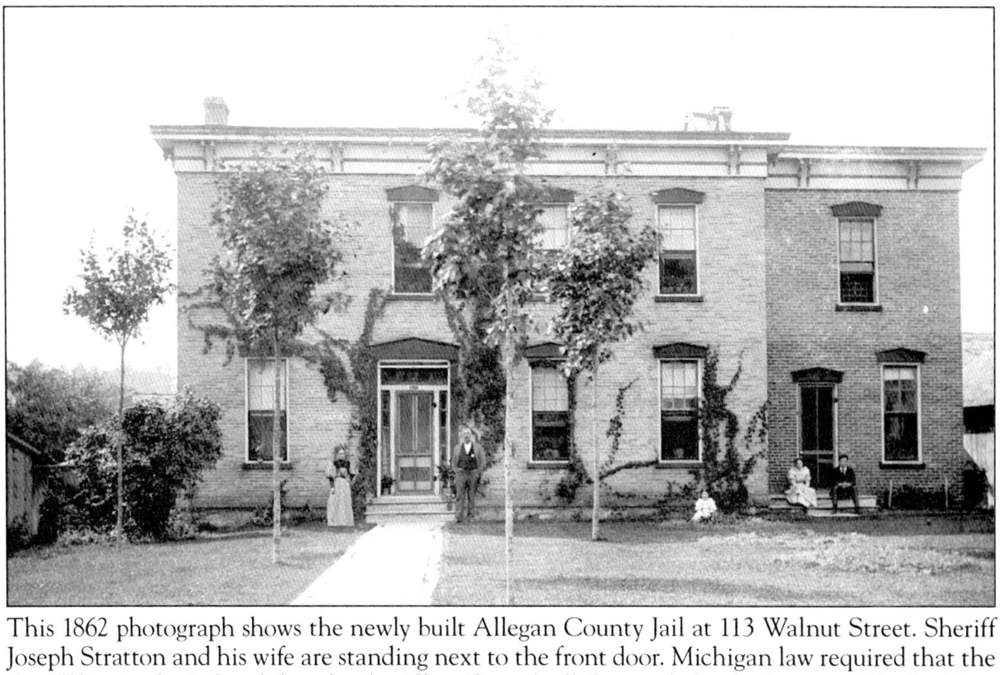

This 1862 photograph shows the newly built Allegan County Jail at 113 Walnut Street. Sheriff Joseph Stratton and his wife are standing next to the front door. Michigan law required that the sheriff live in the jail and that the sheriff's wife cook all the meals for the inmates. The building was torn down and replaced in 1906.

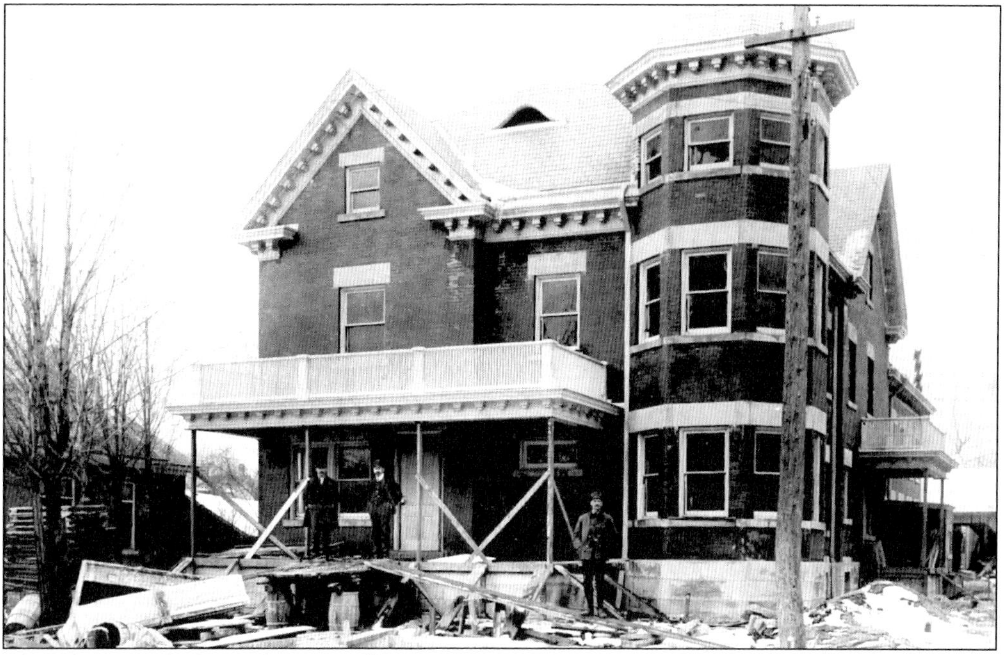

This photograph shows the new Allegan County Jail in its final phase of construction in 1906. Sheriff Allen Whitbeck, elected in 1906, is on the right, and the two men on the left are unidentified. The front of the building was a two-story, four-bedroom home for the sheriff, with a parlor, dining room, kitchen, and private front entrance on the first floor and four bedrooms upstairs.

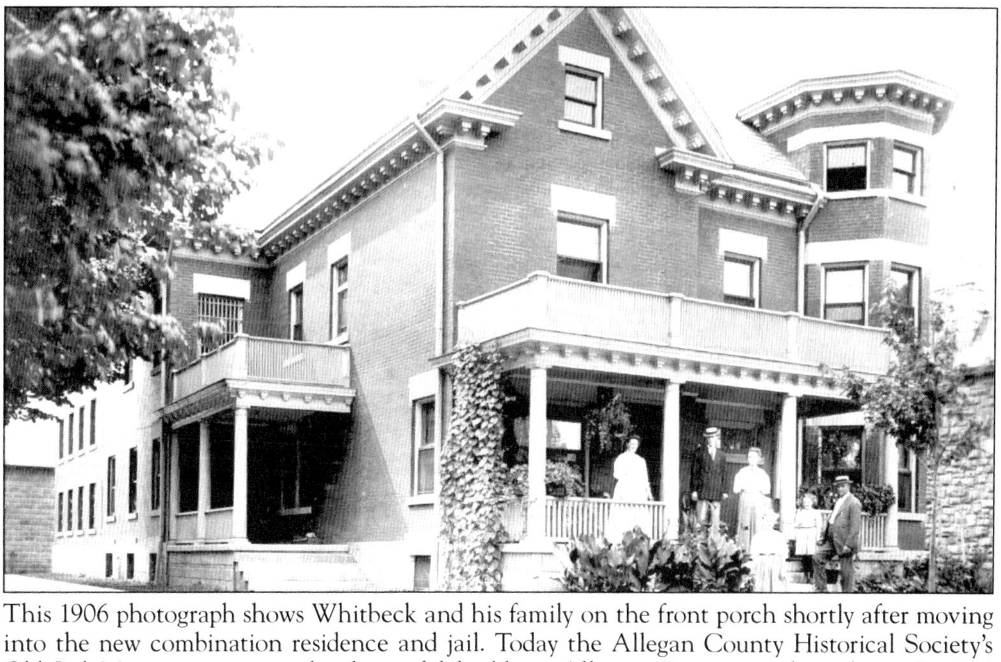

This 1906 photograph shows Whitbeck and his family on the front porch shortly after moving into the new combination residence and jail. Today the Allegan County Historical Society's Old Jail Museum occupies this beautiful building. Allegan County residents have donated over 10,000 artifacts to this museum. Displays are set up in the old cells and in the residence, depicting life in the early 1900s.

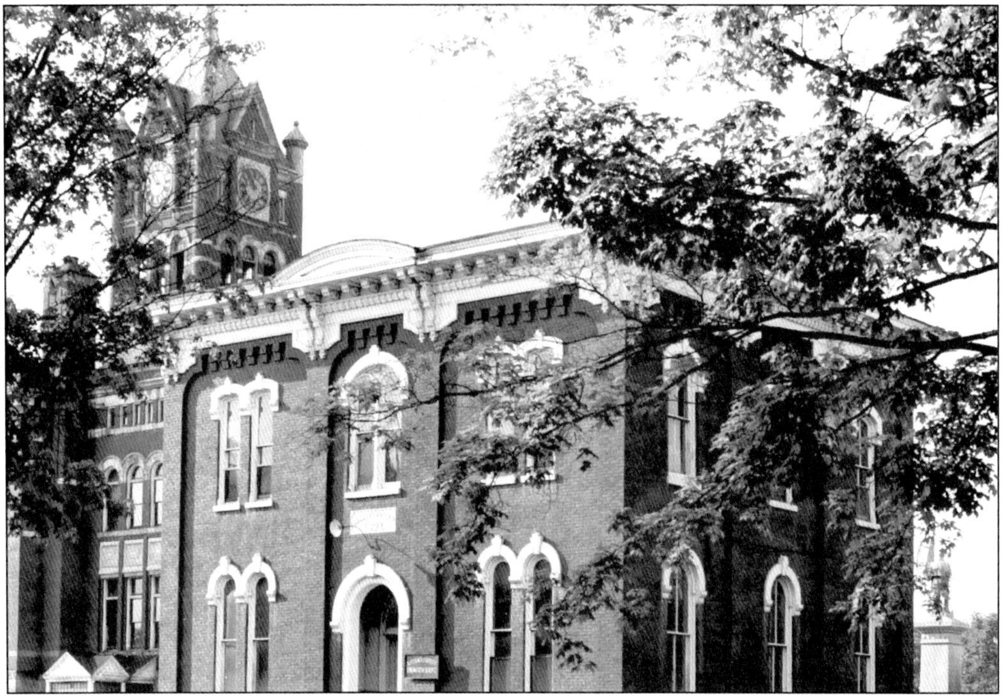

This late-1900 photograph shows the first county building that was erected in Allegan. It was built in 1871 on the corner of Walnut and Trowbridge Streets. In its later years, it served as the office of the superintendent of Allegan's schools. In the right corner, behind the building, the Soldier's Monument, which later looked on in frustration as this building and the courthouse were torn down, is seen.

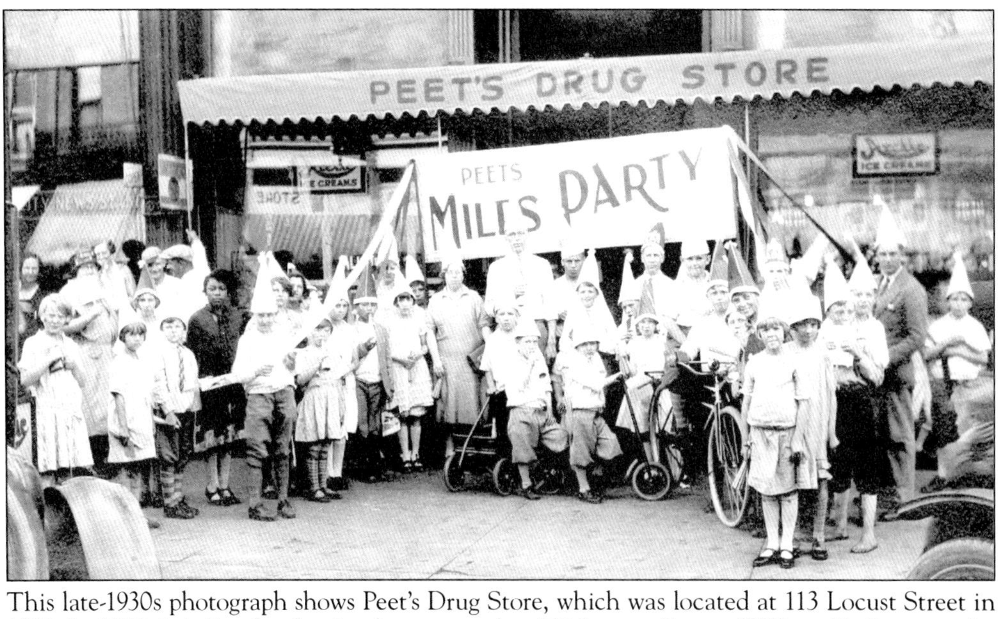

This late-1930s photograph shows Peet's Drug Store, which was located at 113 Locust Street in 1930. In 1938, it is listed as having been moved to 121 Locust Street. William H. Peet was the proprietor. This photograph was found by Doreen Peet-Kieling when she cleaned out a desk, and it was sent to the *Allegan News*, which in turn donated it to the Old Jail Museum.

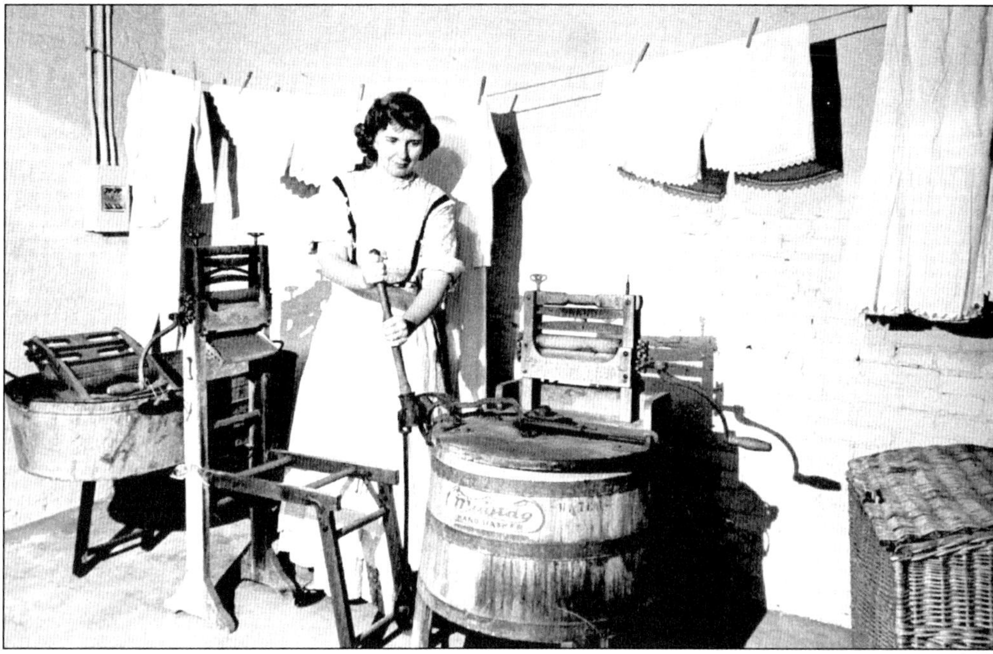

Mary Alice Pahl demonstrates wash day in early times at the Old Jail Museum. Caricatures drawn by Mary of others who contributed to the transformation of the jail into a museum are on the walls of a hallway leading from the museum gift shop. Mary and her husband, John Pahl, were founding members of the Allegan County Historical Society.

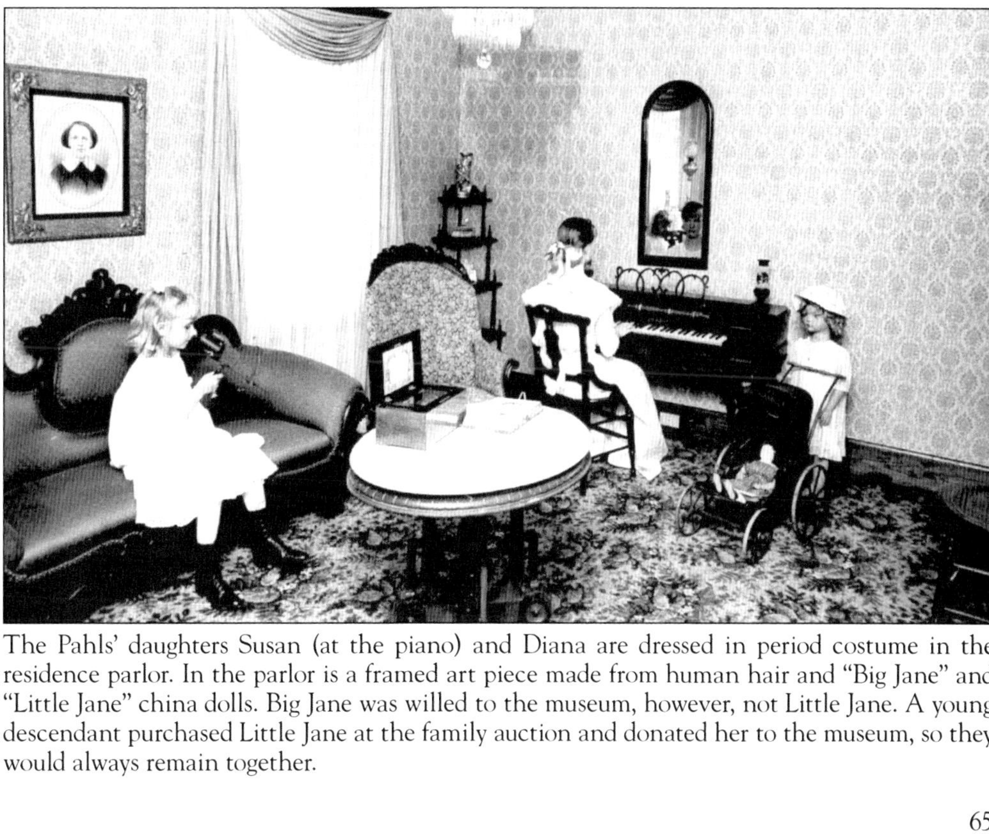

The Pahls' daughters Susan (at the piano) and Diana are dressed in period costume in the residence parlor. In the parlor is a framed art piece made from human hair and "Big Jane" and "Little Jane" china dolls. Big Jane was willed to the museum, however, not Little Jane. A young descendant purchased Little Jane at the family auction and donated her to the museum, so they would always remain together.

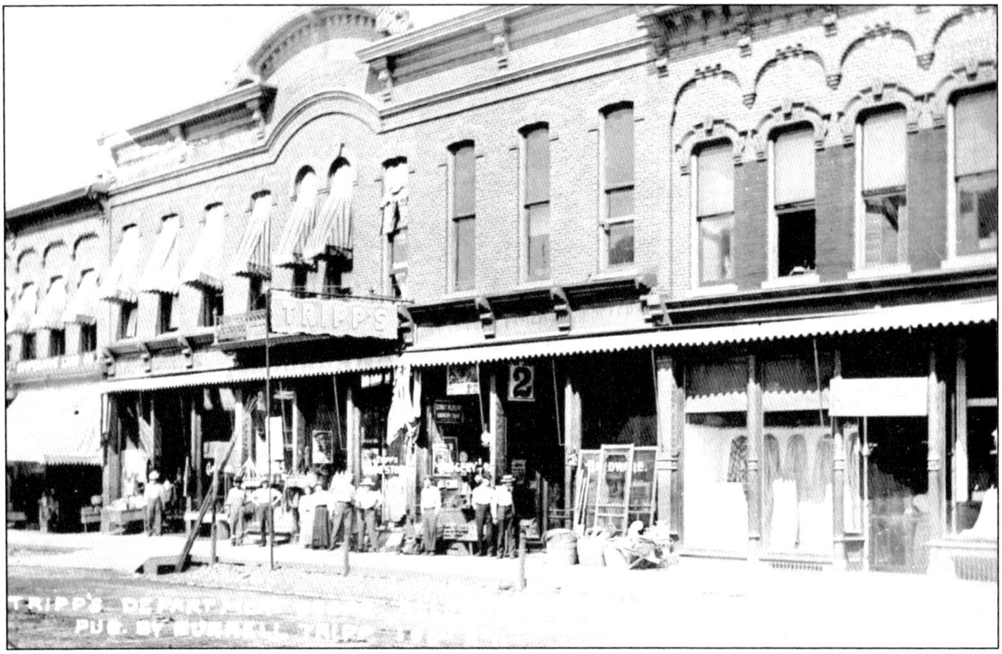

Tripp's Department Store on Locust Street was Allegan's original one-stop shopping venue. Window signs proclaim that it included a drug, hardware, and grocery store, along with books and clothing. The proprietor was Burrell Tripp. In later years, different department stores would come and go in Allegan; however, the Grange store lasted for the longest number of years.

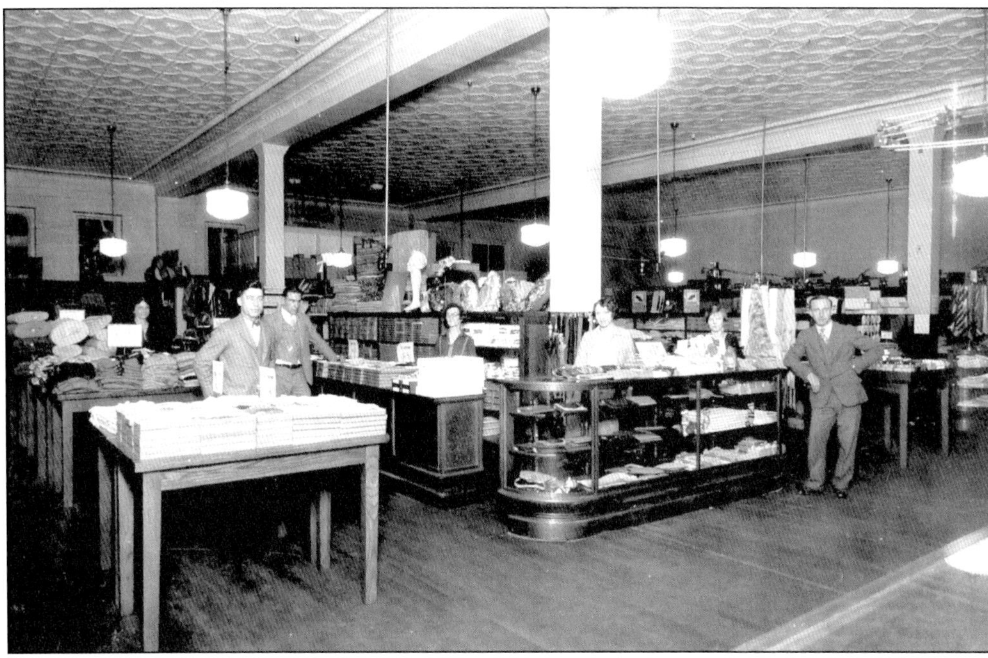

Manager Dan Conroy (left front) of the J. C. Penney store on Locust Street poses in the store in 1927. The two other men are unidentified, but the women are identified in no particular order as Marion Green, Metabelle Weaver, and Naomi Peabody. The fascination of the pneumatic tubes conveying cash and paperwork to the office upstairs is a vivid memory of this store for many.

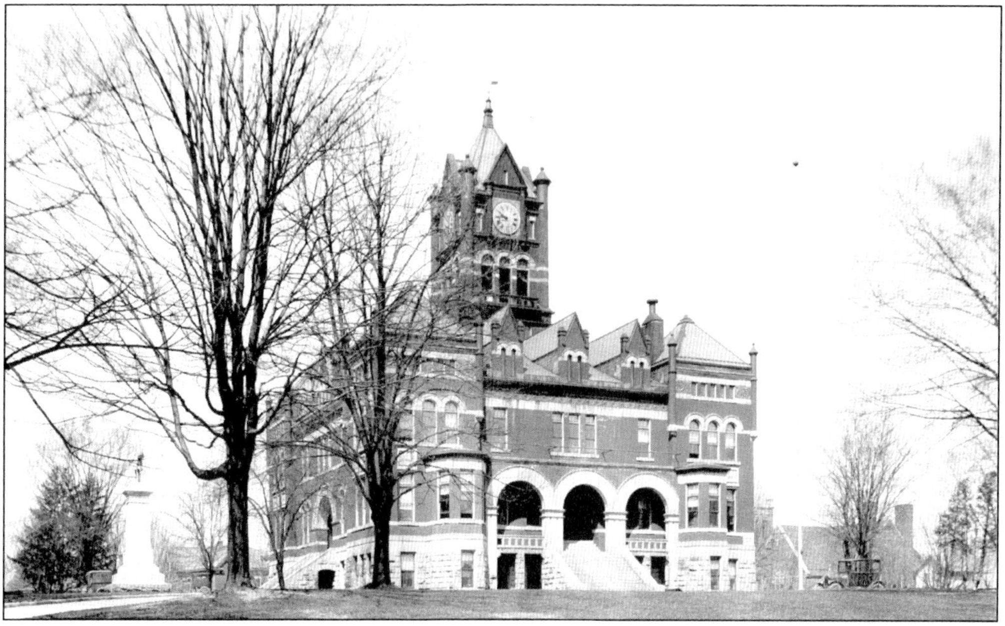

Built in 1890 in the center of the public square, the old courthouse towered regally over Allegan for 71 years. In 1903, the four-sided tower clock was installed for $1,200. On Saturday mornings children gathered to watch the clock being wound. By 1960, outgrown and having fallen into a state of such disrepair that the county did not feel it could afford to remedy, it was sadly demolished.

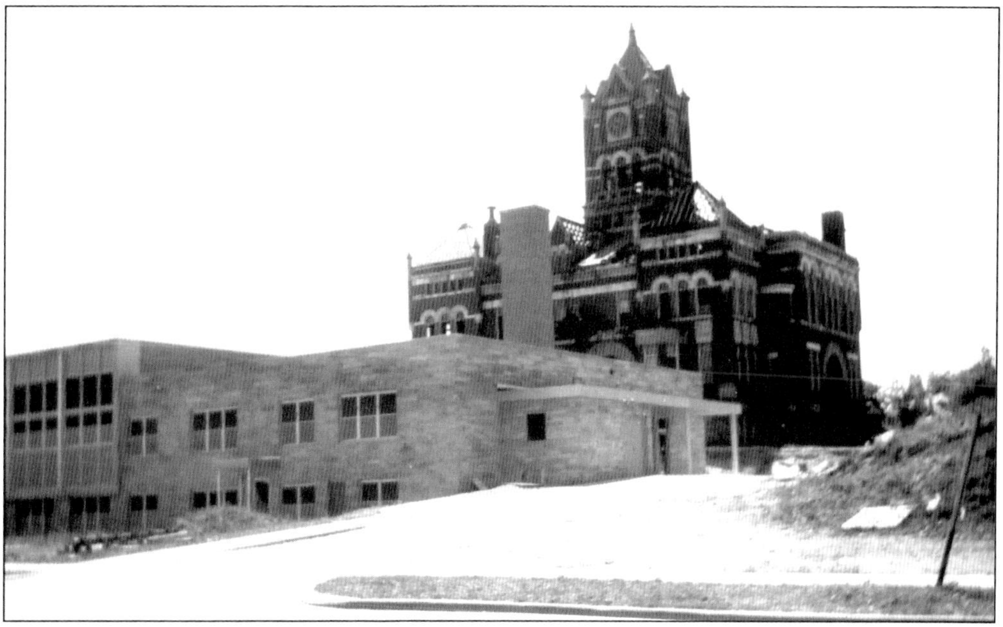

With demolition underway, the new Ralph B. Sytsma county building rises in the shadow of the old courthouse. Demolition was completed in 1961 at a cost of more than $45,000, which exceeded the cost of the beautiful old building by at least $2,000. The clock was saved and remains under the care of the Allegan County Historical Society. The people of Allegan still talk about and mourn the loss of the old courthouse building.

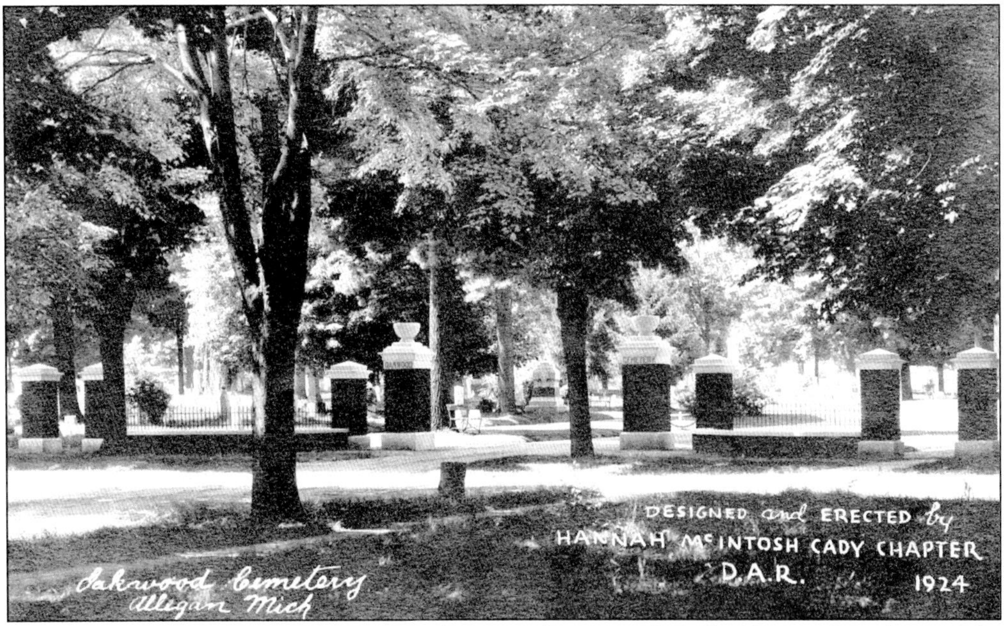

At a sunset ceremony on August 3, 1924, the Hannah McIntosh Cady Chapter, Daughters of the American Revolution, dedicated their gift to the city. Through various fund-raising ventures, they earned money to construct the brick entrance columns at Oakwood Cemetery. They were formally accepted by Mayor William Vosburgh. Two years later, a bronze marker was placed to commemorate the gift.

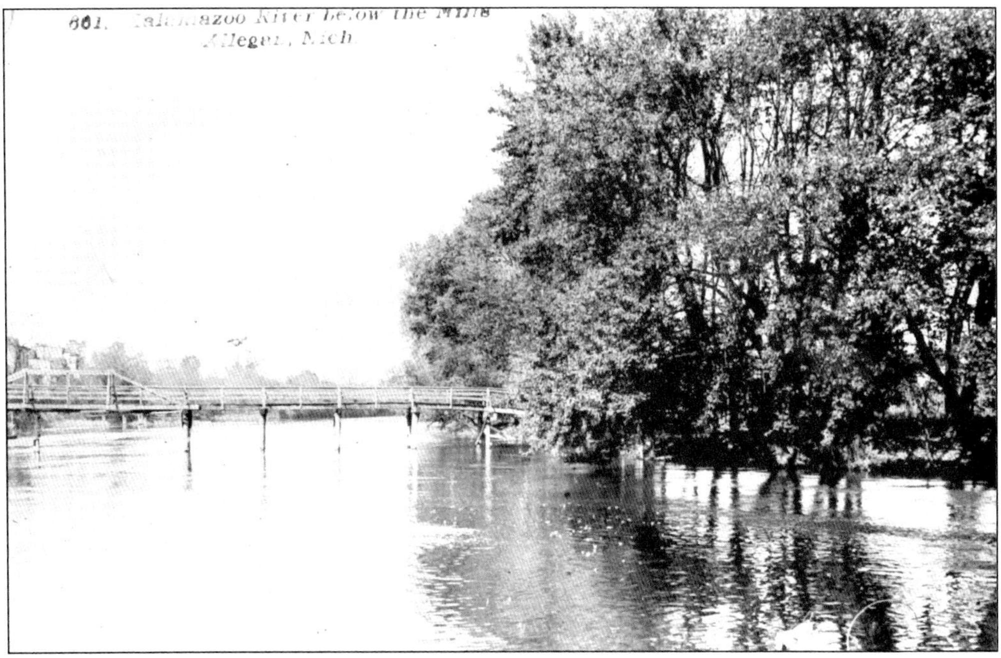

A stroll through Allegan in the late 1800s and early 1900s would have surely taken residents across the wooden footbridge over the Kalamazoo River from Water Street and into Pingree Park. The park was located along the riverbank below the mill district. This was a major recreation area for the people of early Allegan.

Five

PILLS, POTIONS, AND BLOOD (BROTHERS)

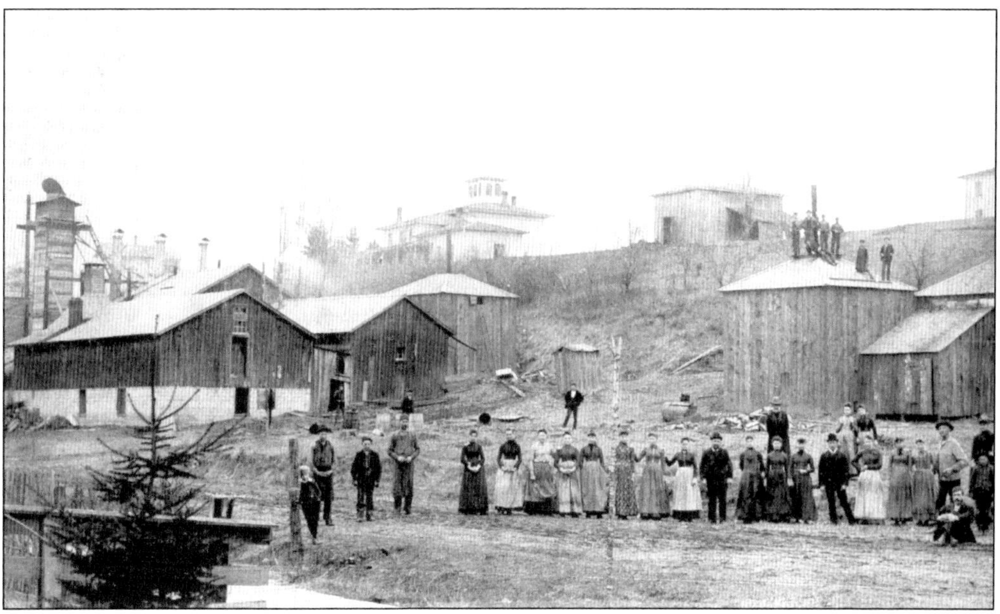

Luther Perrigo's first business venture in Allegan was an apple-drying business in the 1800s. It was located on Park Avenue at the foot of Priest Hill, until destroyed by fire at the beginning of the 20th century. The white house on the hill belonged to Willard Priest, a local builder for whom the hill was named. Leaning against the post in the forefront (left) is Luther's son Ray.

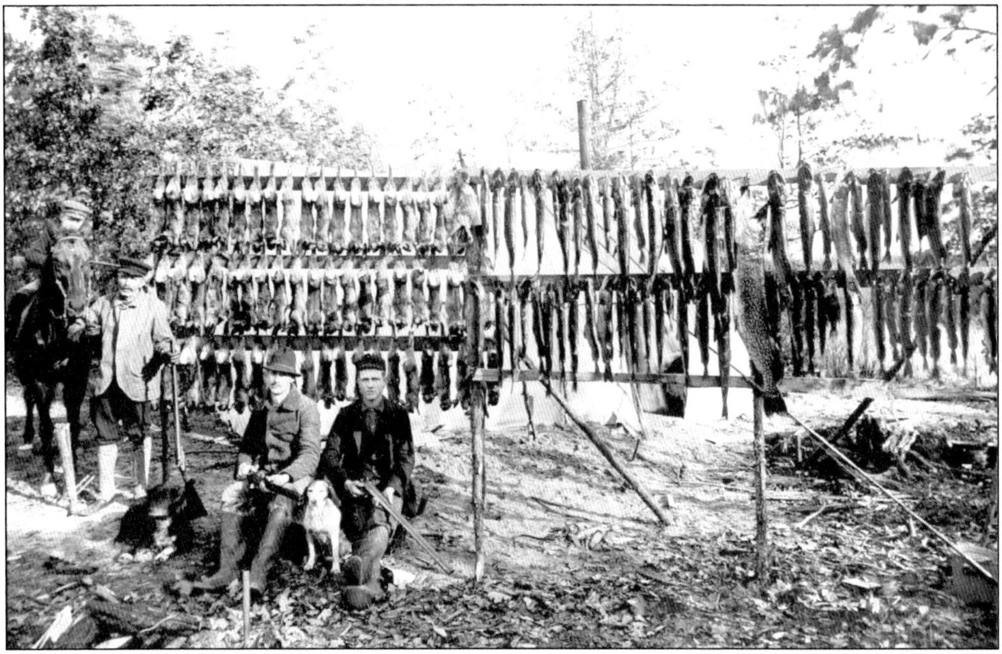

Hunting and fishing camps were common in the Allegan area. This spot was Smith's Mill Pond at Swan Creek. In this 1899 photograph, a young Ray Perrigo sits astride a horse, while father Luther holds the reins. Seated with the dogs are Frank Marty (left) and Frank Switzenberg (right).

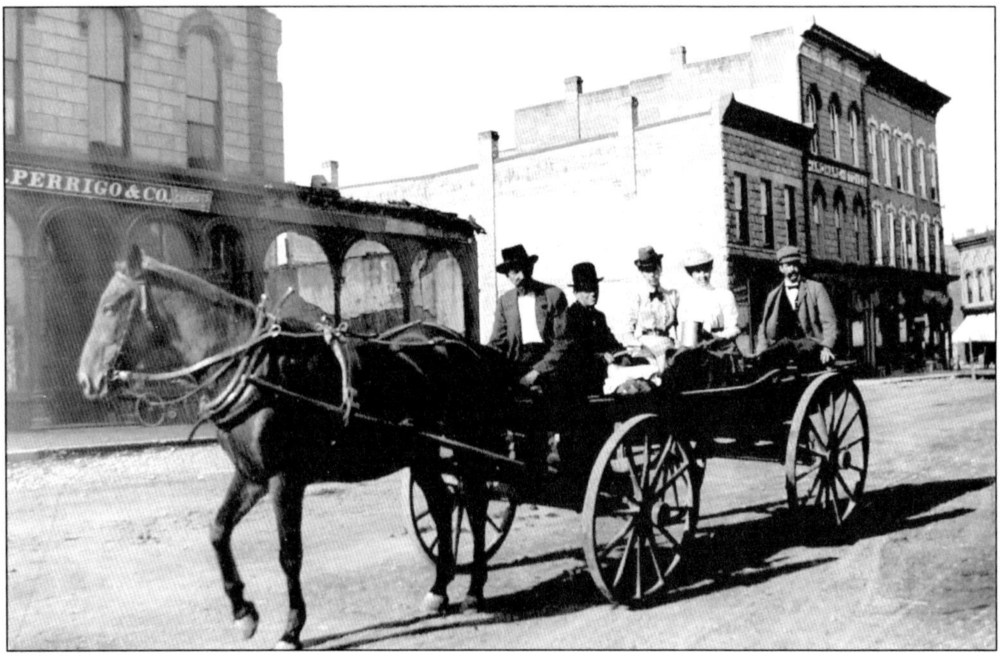

Members of the Perrigo family pose in front of the family store in the late 1800s. Luther's innovative idea to package and distribute patented medicines for home use has grown into the world's largest manufacturer of over-the-counter pharmaceutical and nutritional products for various store brands. (Courtesy Perrigo family.)

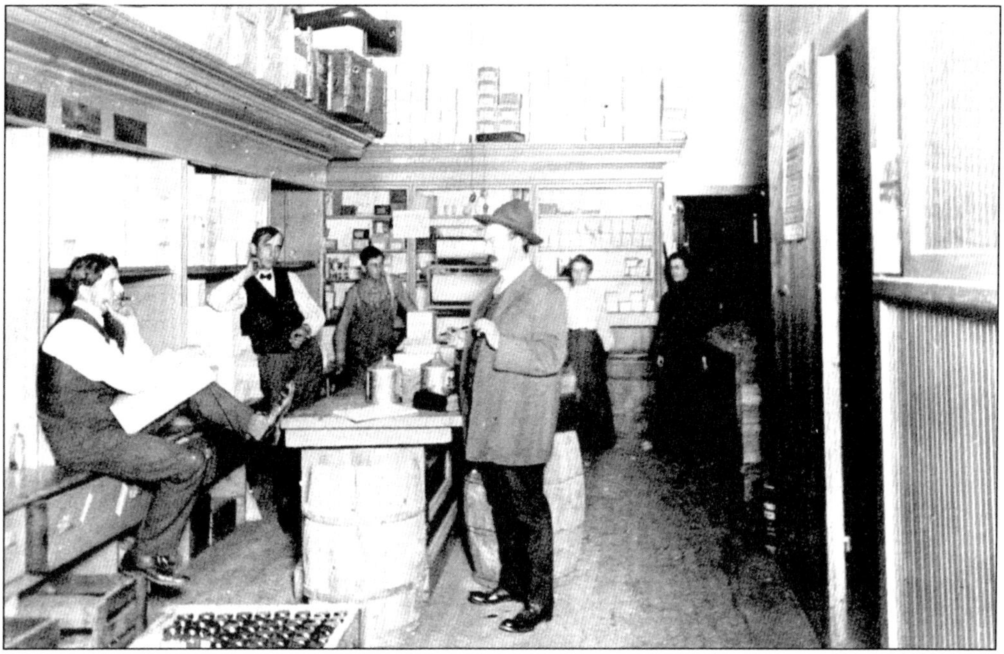

The Perrigo Company's humble beginnings in this small store on Brady Street are in sharp contrast to its world-class status in the pharmaceutical world today. The store was located on the site of the driveway that leads to the parking lot adjacent to the Dr. Mahan Memorial Gazebo. The company now occupies seven buildings in the Allegan area.

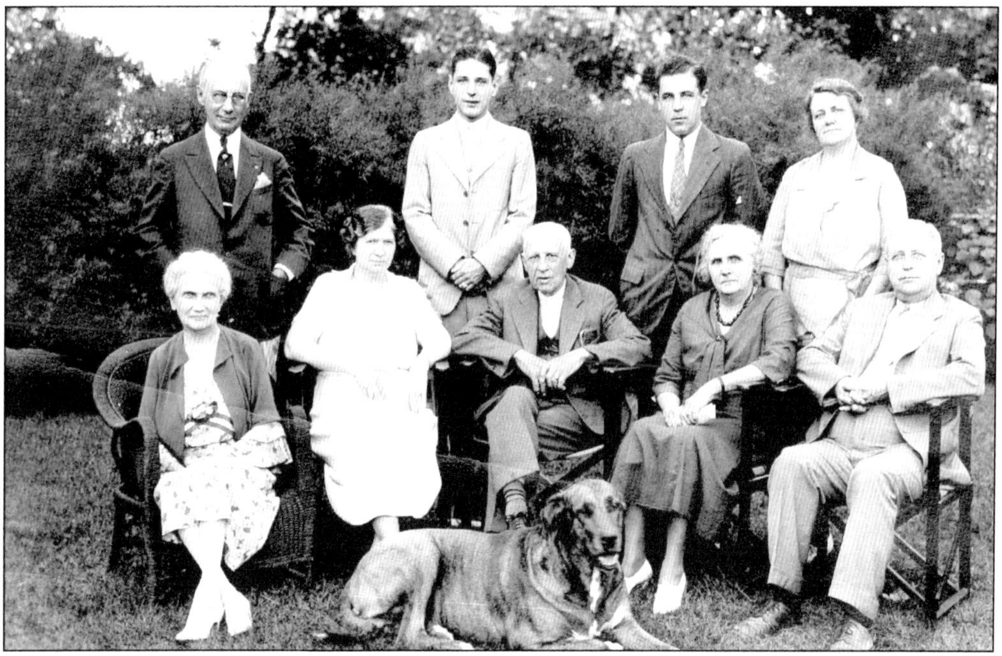

This 1933 photograph shows the immediate family of the Perrigo descendants currently residing in Allegan. Pictured with the family dog Duke are, from left to right, (first row) Mrs. Glenn Smith, Mrs. Charlie Smith, Charlie Smith, "Grandma" Buchanan, and Harry Perrigo; (second row) Glen Smith, Blake Perrigo, Paul Perrigo, and Louise Perrigo. (Courtesy Perrigo family.)

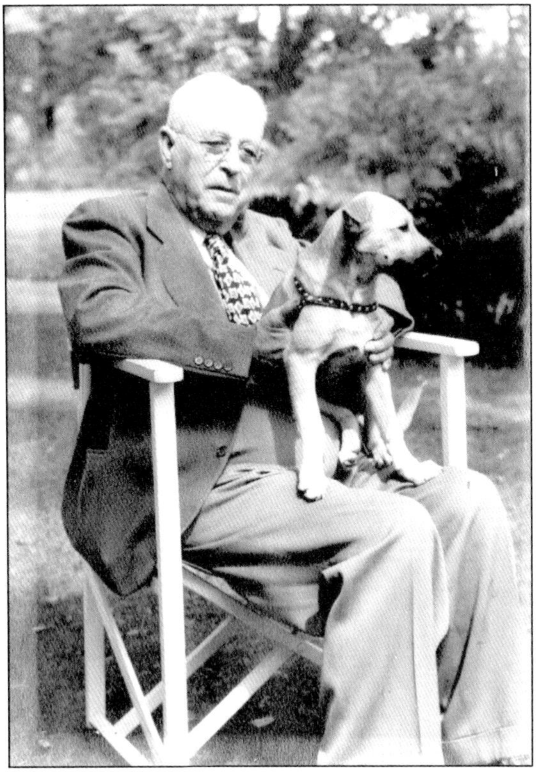

Harry Perrigo, grandson of Luther Perrigo, is shown relaxing with his dog Midge in his yard on Davis Street, about 1951. Harry was the retired president of Perrigo Company and was very active in community affairs throughout his life. His granddaughter Ann Perrigo, director of the Allegan Public Library, believes this may have been one of the last photographs taken of her grandfather. (Courtesy Perrigo family.)

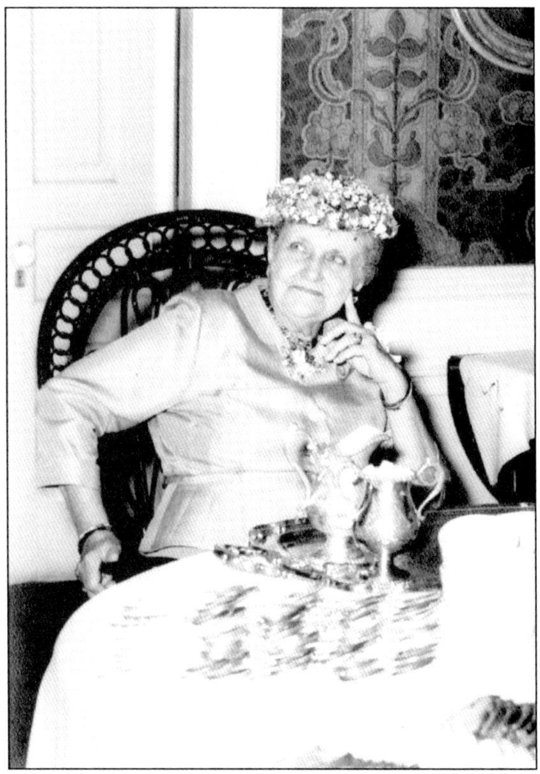

Harry's wife, Louise Perrigo, is shown at the Pritchard home, just south of the Perrigo home on Davis Street, pouring at a Daughters of the American Revolution tea. Like her husband, Louise was also very active in various organizations around town and was easily recognized by her stylish wardrobe and friendly smile. (Courtesy Perrigo family.)

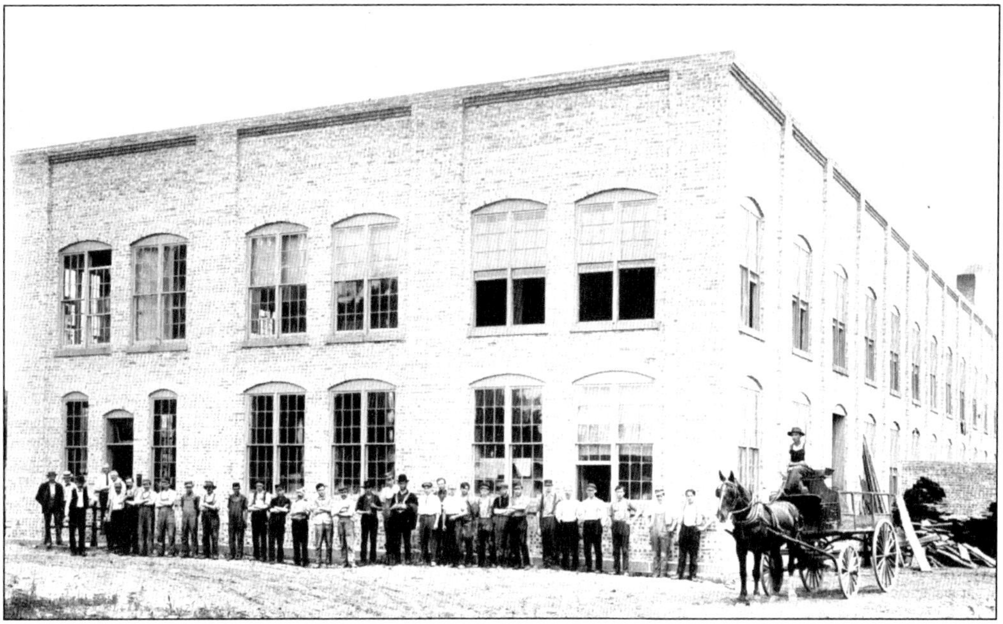

This 1906 photograph shows the Allegan Mirror and Plate Glass Company. In 1914, just after Kalamazoo's Blood Brothers introduced their Cornelian car, Ray Perrigo urged them to relocate to Allegan. Allegan residents purchased stock as a condition of the relocation, and soon Blood Brothers was producing the Cornelian automobile and universal joints in the factory on Glass Street.

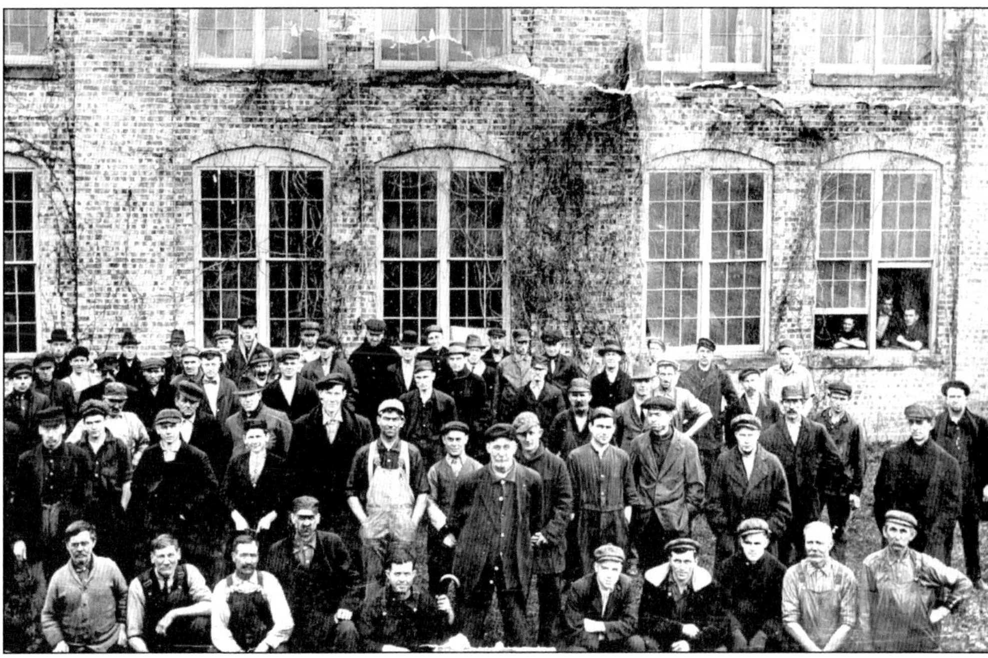

This 1917 photograph shows early employees of Blood Brothers Machine Company on the lawn in front of the plant. The only identified person is, first row squatting, sixth from left, Dewey Huitt. Allegan photographer Joe Ashley was a Blood Brothers employee. Over the years he created a large pictorial history of this important place of business in Allegan's history.

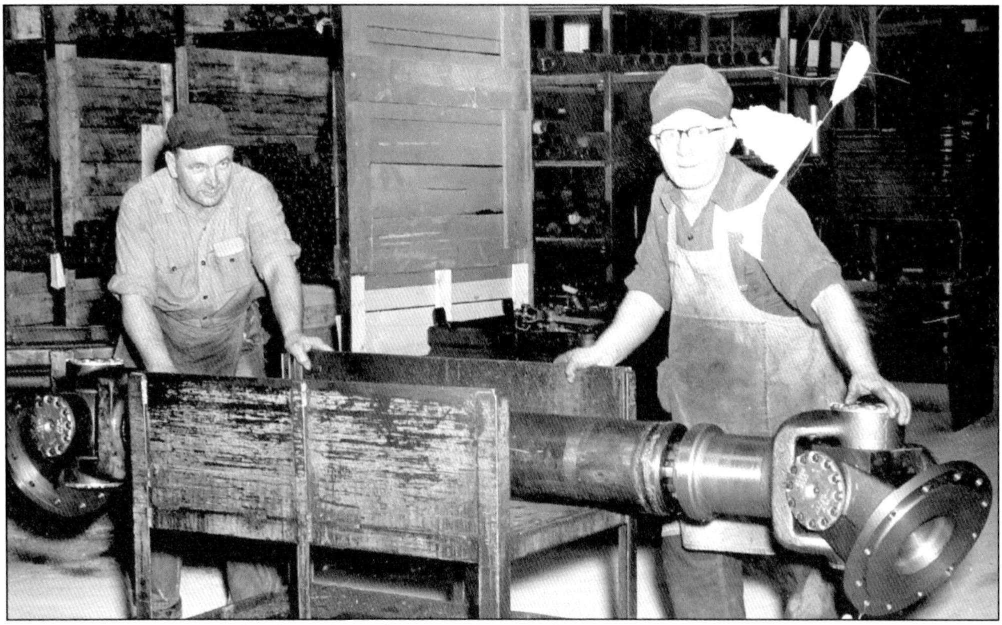

Ival Adams (right, with glasses) and an unidentified man pose with the B-W9 universal joint manufactured at the Blood Brothers Machine Company plant. This part was used to launch planes from aircraft carriers during World War II. Allegan County residents dutifully closed their blackout curtains every night after captured German documents indicated this vital part put our area on the list of German bombing targets.

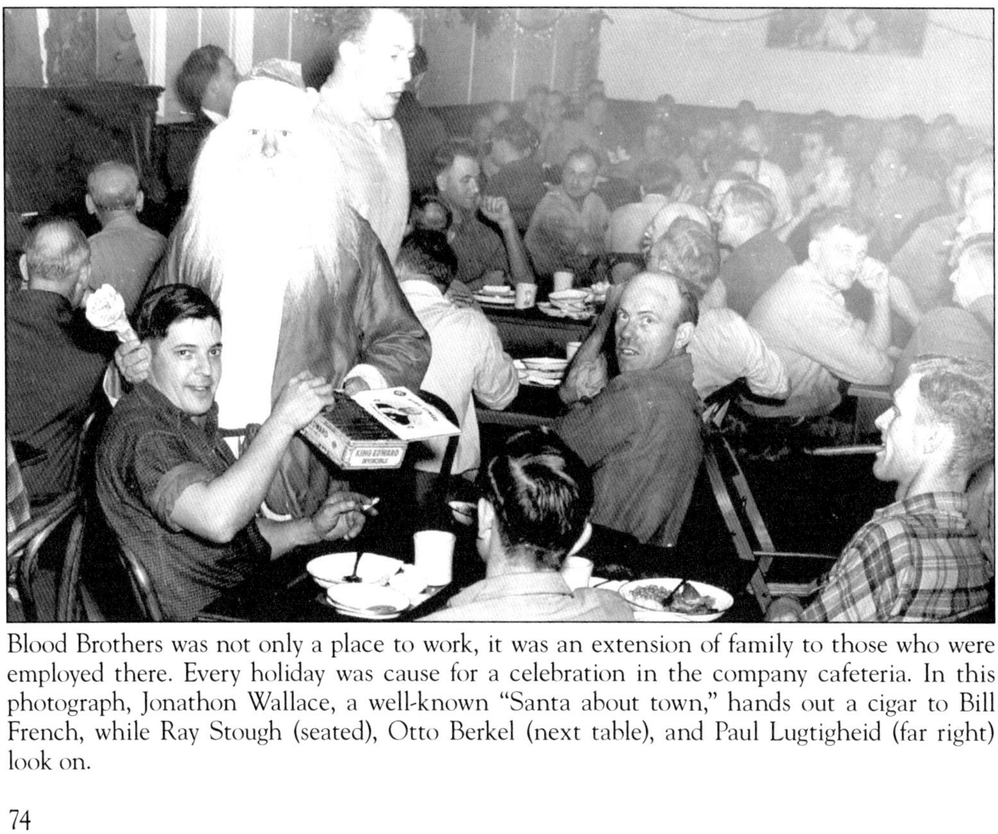

Blood Brothers was not only a place to work, it was an extension of family to those who were employed there. Every holiday was cause for a celebration in the company cafeteria. In this photograph, Jonathon Wallace, a well-known "Santa about town," hands out a cigar to Bill French, while Ray Stough (seated), Otto Berkel (next table), and Paul Lugtigheid (far right) look on.

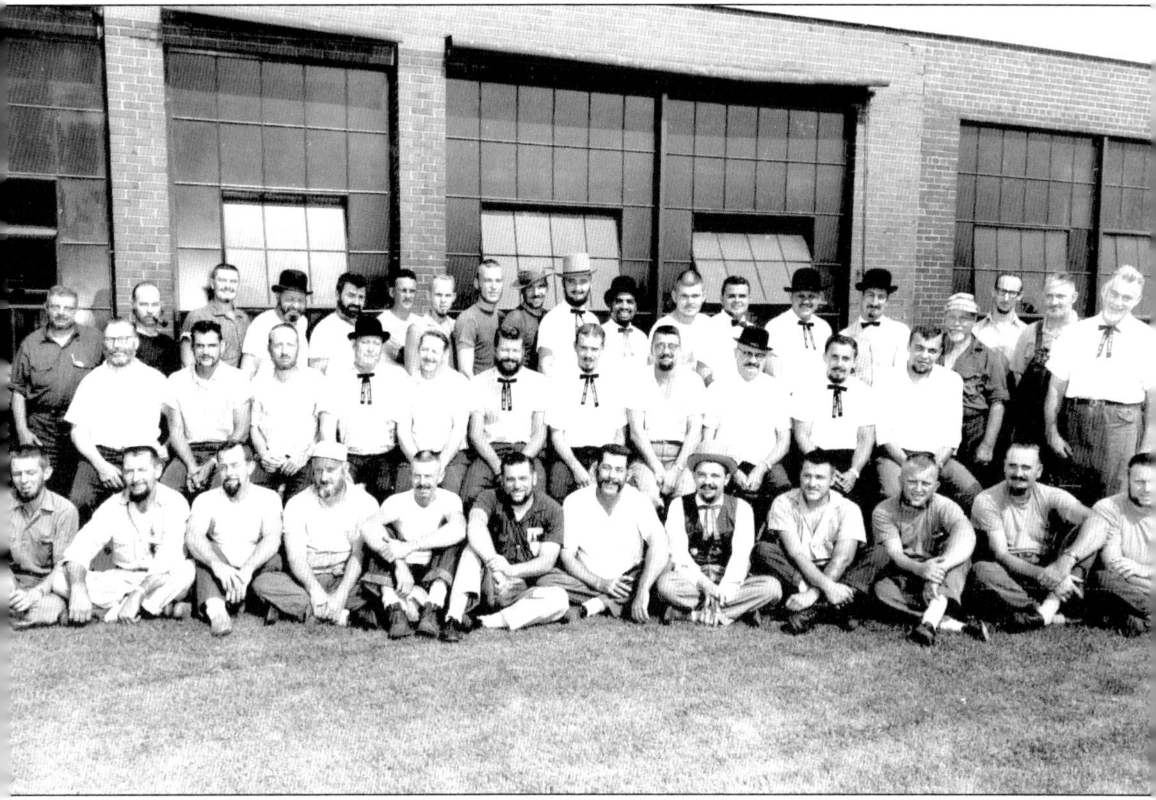

In August 1963, male residents of Allegan were encouraged to grow a beard in celebration of the town's 125th anniversary. Hundreds of men from all walks of life answered the call. Pictured above, in all their tonsorial glory, are Rockwell's "bearded gents." They are, from left to right, (first row) Roger Knoblock, Buck Melvin, Jon Stough, Ken Stewart, Jack Hale, Bud Smith, Ken Plotts, Ray Meiser, Jim Damber, Denver Anderson, Erv Fargo, and Bob Kizer; (second row) Lloyd Martin, Boyd Blain, John Foster, Max Plotts, Red Fuller, Leroy Austin, Dave Flora, Ken Meiser, Bob Gavin, Dan Goodacre, and Tom Goodwin; (third row) Wilber Walters, Gerald Hitchcock, Spike Hilaski, Levi Knobloch, John Crcatovich, Bill Hayes, Hal Truax, Jim Wilson, Robert Nimke, Ron Callender, Charles Butler, Tom Locatis, Bob Earl, Bud Mankins, Herk Banks, Sherm Oisten, Don Parker, Howard Enders, and Russ Rice.

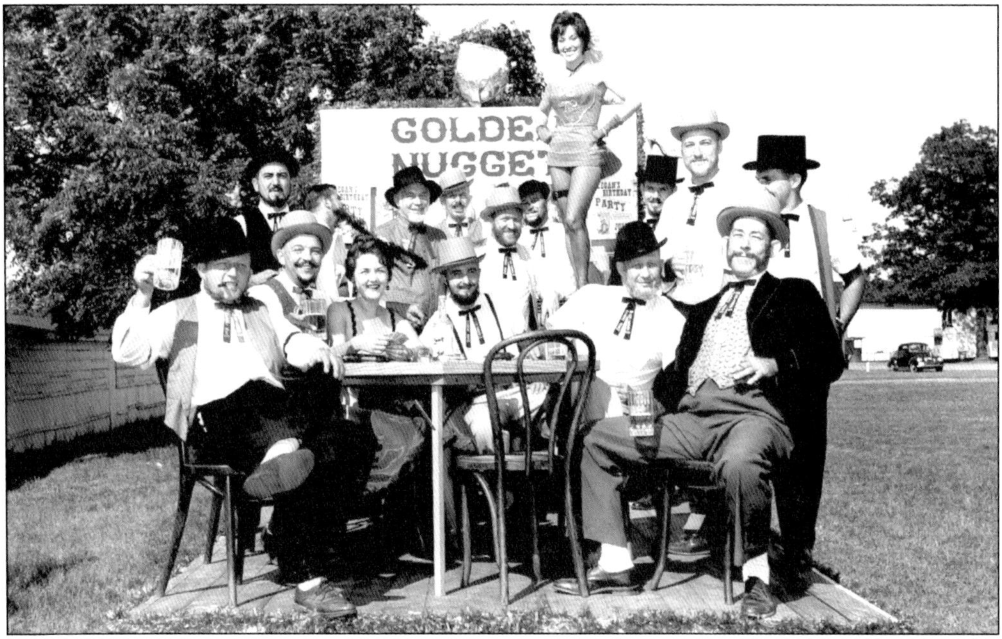

The 1963 Rockwell plant's UAW (United Auto Workers) Local 709 float for the 125th anniversary parade simulated the Golden Nugget saloon on wheels. Posing on their float before joining the parade are, in no particular order, Denver Anderson, Ray Meiser, Ron Callender, Max Plotts, Ken Plotts, Jim DeSmit, and Floyd Miller. Can anyone identify the lovely saloon girls?

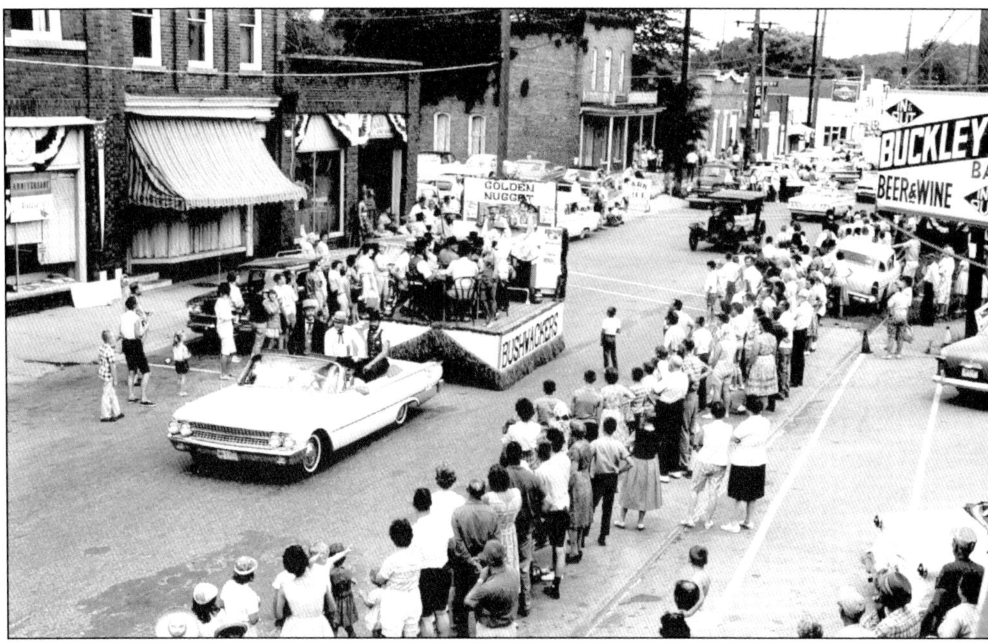

This photograph was taken as the "Bushwacker" float manned by members of UAW Local 709 passed in front of the Oddfellows hall and across from the anniversary celebration headquarters on Water Street. Citizens lined the streets to see the parade, which was one of a number of activities held in conjunction with the anniversary. The Griswold auditorium was kept busy with performances to celebrate the 1963 event.

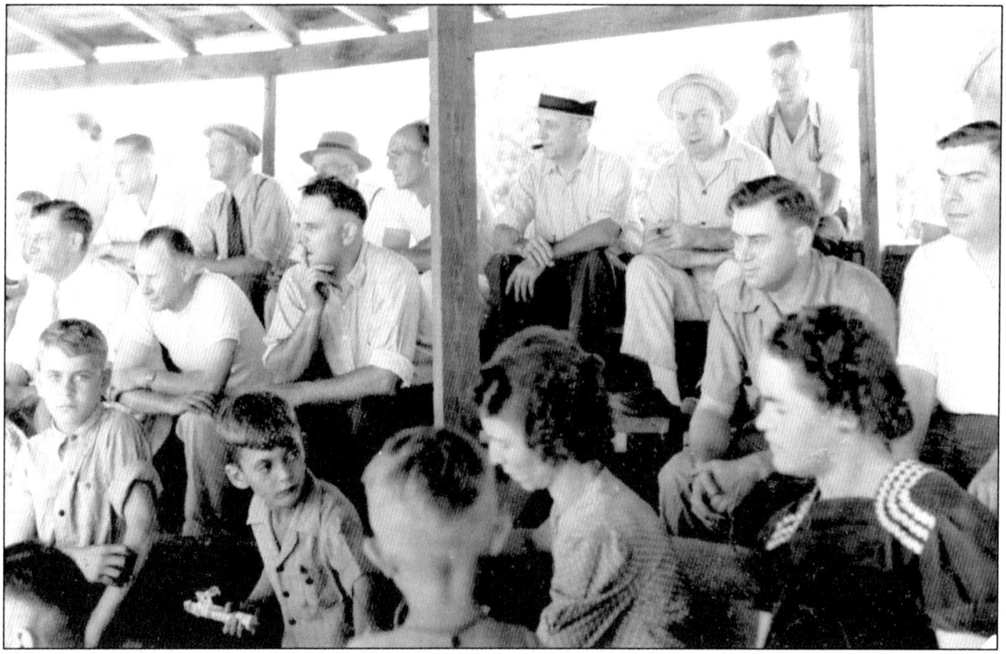

Baseline Lake at the Allegan and Van Buren county line was the site of many Blood Brothers company picnics. The company would plan a day of events, entertainment, and food. The above 1945 photograph, shows employees and family members gathered in the stands, possibly watching a softball game in progress. Lucille Ingalsbee (front right) is the only person identified. Her husband, Leon, was a longtime employee of Blood Brothers.

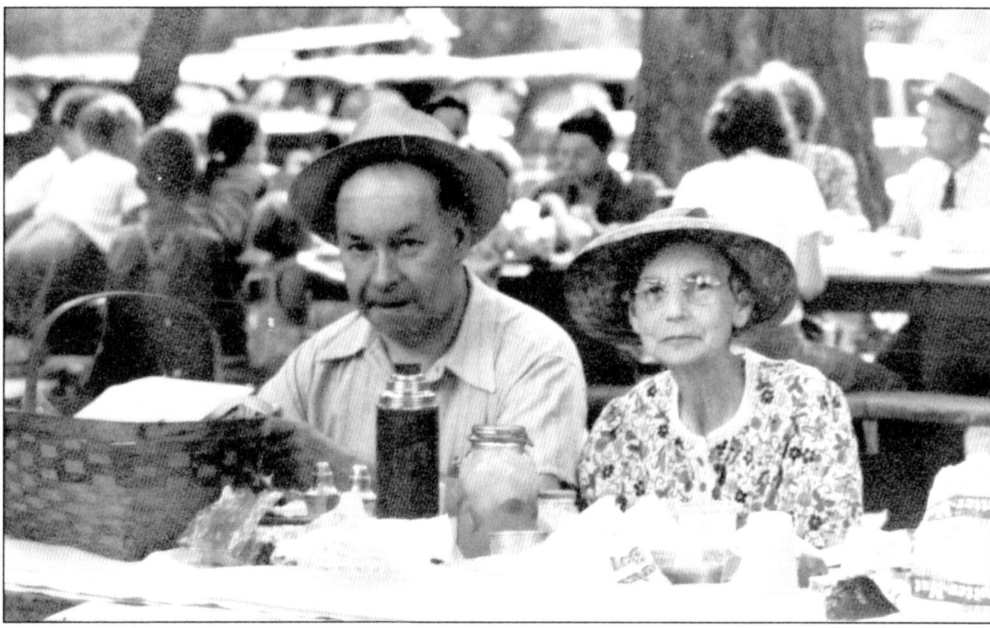

Mr. and Mrs. Charles Hubbell are shown here enjoying their picnic lunch on this lovely summer day in 1945. Charlie was a union leader at Blood Brothers for many years. The Baseline Lake park was perfect for the company picnic, with its baseball diamond, bleachers, and a shaded area with picnic tables.

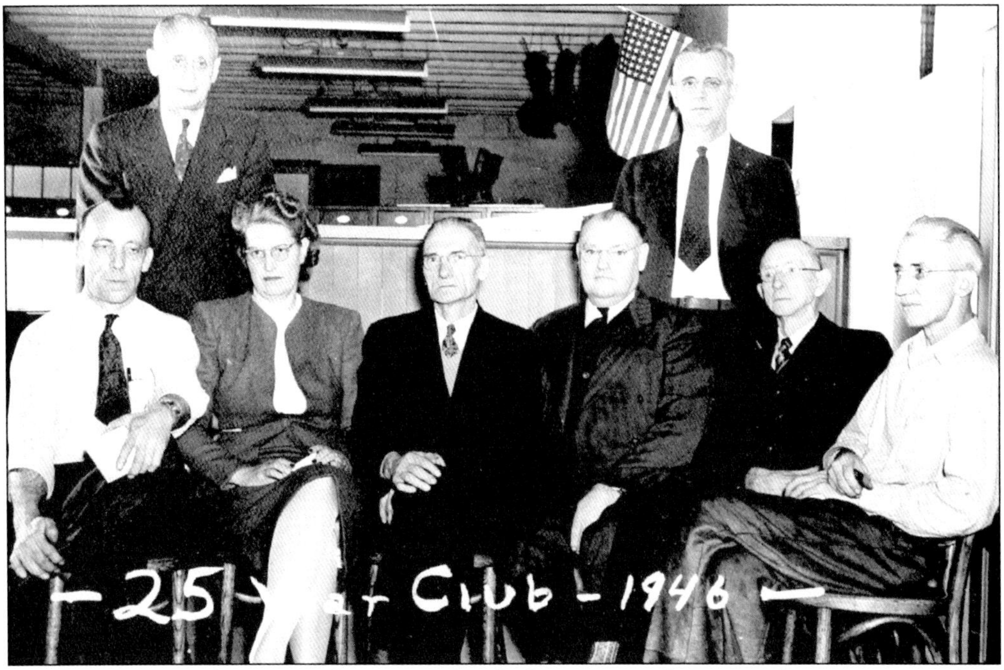

Blood Brothers employees usually remained with the company for years. The company regularly recognized long-term employees. In this 1946 photograph are new members of the 25-year club, from left to right, (first row) Jay Marshall, Marge Cole, Walt Bussey, Corlan Wood, Frank Reams, and Walt Hitchcock. Eventually Marge Cole would receive a 45-year pin before retiring in the 1960s. Standing behind them are Glenn Wilbur (left) and Rock Myers (right).

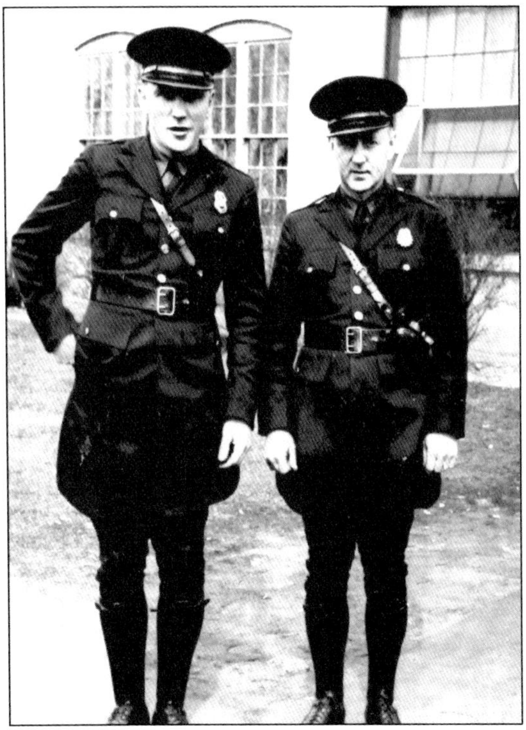

During World War II, due to the perceived threat from manufacturing important war effort parts, Blood Brothers was designated a war defense plant. Visitors were required to obtain a permit at the guard gate before entering the plant. The guards were also issued uniforms as added security. In this 1942 photograph are Ernest Wilson (left) and Roy Ellis (right), dressed in the newly issued uniforms for Blood Brothers watchmen and guards.

This c. 1950 photograph shows Blood Brothers management personnel handing Allegan's well-known and respected Dr. J. E. Mahan donations for an unidentified charity. From left to right are Mildred Brackett, Dr. Mahan, Bob Gibson, and John Katherler. Blood Brothers and its employees were always ready to step forward when there was need for charitable contributions.

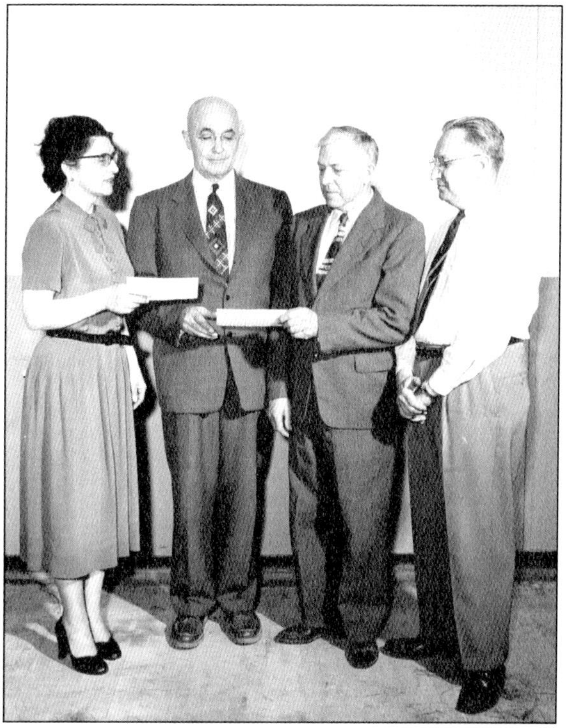

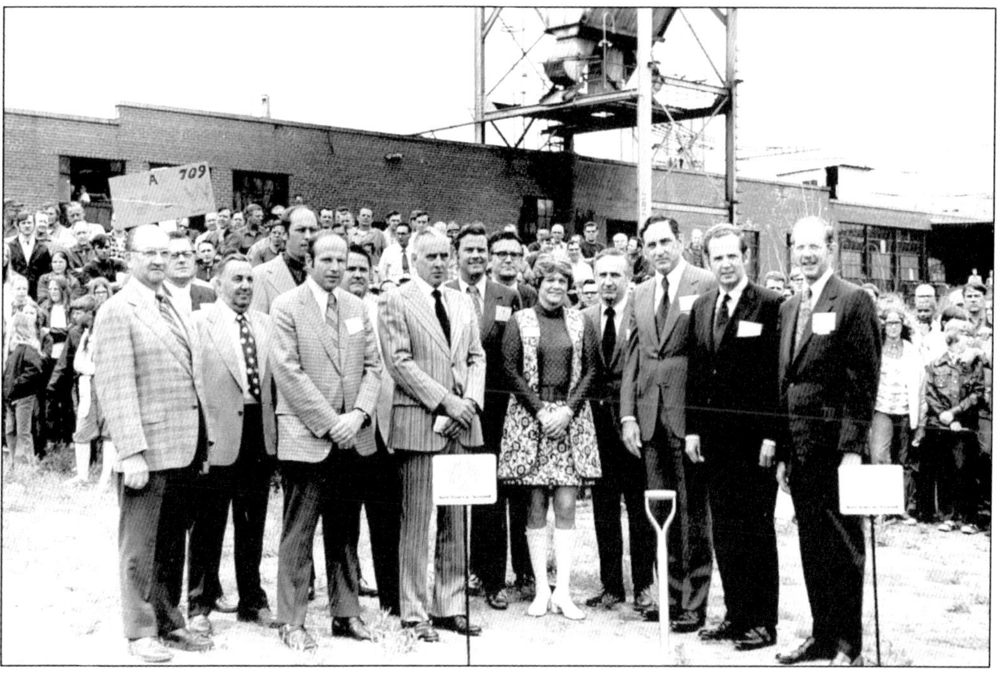

In this 1972 photograph, Michigan governor William Milliken, second from right, has come to Allegan to wield the gold groundbreaking shovel for a 100,000-square-foot expansion to Blood Brothers plant. All Blood Brothers employees were invited to attend. Others identified, in no particular order, are T. E. Malila, James Rolfe, ? Bollinger, Hank Barber, Don Wilbur, James Green, Mrs. Stone, and Joe Armstrong. The shovel used was donated to the museum.

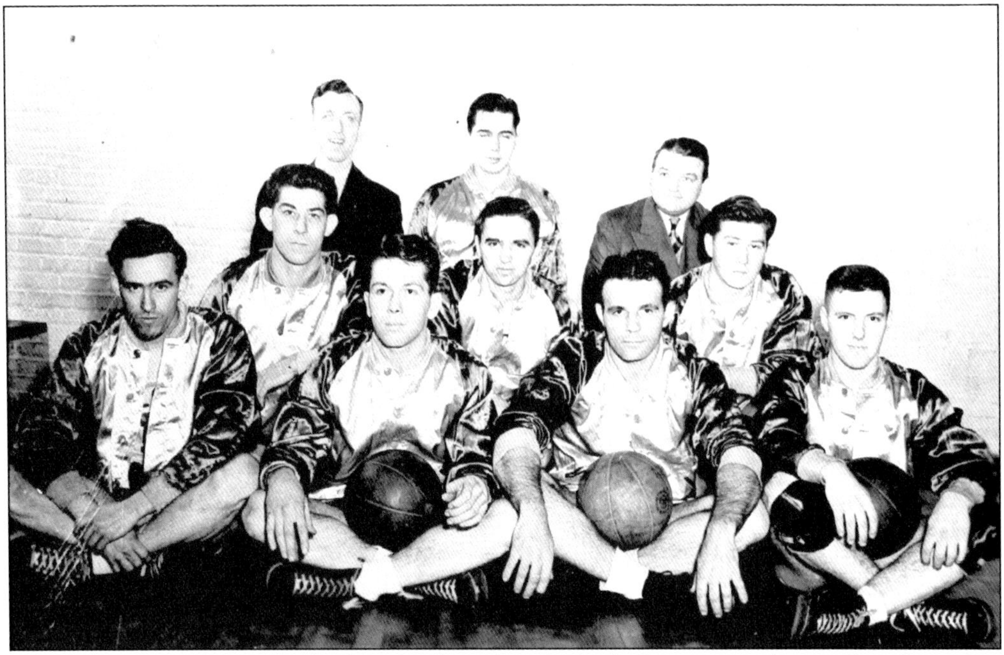

This c. 1950 photograph shows the Blood Brothers basketball team suited up and ready to play. Shown are, from left to right, (first row) Walt Smith, Bill Collins, Zeb Jones, and Basil Ellis; (second row) Ken Plotts, ? Shaffren, and Stan Brokus; (third row) coach Hugh Bridgeman, player Jerry Vahue, and coach Norm Kirk.

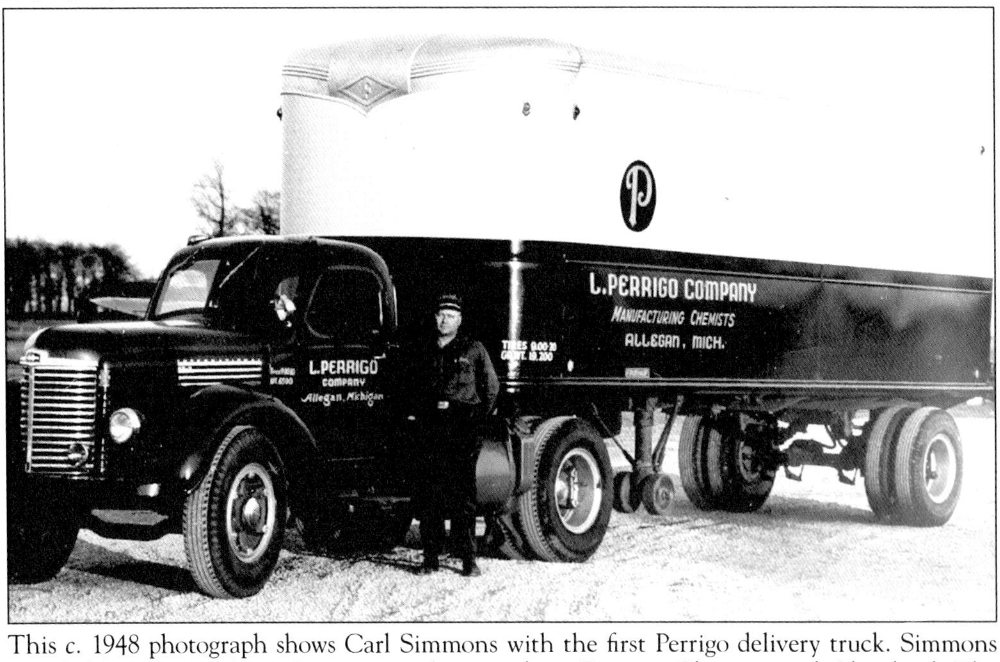

This c. 1948 photograph shows Carl Simmons with the first Perrigo delivery truck. Simmons traveled locally and long distance to places such as Detroit, Chicago, and Cleveland. The Perrigo Company began using its own trucks for local delivery only in the 1970s. Today Blood Brothers is gone, however, Perrigo is still a major factor in Allegan with seven plants and over 2,800 employees locally.

Six

Grand Homes

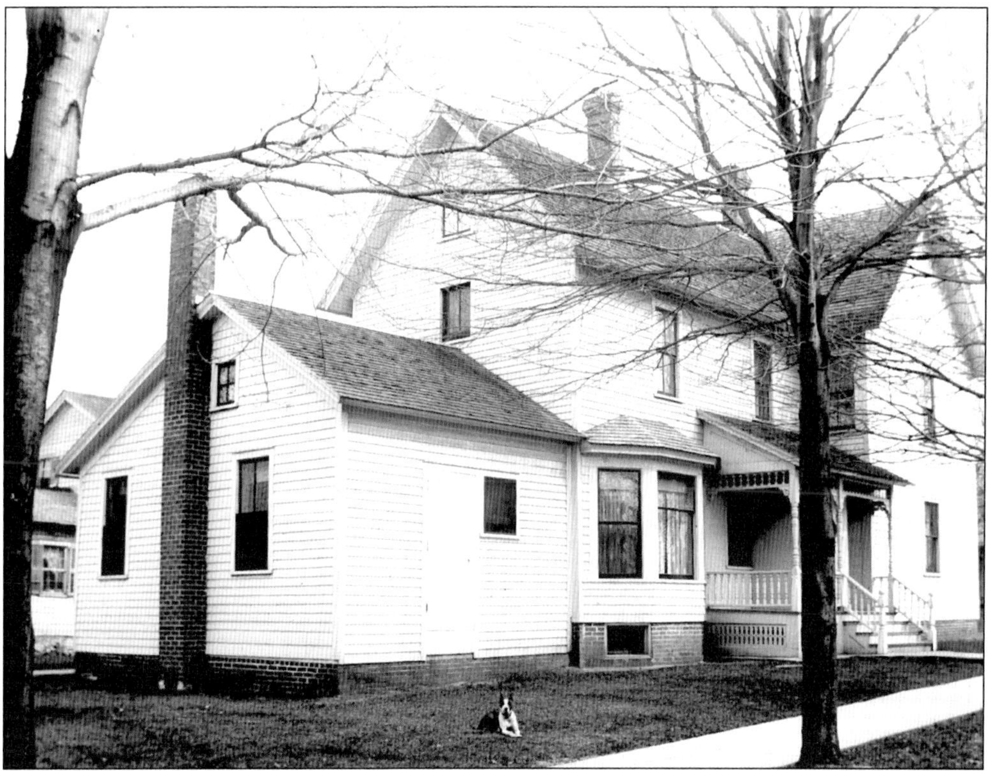

This 1888 home at the corner of Cutler and Cedar Streets was built for shoe salesman George F. Peck with his grand prize winnings from the Louisiana State Lottery. Built-in closets were a rarity then, with wardrobes and armoires serving the purpose of household storage. Ahead of her time, Ella Peck demanded that each room have a closet.

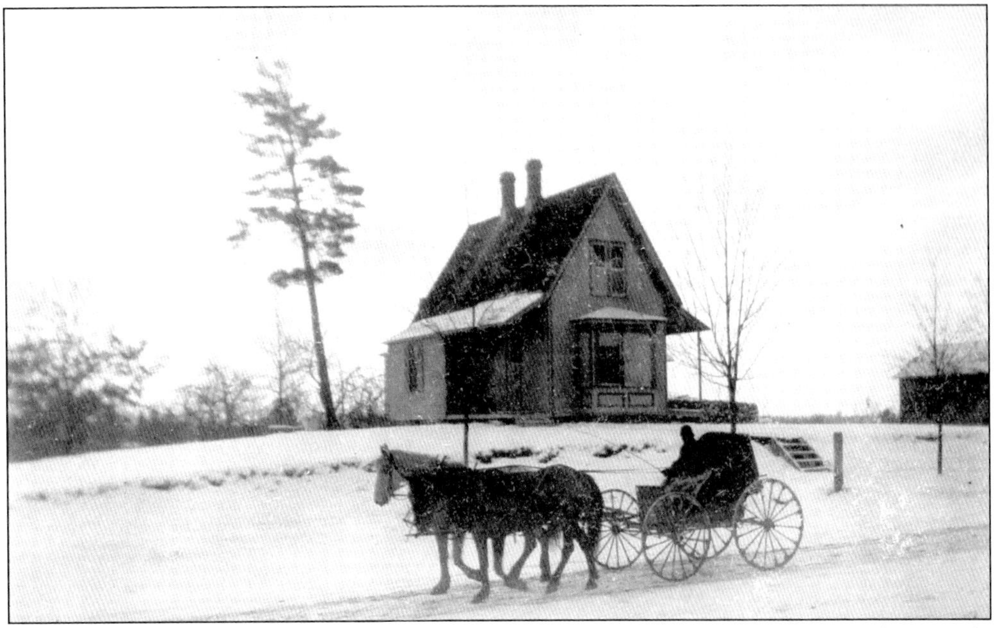

The 1858 Theron Hudson home is shown at the top of Ely Street hill in this early photograph. Hudson was a bookkeeper for Nathaniel West, owner of a sash, floor, and blind factory. Today this home still stands, surrounded by neighboring homes and showing little exterior modification. In the mid-20th century, it was the home of Elmer Rewalt, who taught driver education at Allegan High School.

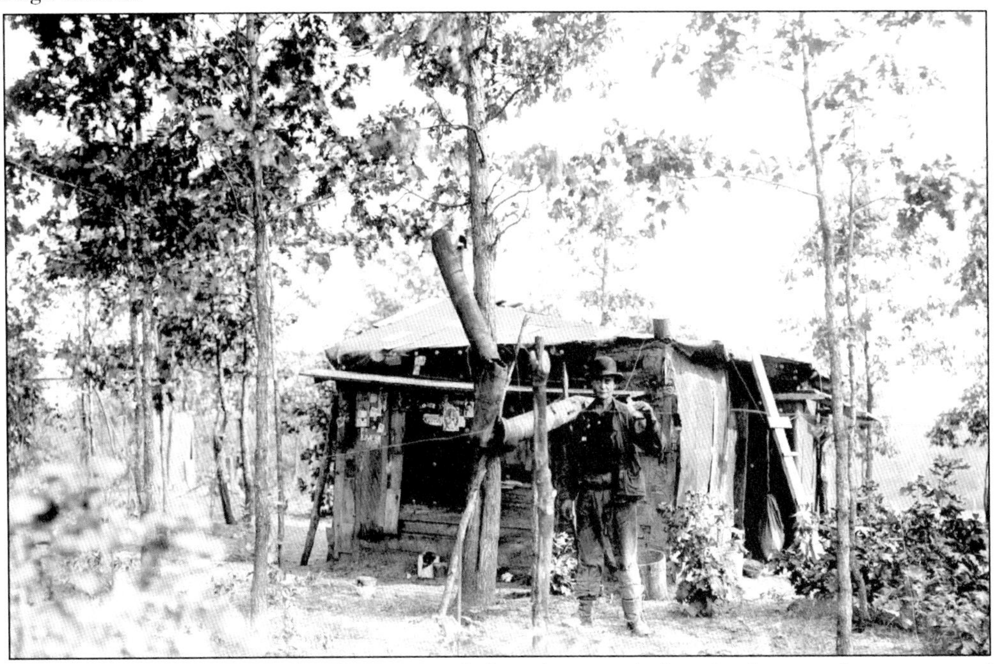

Photographer William Vosburgh captioned this photograph "a suburban residence—city of Allegan." Although the gentleman standing in front of his home is unidentified and the date is not available, his attempt to personalize it with signs and photographs is evident. An interesting architectural feature is the stovepipe protruding from the front of the residence.

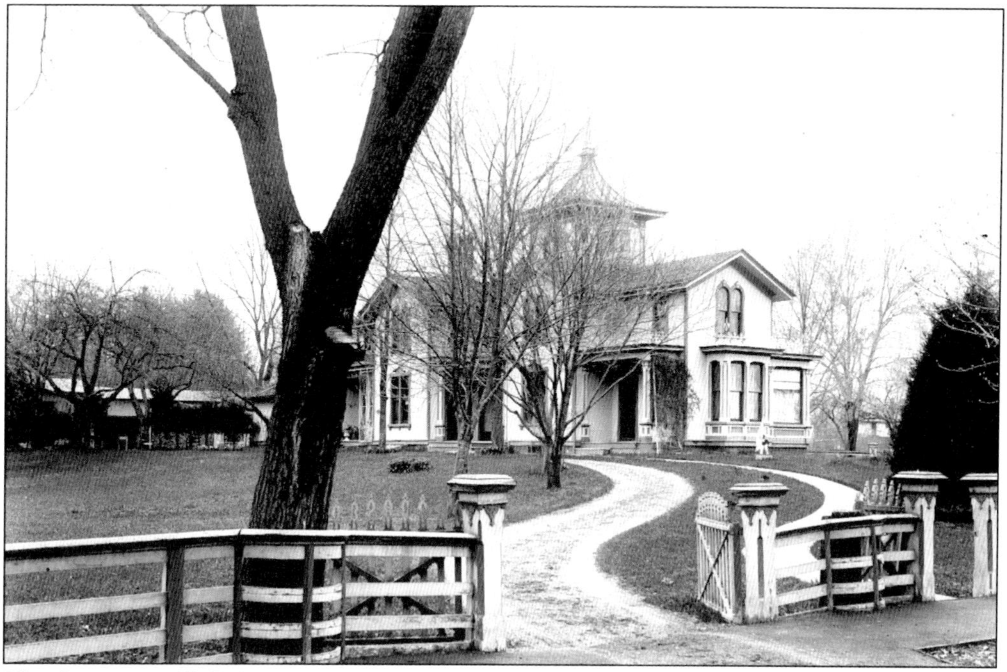

This home at 107 DeLano Street was originally the home of lumberman O. T. Booth. An amateur architect, Booth designed and built this home in 1868–1871. He designed several other homes in the area, specializing in corner lot designs. Hollister Marsh became owner in 1881, followed around 1921 by Siebe Baker, founder of Baker Furniture Company, and Ray Perrigo, son of Luther Perrigo, around 1940.

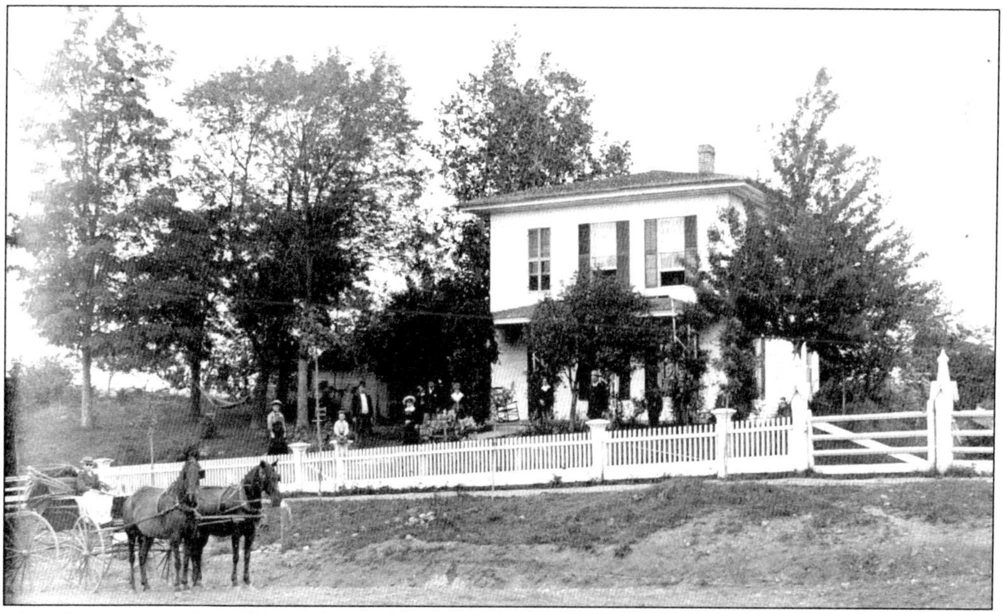

This home, which still stands at the top of Marshall Street hill, once was the home of Dr. Charles C. Flinn. It was built by Nathaniel Dickinson, a relative of Alby Rossman, and was also the home for many years of the Oliver family. The Oliver brothers, George and Andrew, founded a furniture business that was family-run for years.

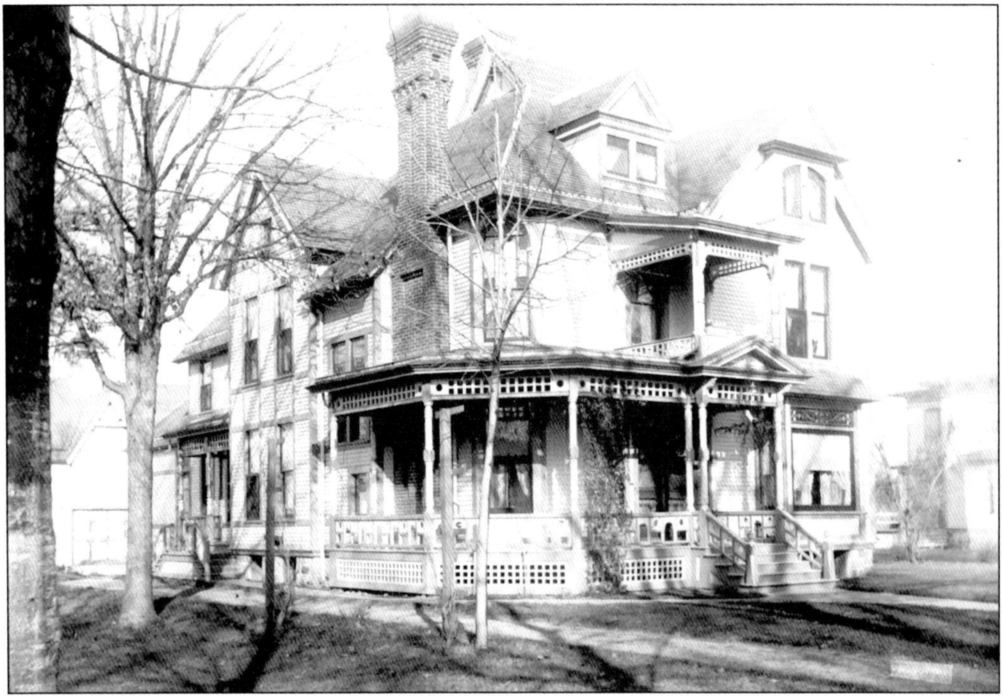

This lovely 1886 home, located at 330 Monroe Street, was originally the home of local merchant M. C. Sherwood. In later years, it was the home of the Armintrout family. This photograph, taken in 1934, shows a more intricate design than the home today.

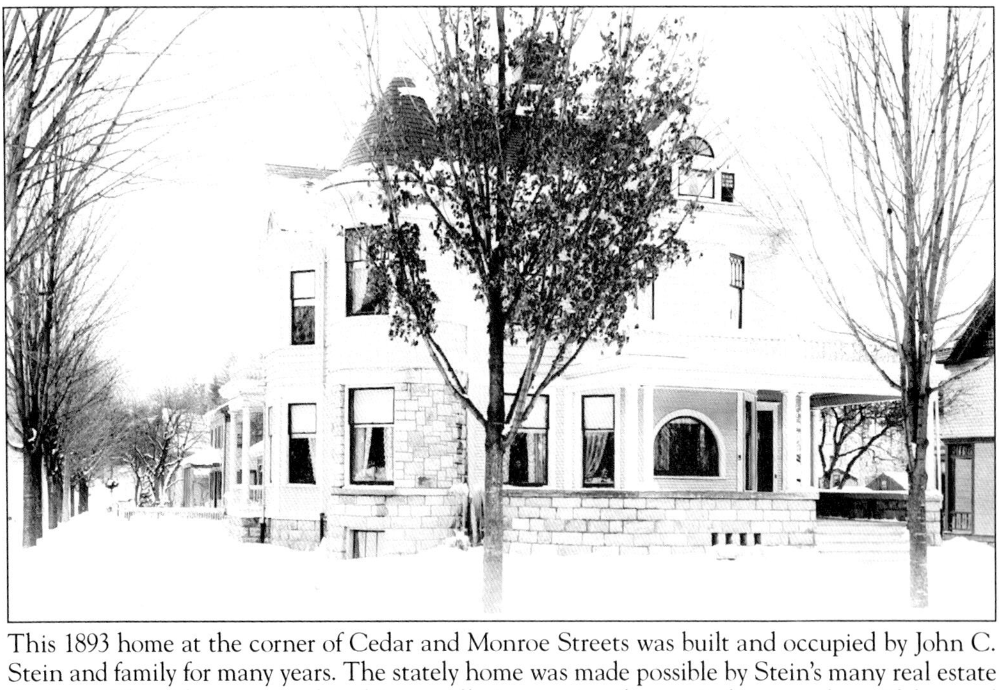

This 1893 home at the corner of Cedar and Monroe Streets was built and occupied by John C. Stein and family for many years. The stately home was made possible by Stein's many real estate dealings. The side turret and architecturally interesting front windows are beautiful period features of the home, which still stands on this historical intersection.

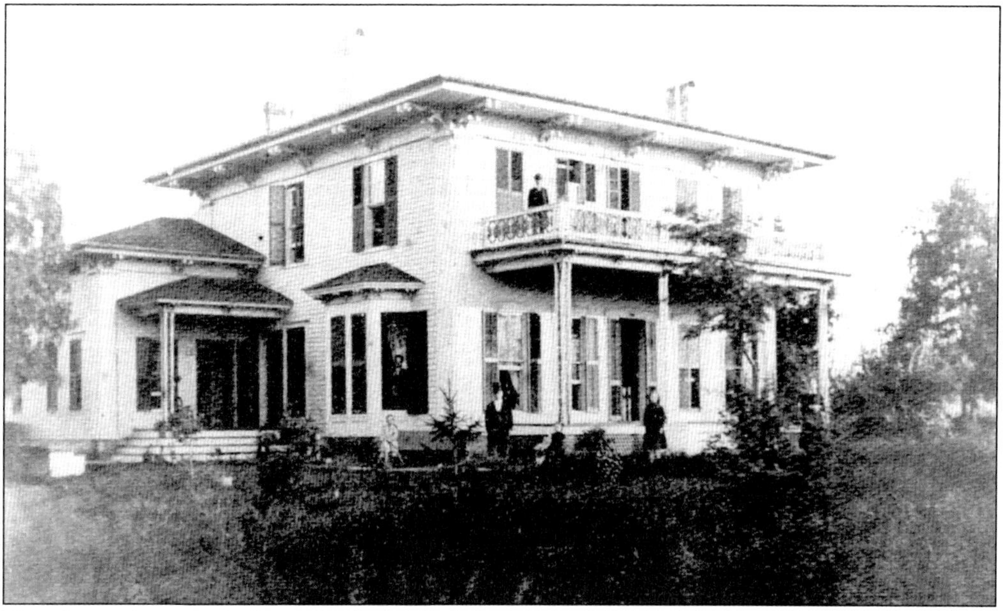

The above photograph shows the home built and designed in 1863 by James R. Rockwell for the Jenner family. Rockwell also built the identical Wetmore home in Monterey Township at around the same time. The Ely Street home was later occupied by Judge Ford Stratton, Nyberg Funeral Home, and most recently the Church of the Latter Day Saints.

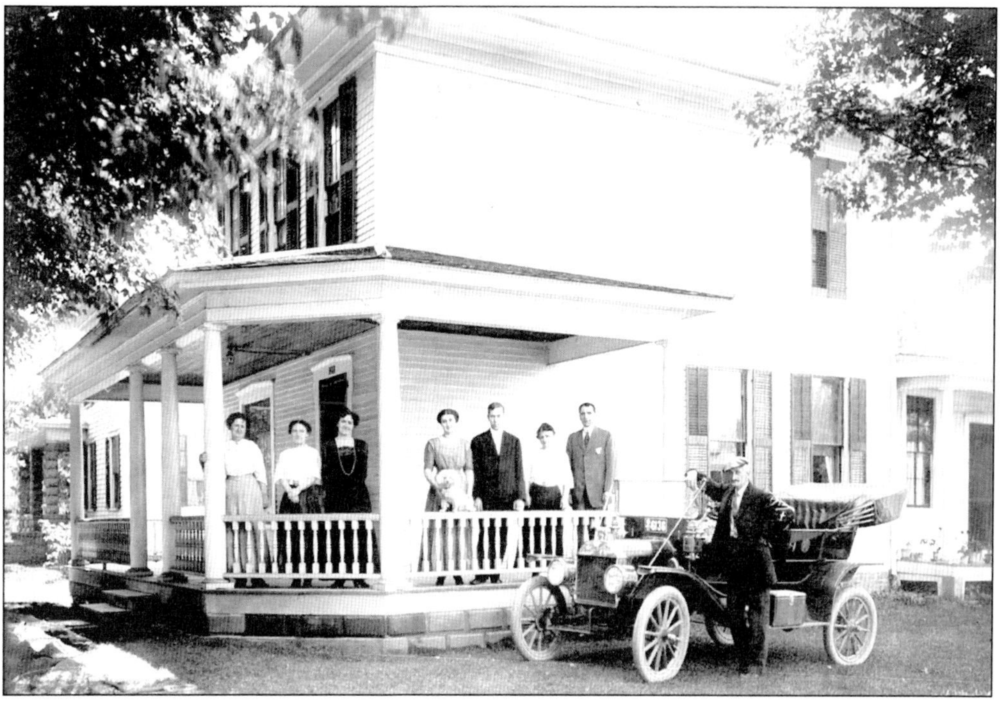

Local merchant, photographer, and mayor William Vosburgh built this home at 123 Grand Street from deadhead logs discarded by nearby Dewing sawmill. Vosburgh is shown here beside his prized automobile. According to the notation on the photograph, his wife was accustomed to sitting in the back seat and telling him how to drive. This later became the home of Ralph Ream.

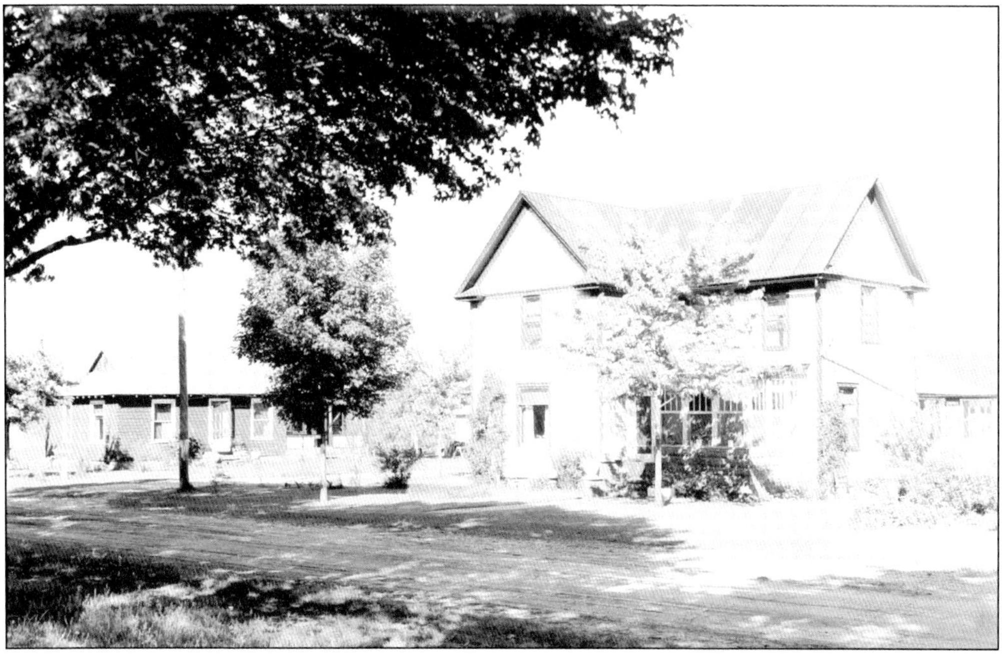

The above photograph shows two Allegan homes. The home on the left is on Kalamazoo Street with the river directly behind it, and was built in 1927 by Ed Whitney and his son Irvin. The home on the right is on Fourth Street and was also owned by Ed Whitney. He operated his Whitney Burial Vault business in a building in the rear.

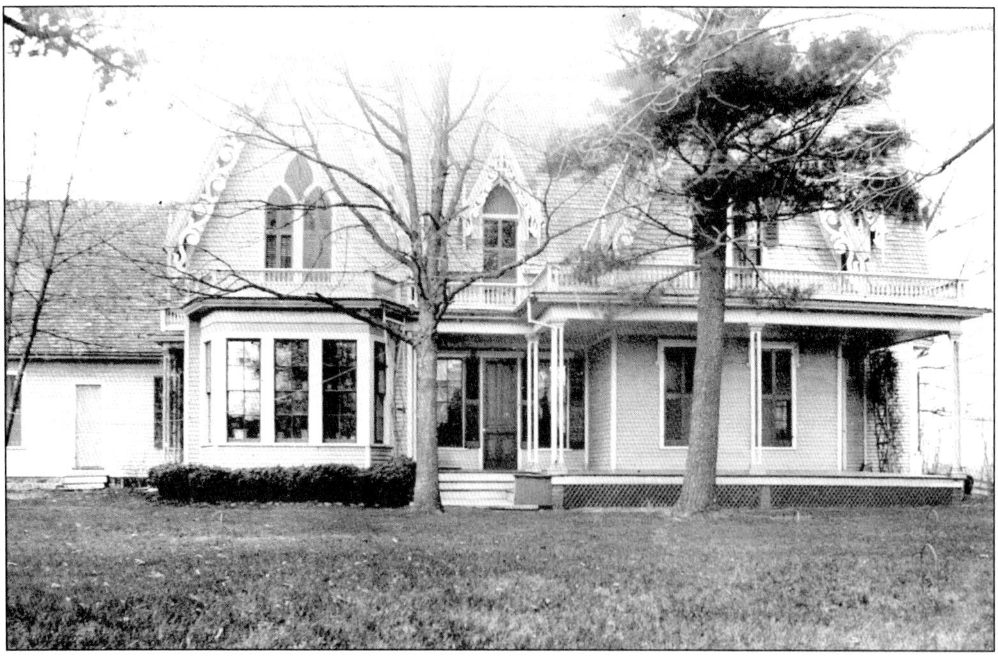

Shown above is the 1866 Davis Street home of Gen. Benjamin Pritchard. Mary Pritchard had been injured in a train accident in the early years of their marriage and spent most of her time in a wheelchair. Painting became her passion. The general added the long windows on the left to provide her with natural sunlight in the room where she spent many hours painting.

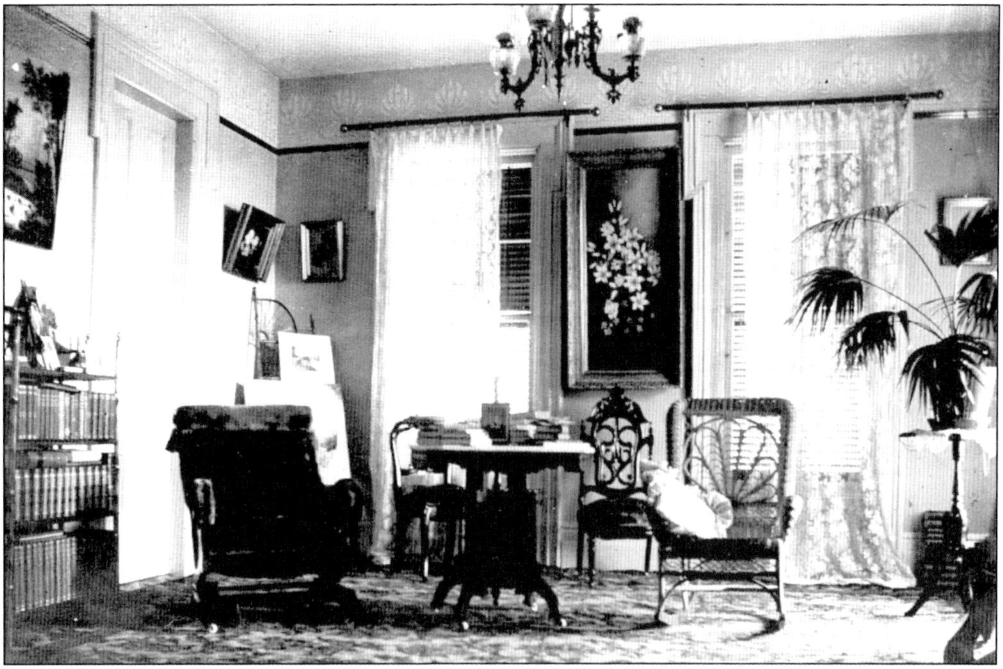

This c. 1900 photograph shows the interior parlor of the Gen. Benjamin Pritchard home at the time his grandson Dudley Pritchard lived in the home. General Pritchard built the home himself, and there is a lovely curved staircase in the front hall. Nearly the entire town of Allegan can be seen from the hilltop where the Pritchard home is located.

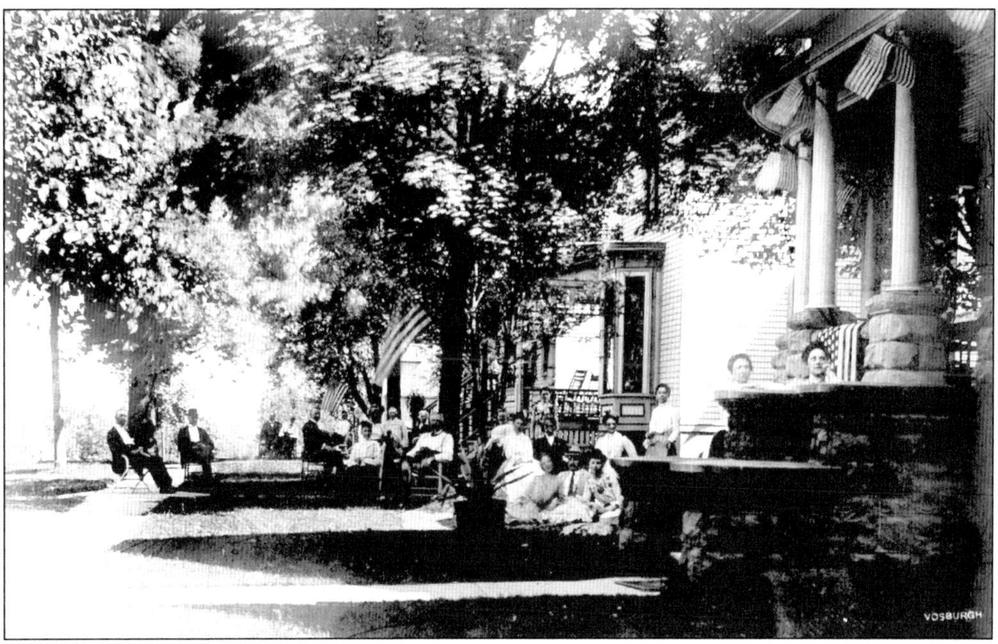

Harold C. Weeks had a successful land abstract and real estate office. He built this home (foreground) on Crescent Street in 1894, near the homes of attorney Hannibal Hart and the first home of Judge Philip Padgham. Neighbors along the street are enjoying an early-20th-century Fourth of July celebration, with each home decorated appropriately with American flags.

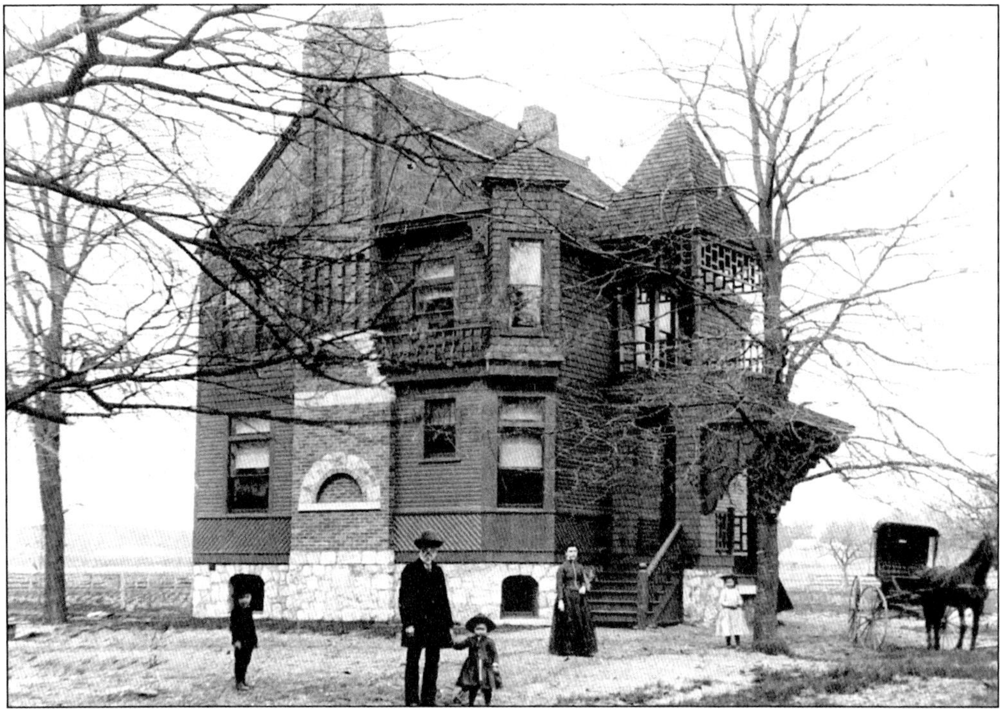

Harlow Higginbotham personally designed this home for his family. It was built in 1887 and was originally located on River Street. In 1991, it was moved to North Main Street. Elizabeth Higginbotham refused to "leave civilization" in New York unless she could bring her piano. It was loaded on an ox cart for the 1840 trip and later was donated to the Old Jail Museum.

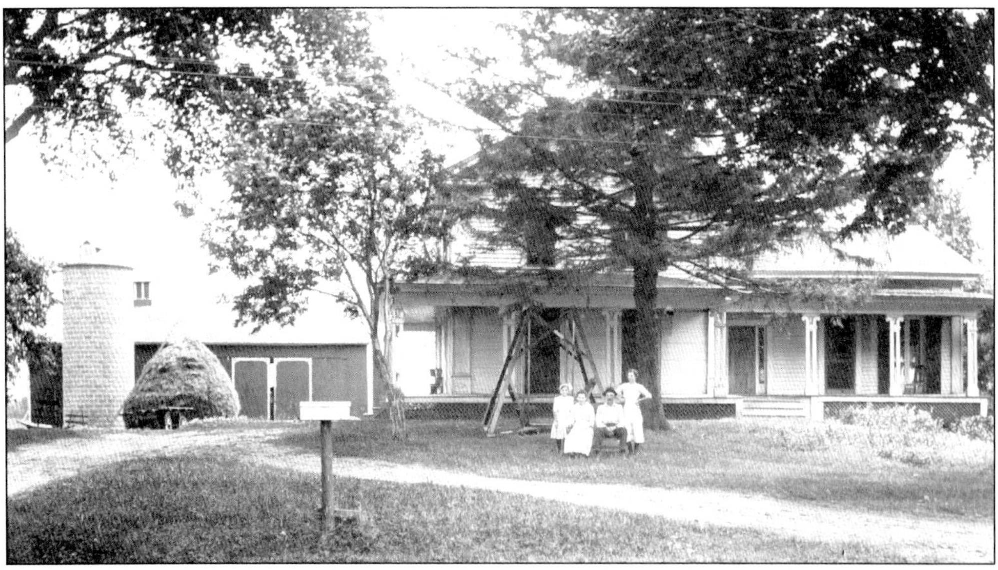

Samuel Hubbard, a member of the Boston Company group that developed Allegan, built this farmhouse in Trowbridge Township in 1836. Local legend tells of a lumberjack, killed in a barroom knife fight and buried on the property, who still returns as a friendly spirit. Today the farmhouse is the Grill House, and the silo pictured is the centerpiece of its conference center and banquet hall.

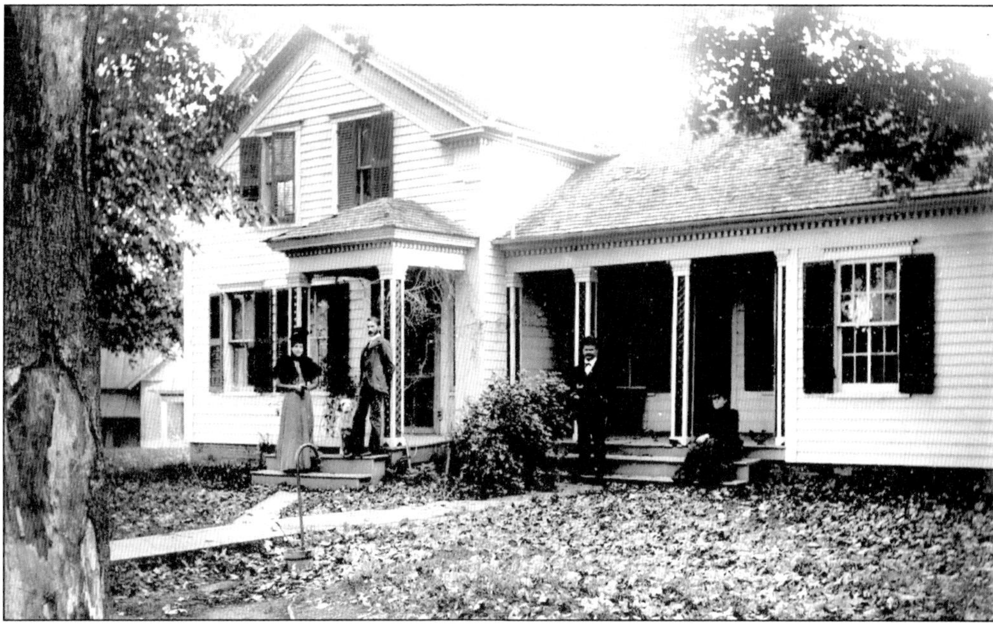

Originally the home of Dr. William Albright, this comfortable abode on Water Street, near where Ken's Tire and Auto Service is now, was home for many years to longtime county surveyor Hugh MacDougall. This son of a Scottish Highlander traveled by horse and buggy when he began his job in 1896. He continued working well into his 80s, setting a record for longevity in the office of county surveyor.

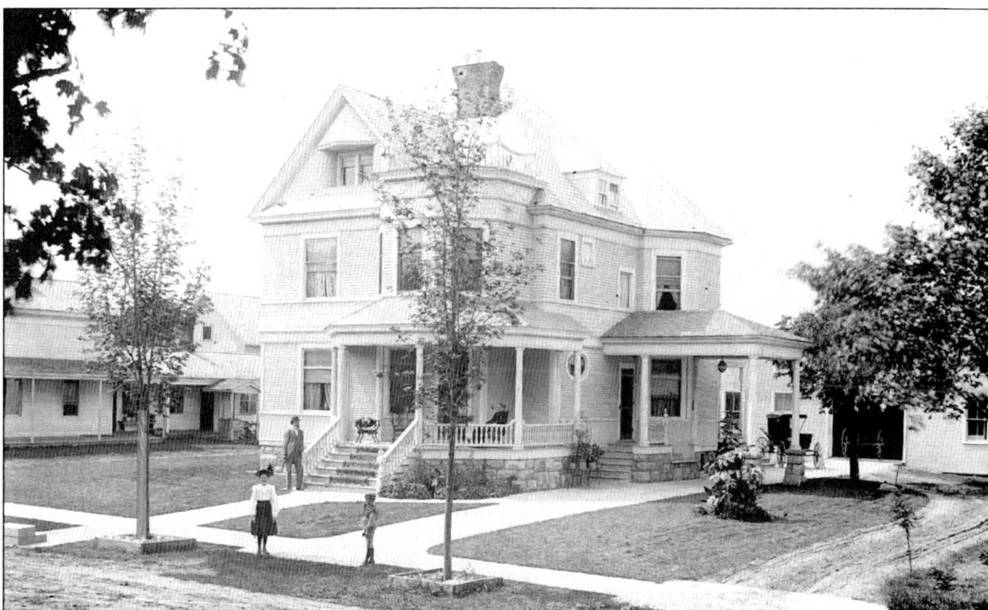

This large home belonged to George Lay, one of the wealthiest men in Michigan. He owned a lumberyard in Hopkins, a buggy factory, and a huge farm outside Allegan where the family resided. When he desired that his children attend a private school, open only to Allegan residents, he built the small home on the left. In later years, he built the large home next door as his retirement home.

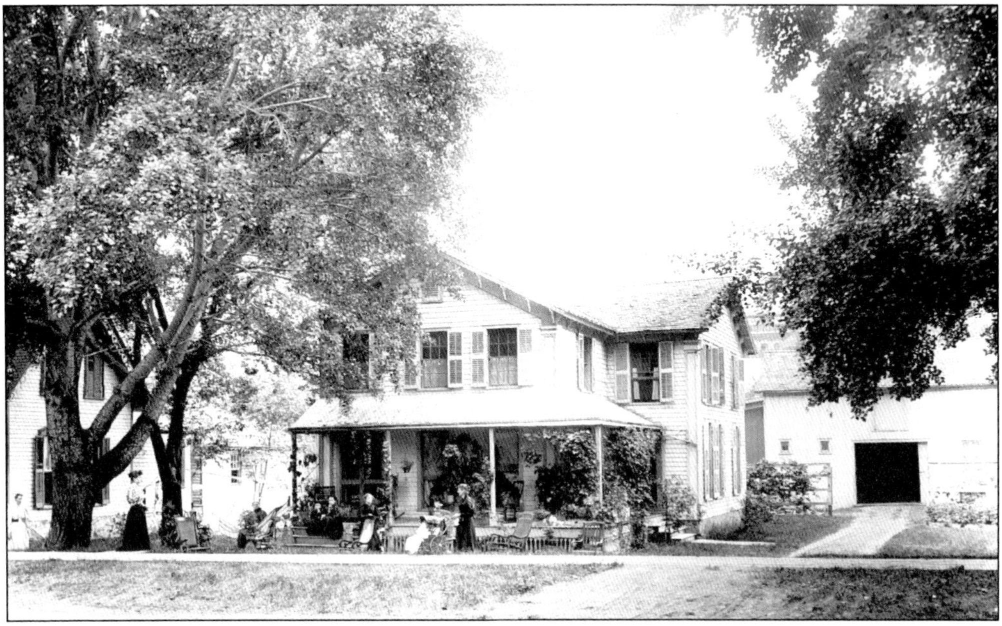

This home in the 200 block of Cutler Street belonged to L. M. Walter, one of Allegan's earliest druggists. The carriage house shown, right, is where the Seventh Day Adventist Church now stands. Neighbor Viola DeLano is identified, far left, and one of the two girls seated on the steps is Louise DeLano. After World War I, the house was owned by fireman and owner of Allegan Hardware, Harry Lutts.

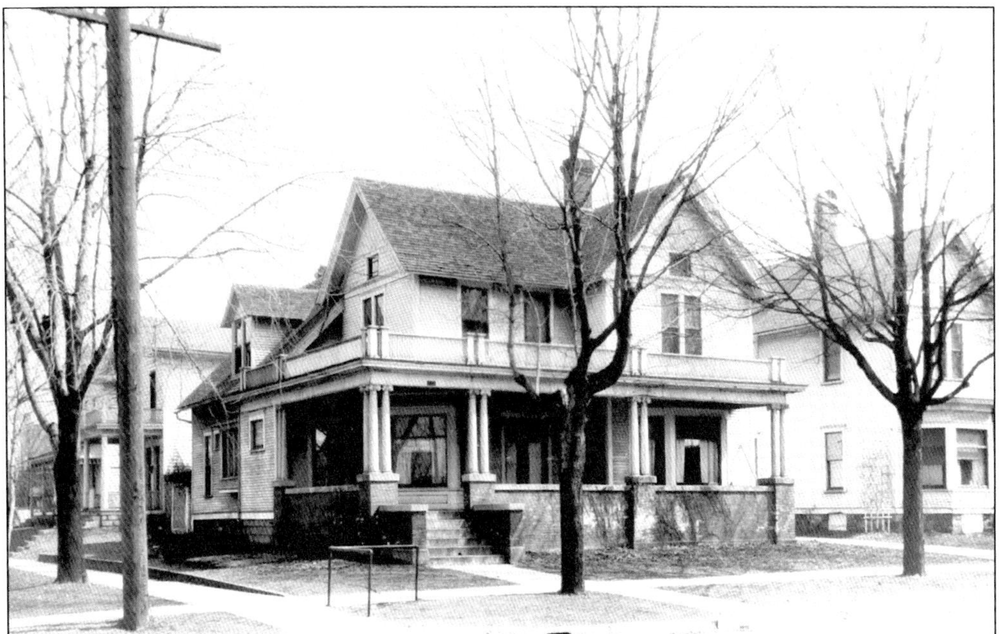

This c. 1920 photograph shows an earlier home of Siebe Baker, founder of Baker Furniture Company, at the corner of Chestnut and Cutler Streets. The large residence would eventually become Frost and Gorden Funeral Home. When Clyde Frost died, his wife wanted to keep the house, so Glenn Gorden started his own business in a large home on Trowbridge Street.

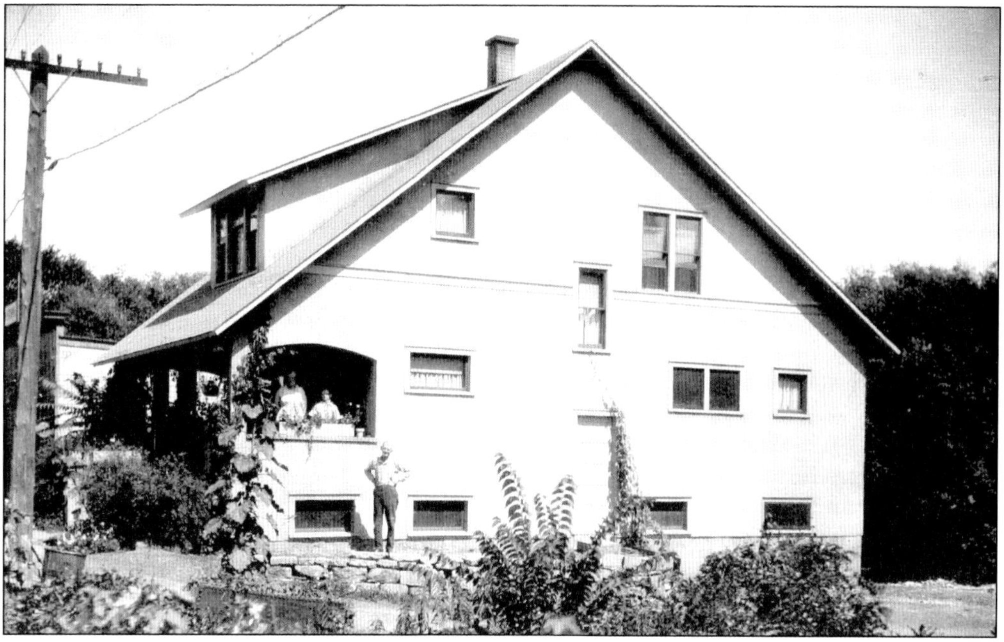

This c. 1930 photograph shows the John and Avada Katherler home at 544 Water Street. John did not have far to walk to work every day, as he also built his Great Lakes Wall Paper Company building right next door at 548 Water Street. Today all the homes on Water Street are gone and only commercial buildings remain.

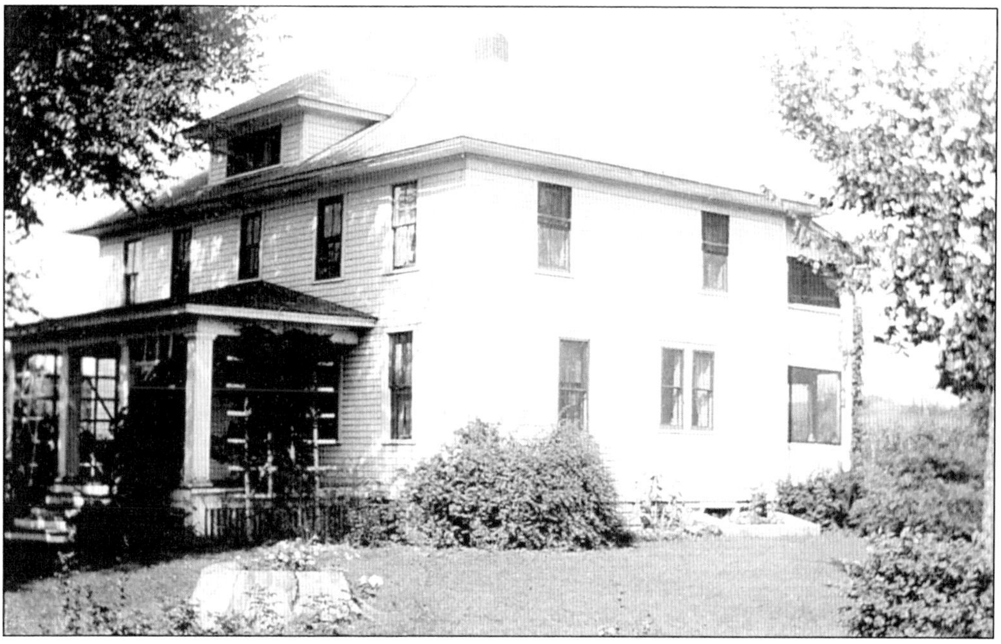

This 1935 photograph is the River Street home that was built by Ruth Berkin's father, Elbert Miller, in 1925, at the site of his original homestead. It was called Shadowhurst, and one of the favorite places for Berkin and her cousins was the sleeping porch, which can be seen off the back of the home. Berkin spent one cold winter night sleeping there, just to say she did. (Courtesy Sally Trabulsi.)

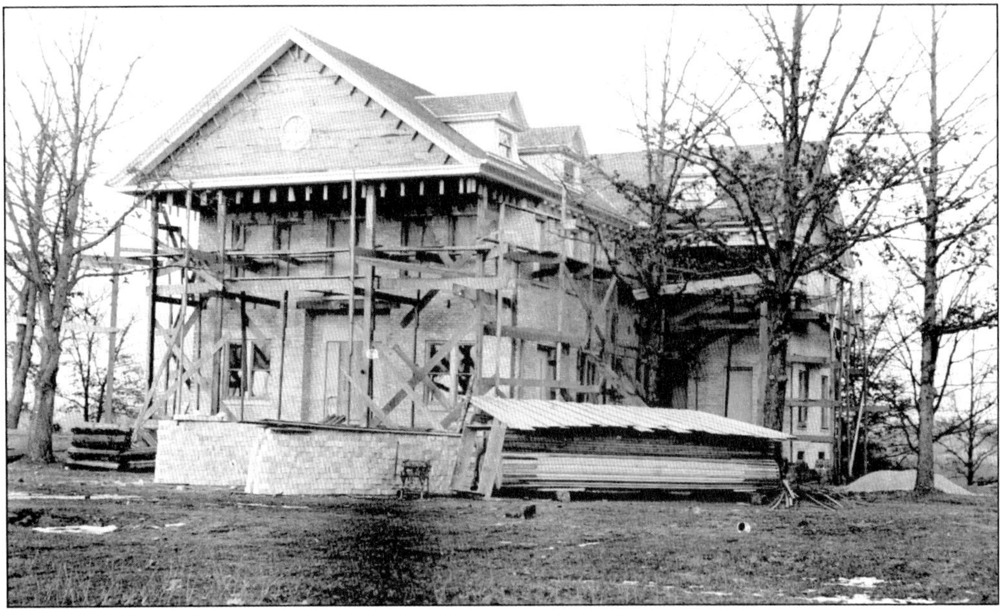

The John Robinson Hospital was built by Dr. Arthur Robinson in 1909 on Marshall Street and was named for his firstborn son. The building combines Greek Revival porch columns with a Georgian Revival overall style. Paranormal investigations are routinely held on the site, as reports that spirits of former patients roam the building are part of local legend.

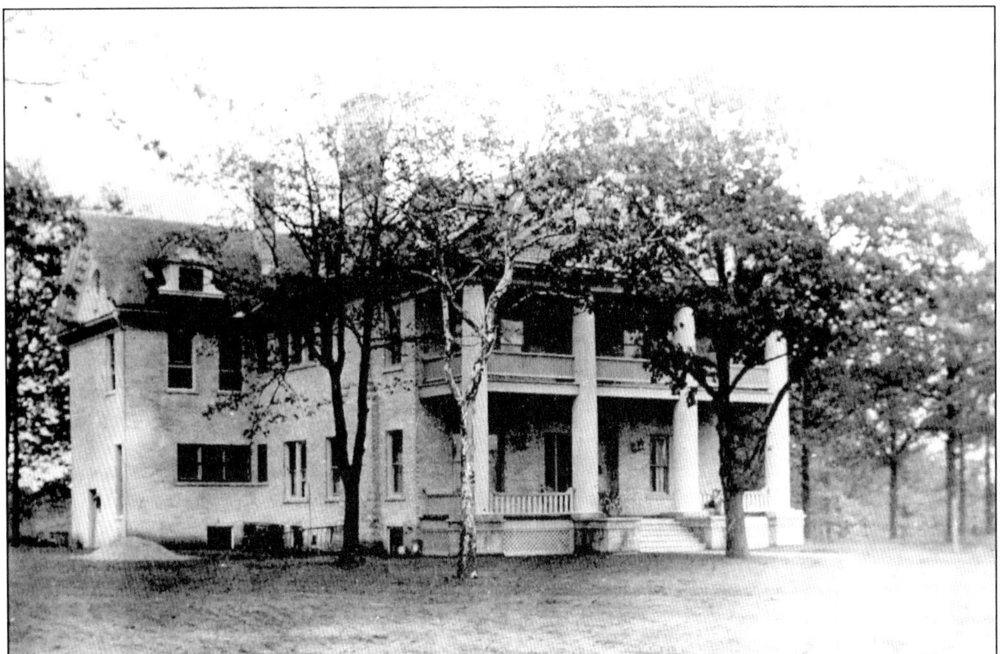

In 1938, the John Robinson Hospital closed upon the completion of the new Allegan Health Center, and the following year the building became the home of the Allegan Elks Lodge 1621. The posted "fallen brothers" roster of the lodge is an assemblage of important names in the 20th-century history of Allegan. The building remains in use today for not only lodge functions but for events open to the public.

Seven

TRANSPORTATION

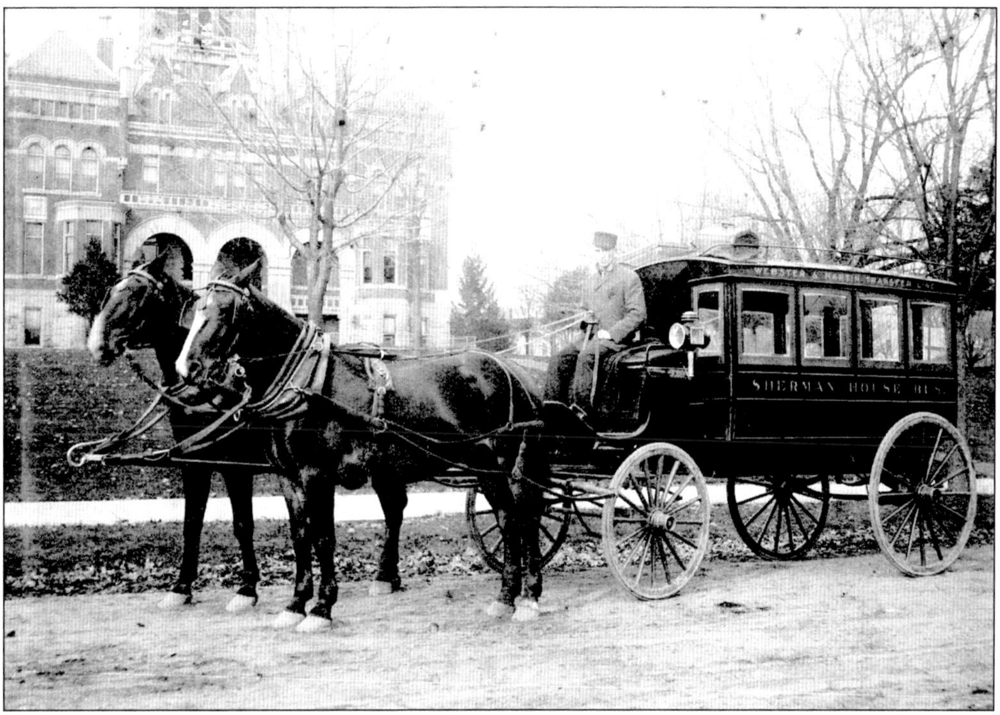

When visitors arrived in Allegan in the late 1800s and early 1900s they were met at the train station by a horse-drawn carriage and taken to their hotel. This beautiful "bus," with its matched team of horses, would deliver visitors to the Sherman House and provide taxi service to customers during their stay.

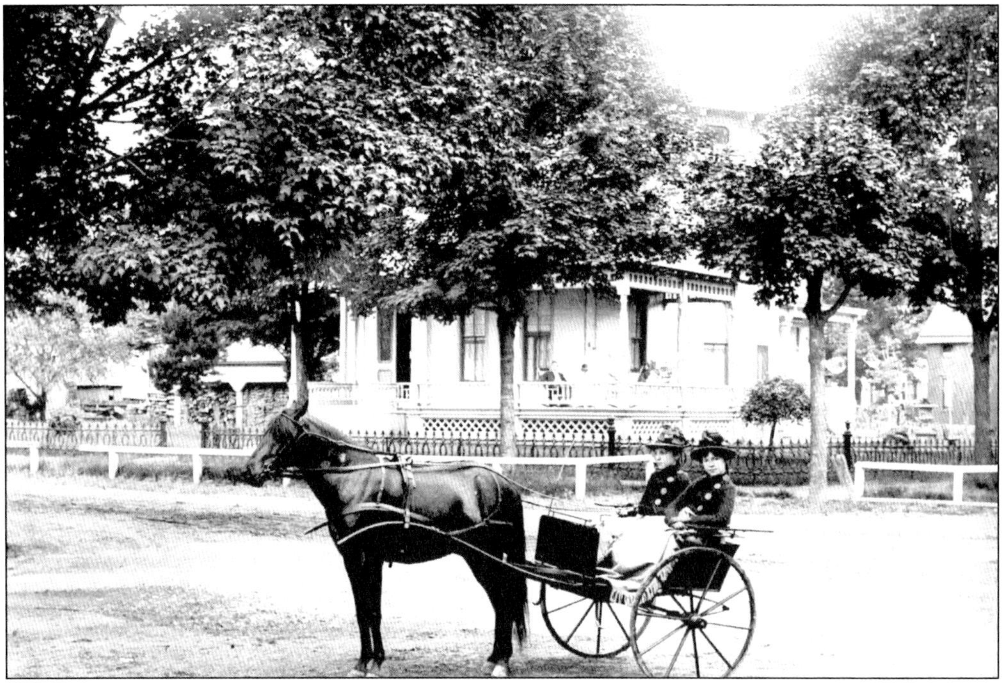

A pony cart was an excellent mode of transportation on the dirt streets of Allegan in 1900. These two young ladies, possibly sisters, pose with their pony at the intersection of Walnut and Cutler Streets. The Davis home, later home to the DeLano family and presently the DeLano Inn, is in the background. The iron fence surrounding the home was forged by Alby Rossman's foundry and still stands today.

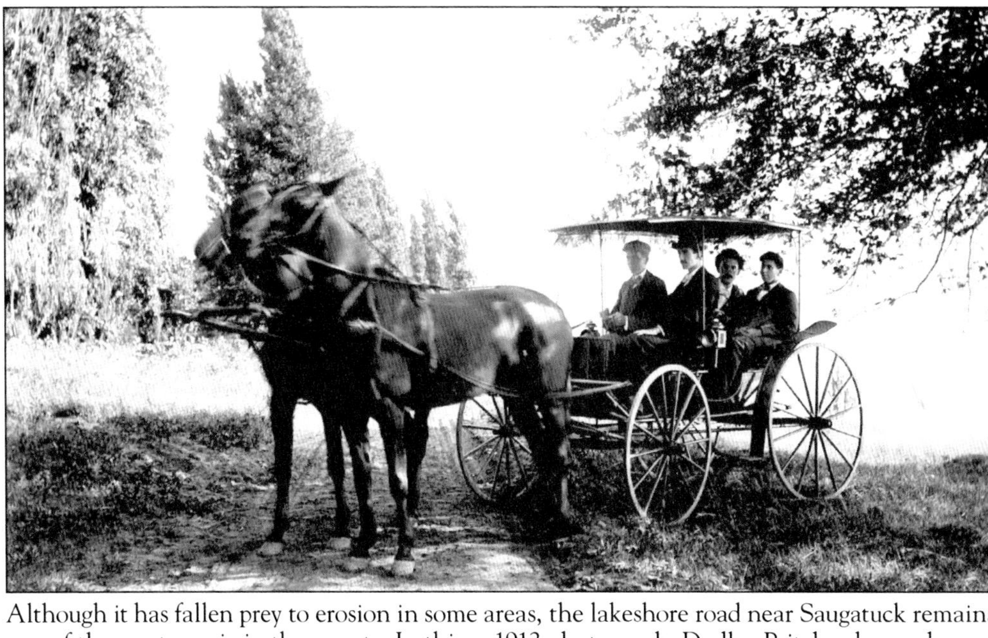

Although it has fallen prey to erosion in some areas, the lakeshore road near Saugatuck remains one of the most scenic in the county. In this *c.* 1912 photograph, Dudley Pritchard, grandson of Civil War general Benjamin Pritchard, drives his father, Harry, and two unidentified men along the one-lane path for an outing in the lakeshore tourist town.

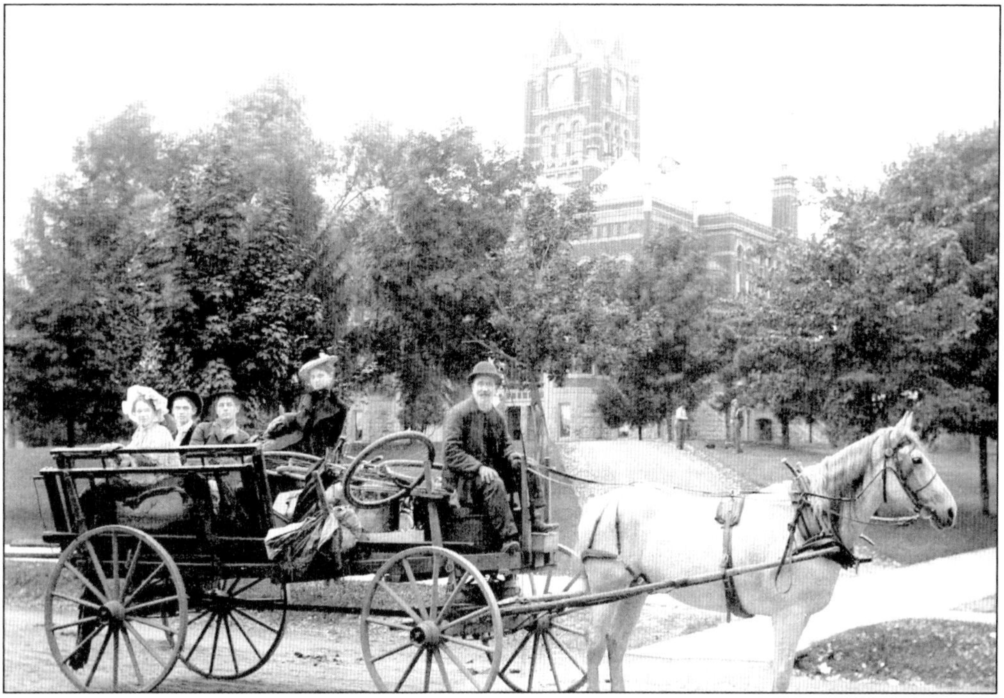

This open-air cart, pulled by only one horse, was carrying two couples, at least two bicycles, and possibly some luggage. In the late 1890s, hackneys such as this would transport people and their large-sized belongings short distances for a nominal fee. All are unidentified, but captured forever in this photograph, they are important figures in Allegan history.

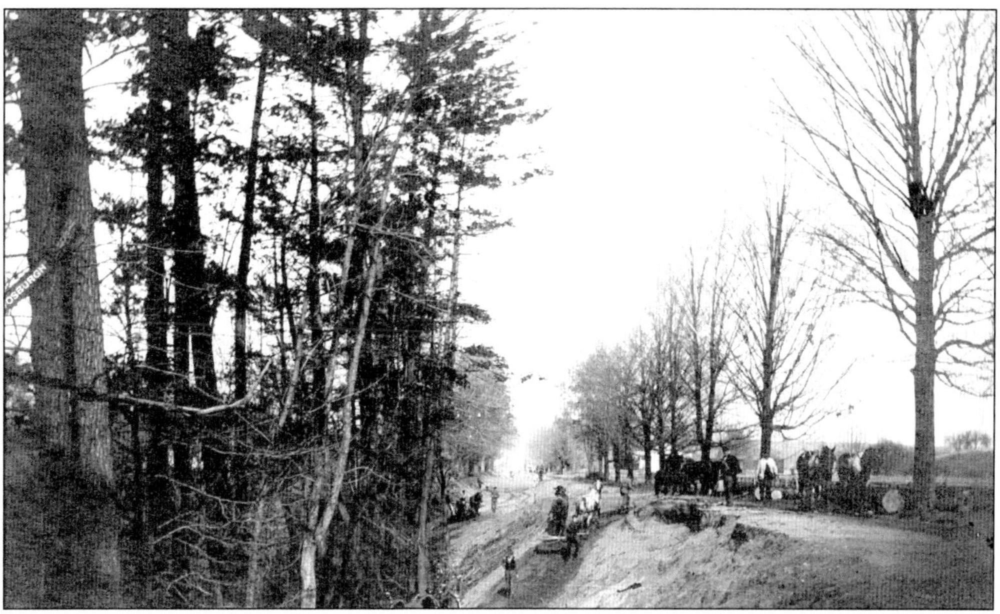

In 1868, the railroad came to Allegan. This photograph shows the beginning of track construction on River Street, with horses a large part of the effort. In the past, the Kalamazoo River was the main artery for goods to travel to local businesses. With the coming of the railroad things would change.

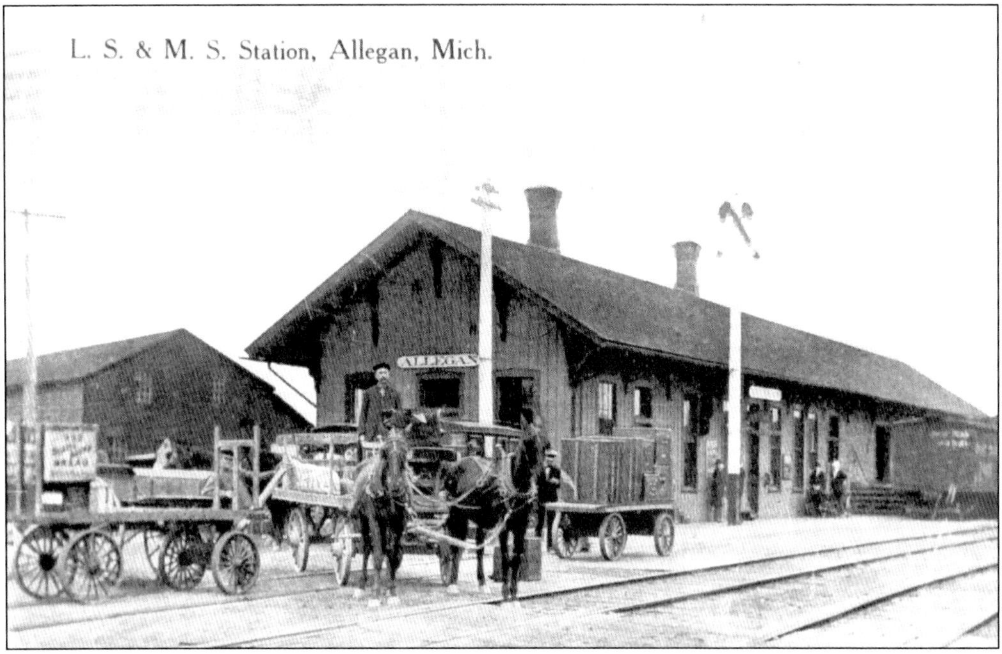

This is the Allegan Railroad Station around 1870. The carts pictured appear to be waiting for the next freight train and a load of goods to deliver to local merchants. Originally the river was the main artery for goods to travel to local businesses, but with the coming of the railroad, the downtown area could expand beyond Hubbard and Brady Streets and the banks of the Kalamazoo River.

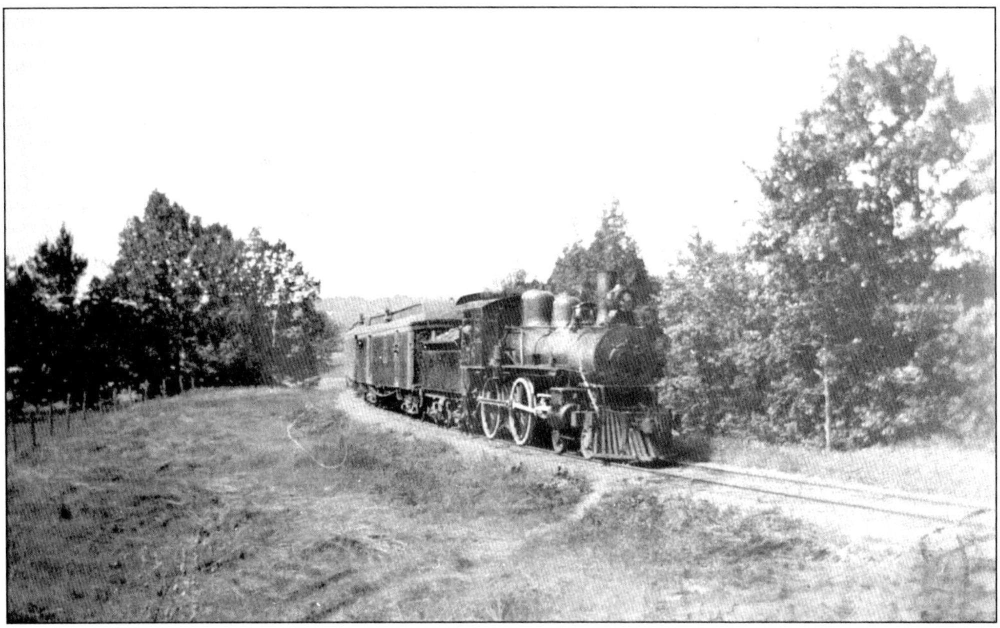

The first passenger train into Allegan was the Lake Shore and Michigan Southern steam engine pulling two Pullman cars. The tracks in Allegan were built swiftly, with approval in March 1869 and the first train arriving in November of that same year. It brought a surge of growth to Allegan; however, it was not a lasting situation as the last train left Allegan on March 24, 1976.

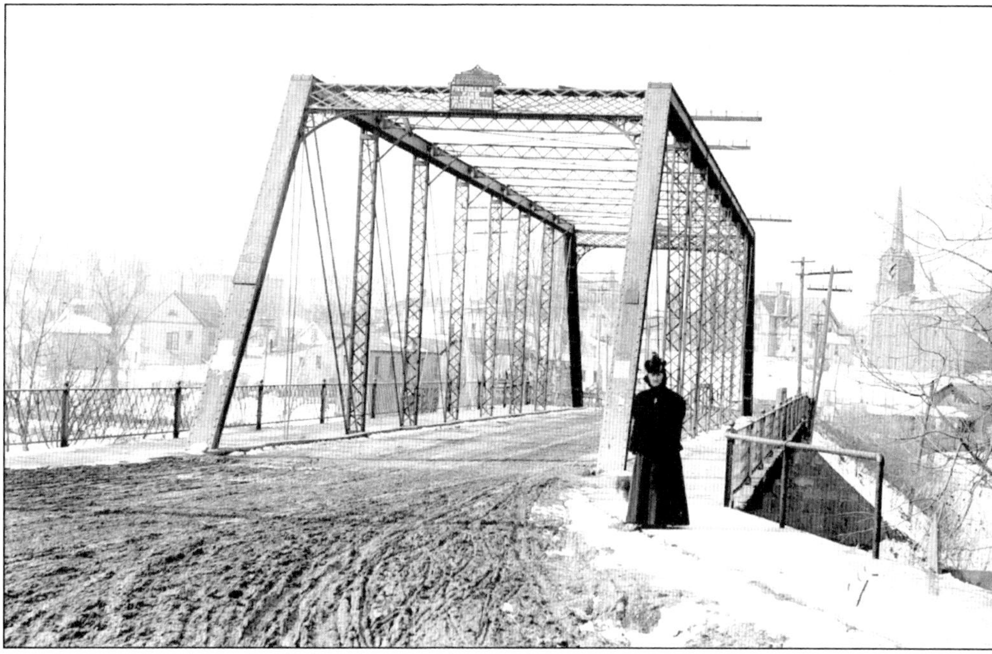

Caroline Vosburgh, wife of the photographer and mayor, poses on a winter day at the North Side Bridge. The 1838 bridge crossed the river on Monroe Street near today's Village Market. Looking west, the Presbyterian church can be seen in the background. The sign atop the bridge warns the public of a $5 fine for crossing this bridge "faster than a walk."

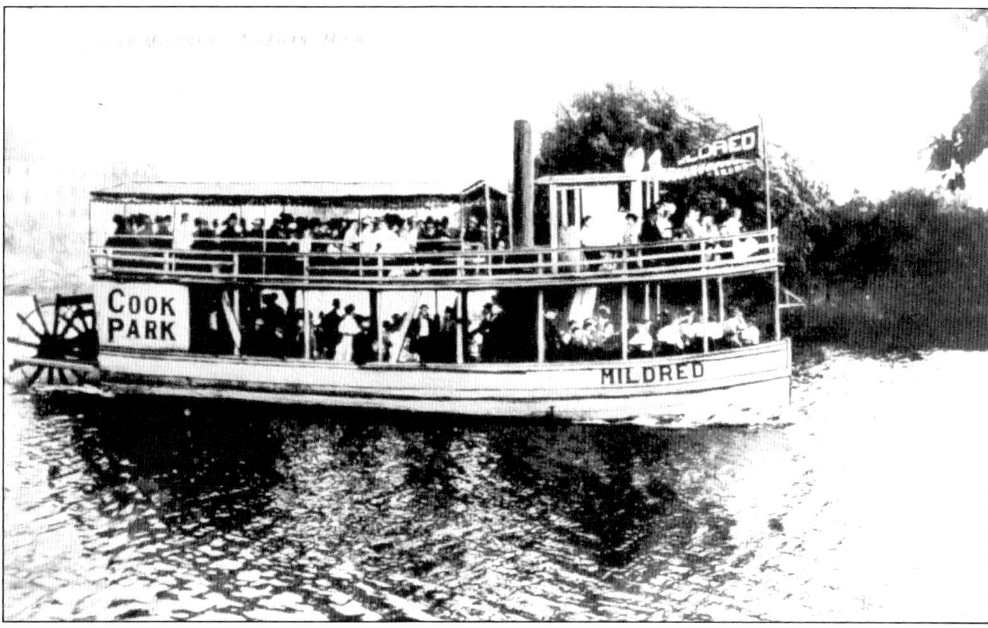

Around the dawn of the 20th century, the steamboat *Mildred* was running excursions from the downtown dock to Cook Park, a lovely spot south of Allegan on the road to Paw Paw. Other steamers made regular trips between Allegan and Saugatuck. Before the advent of steamboats, river transportation consisted mainly of flat-bottomed boats, which had to be poled up and down the river.

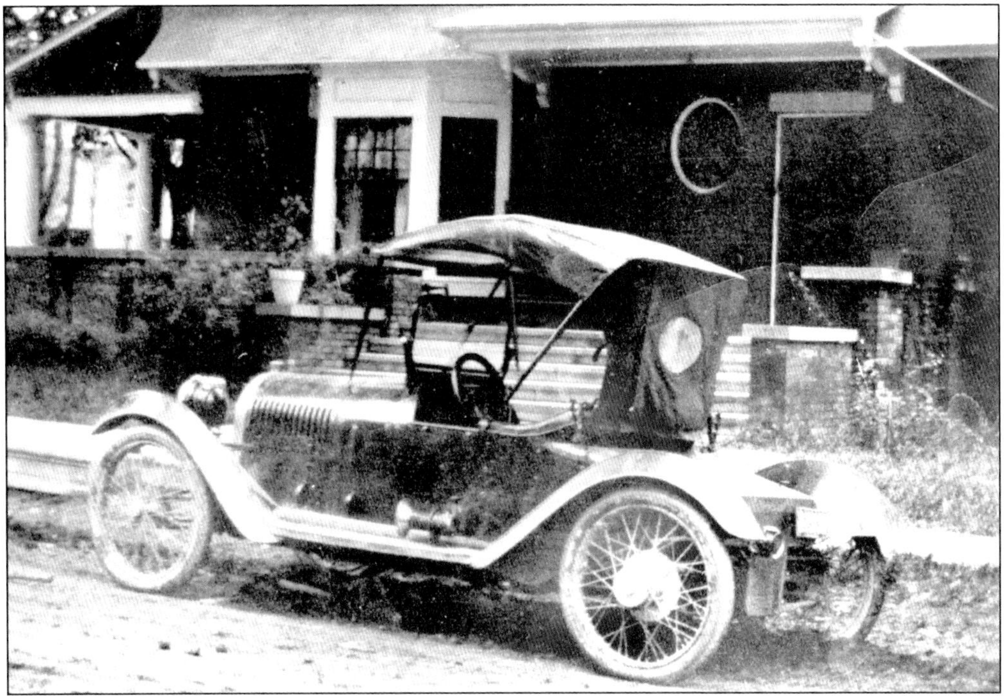

Above is one of the 100 Cornelian automobiles built in Allegan in 1914 by Blood Brothers Machine Company. The designer was Howard Blood, and Cornelian probably seemed to be an apt name. Although it was entered in the 1915 Indianapolis Speedway race, engine problems developed that prevented it from finishing the race. It was driven by Louis Chevrolet; however, Chevrolet had no hand in either the design or the production of the automobile.

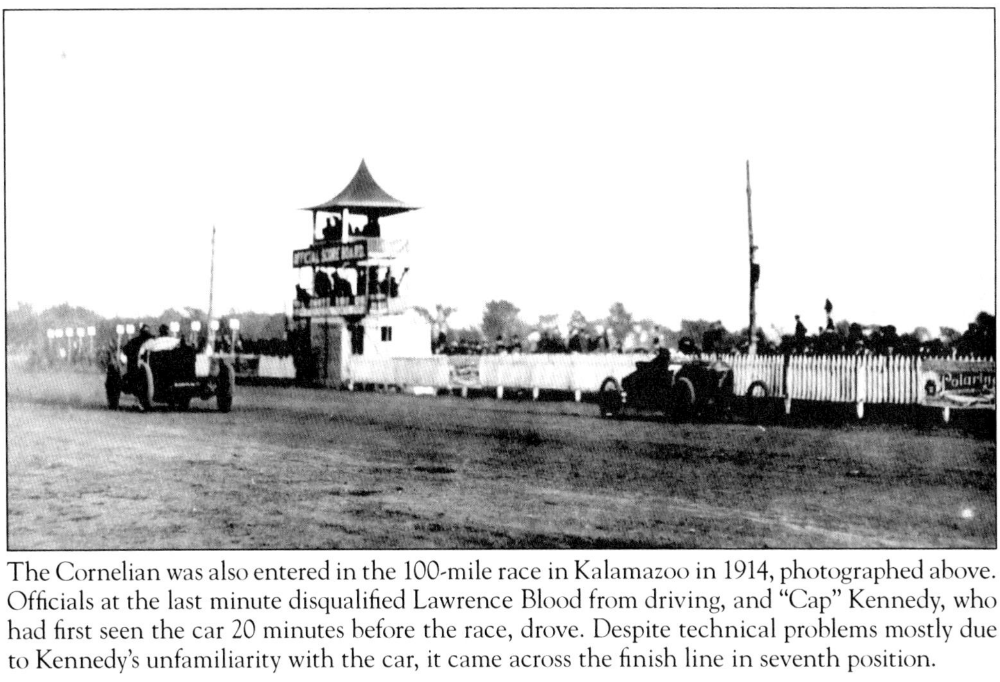

The Cornelian was also entered in the 100-mile race in Kalamazoo in 1914, photographed above. Officials at the last minute disqualified Lawrence Blood from driving, and "Cap" Kennedy, who had first seen the car 20 minutes before the race, drove. Despite technical problems mostly due to Kennedy's unfamiliarity with the car, it came across the finish line in seventh position.

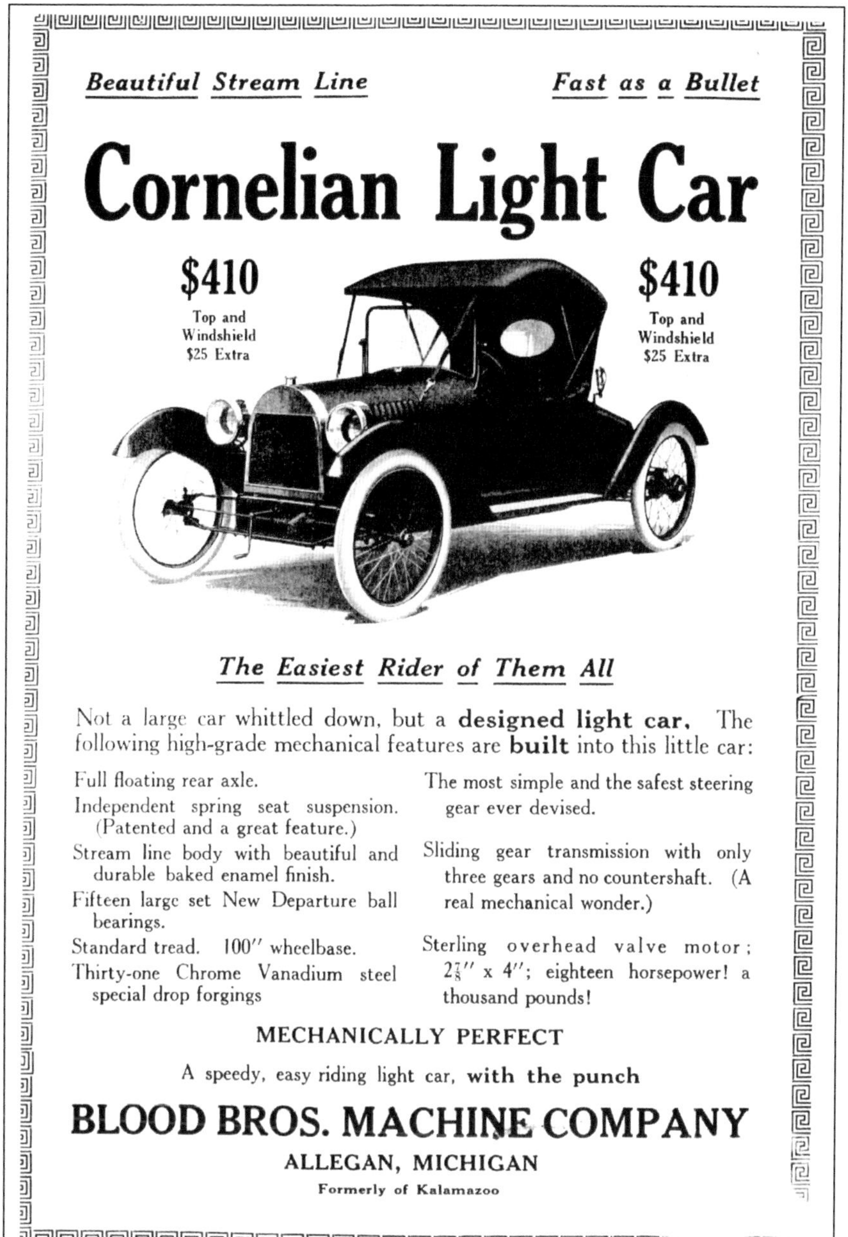

This advertisement for the 1914 Cornelian automobile, built by Blood Brothers, calls it a "speedy, easy riding little roadster." It was a well-designed little light automobile. The frame and body were built in a single unit. This type of construction is what made the Cornelian lighter than the usual separate frame and body automobile construction. It had left-hand steering and special fenders that were designed to cut down on the splashing of mud and water that occurred with most automobiles of the time. Blood Brothers had intended to build 2,500 cars in 1915. The Blood Brothers plant was moved from Kalamazoo to Allegan at this time, and when escalating production costs to produce the automobile arose, they decided to cease production. It is estimated that only 100 Cornelians were built. As far as is known, none remain in existence today.

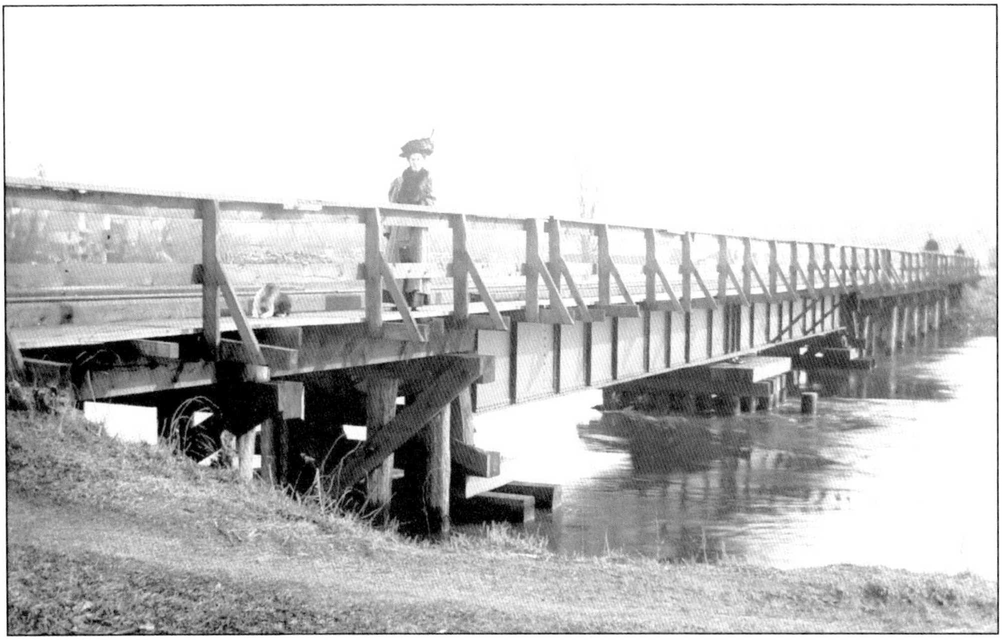

This photograph shows Louise DeLano Peck on the Pere Marquette railroad bridge, built in 1901 to cross the Kalamazoo River. This bridge would turn, allowing large boats to navigate the river. The Pere Marquette went from Petoskey near the Straits of Mackinac to Chicago. A spur line went from Holland to Allegan.

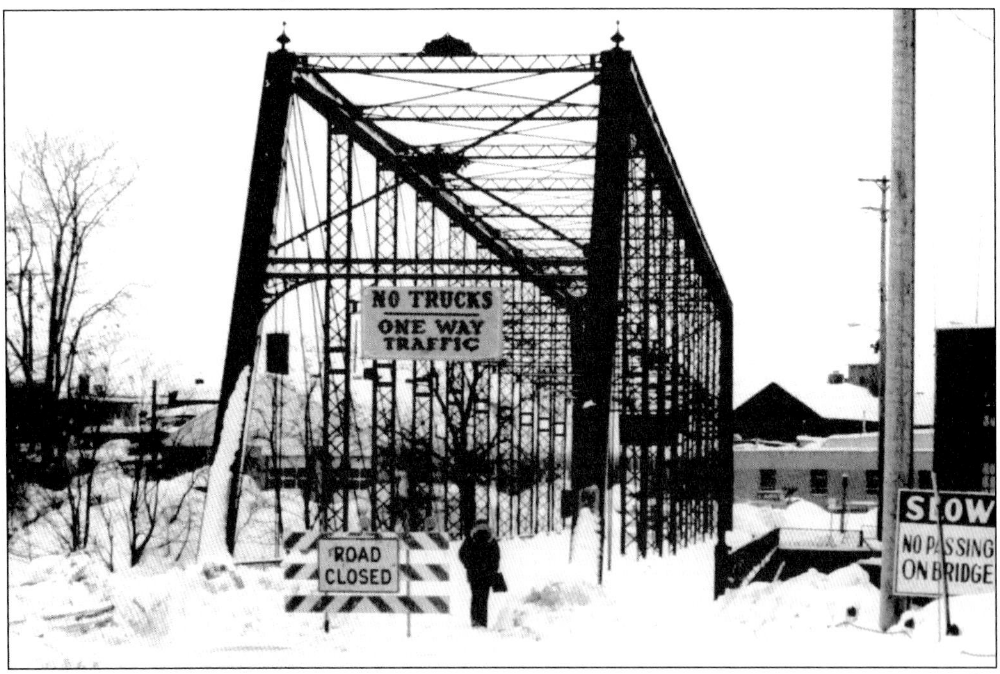

The first wooden bridge was built at this ancient Native American crossing in 1837. In 1886, the old Pratt iron truss bridge was built. Almost a century later, after being closed for safety reasons, ordered replaced by government decree, and subsequently rescued by the people of Allegan, it was lovingly restored by the local firm of H&K Construction Company.

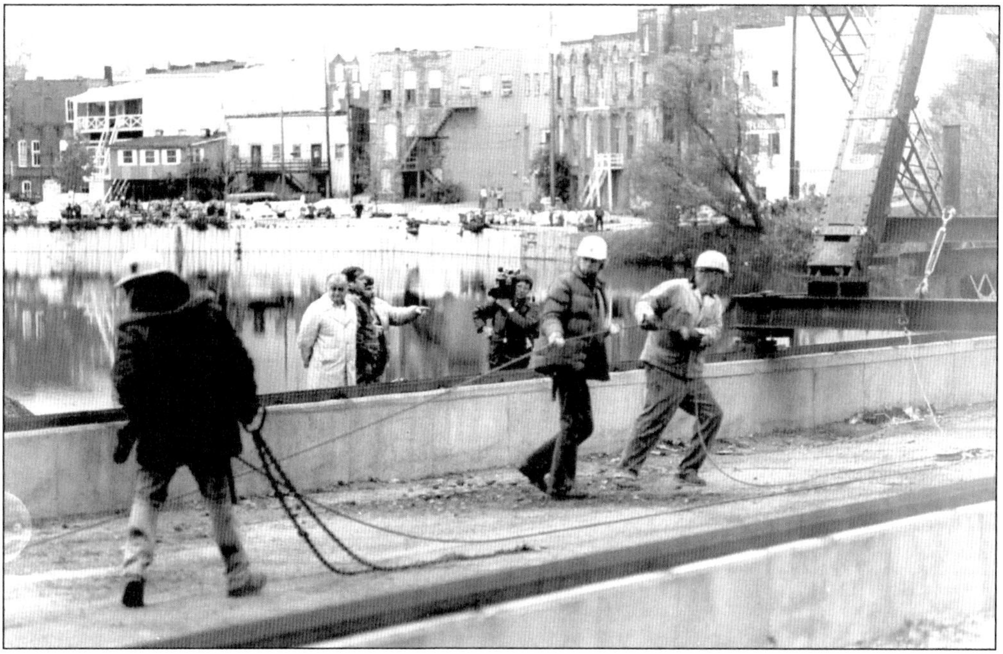

Amid much fanfare, the Second Street bridge was returned to its place on the river in 1983 after extensive restoration by H&K Construction of Allegan and Wilkins and Wheaton Engineering of Kalamazoo. The 225-foot bridge was rolled from its foundation on tracks to a temporary trestle onshore to make the repairs, a maneuver that captured national media attention.

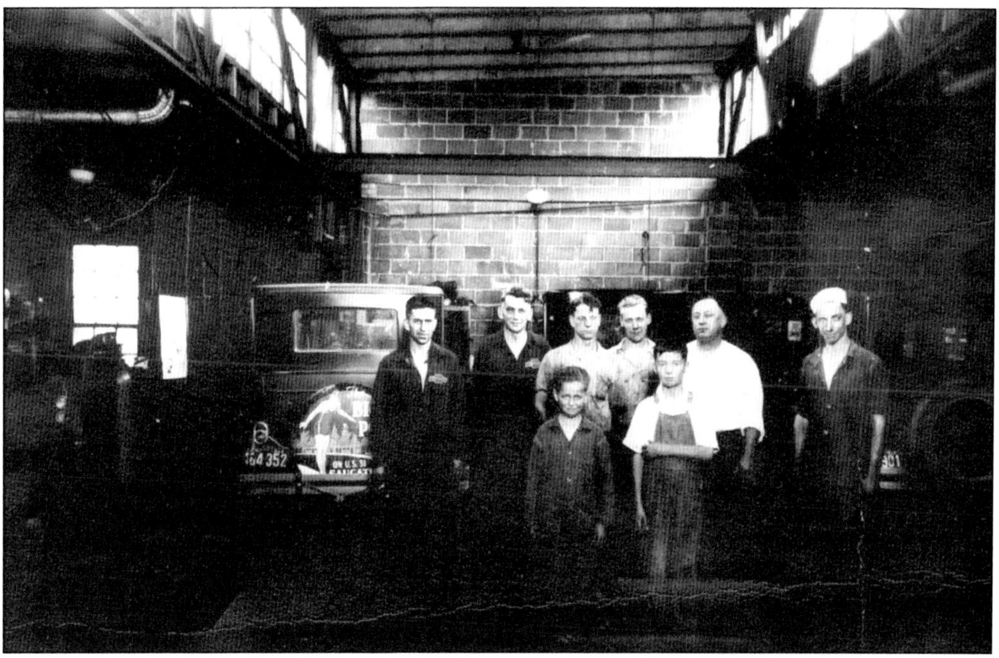

This 1930 photograph shows six employees of the Chevrolet garage on Brady Street owned by Carl Blanz. Shown from left to right are (second row) Howard Wedge, "Pop" Gray, Jerry Krup, Basil Kibby, Carl Blanz, and John Wait. The two young boys in the front, Russell "Bud" Blanz (left) and Raymond Blanz, are Carl's sons.

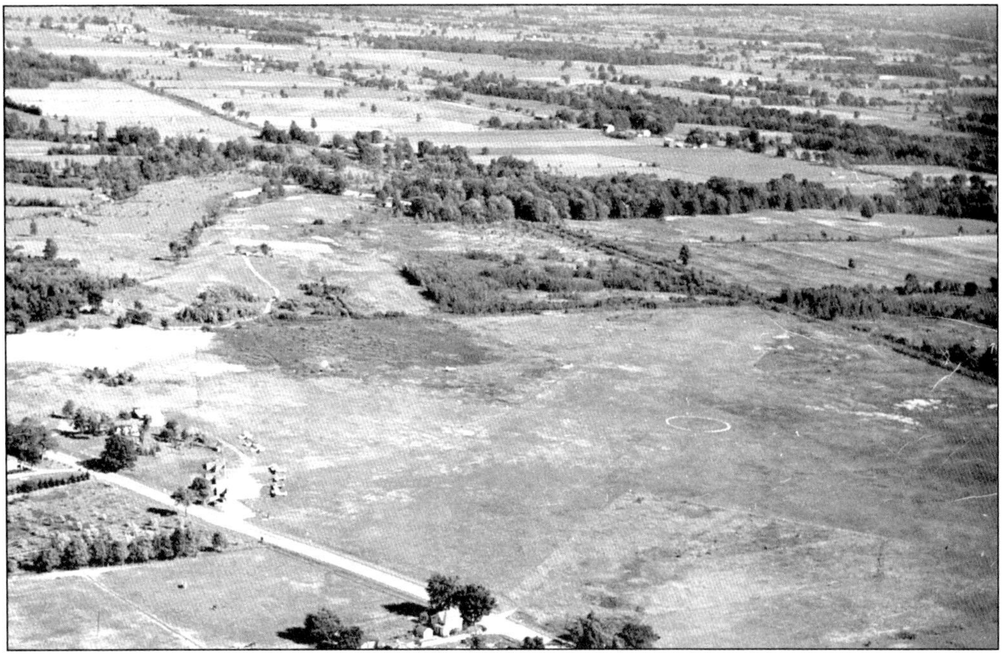

The above photograph, with no date upon it, shows Padgham Field, Allegan's airport. Judge Philip Padgham donated the land, and in 1936, the Public Works Administration began the project of clearing the land and assembling three hangars. William Urfer, who owned property bordering the field, erected the necessary wind sock.

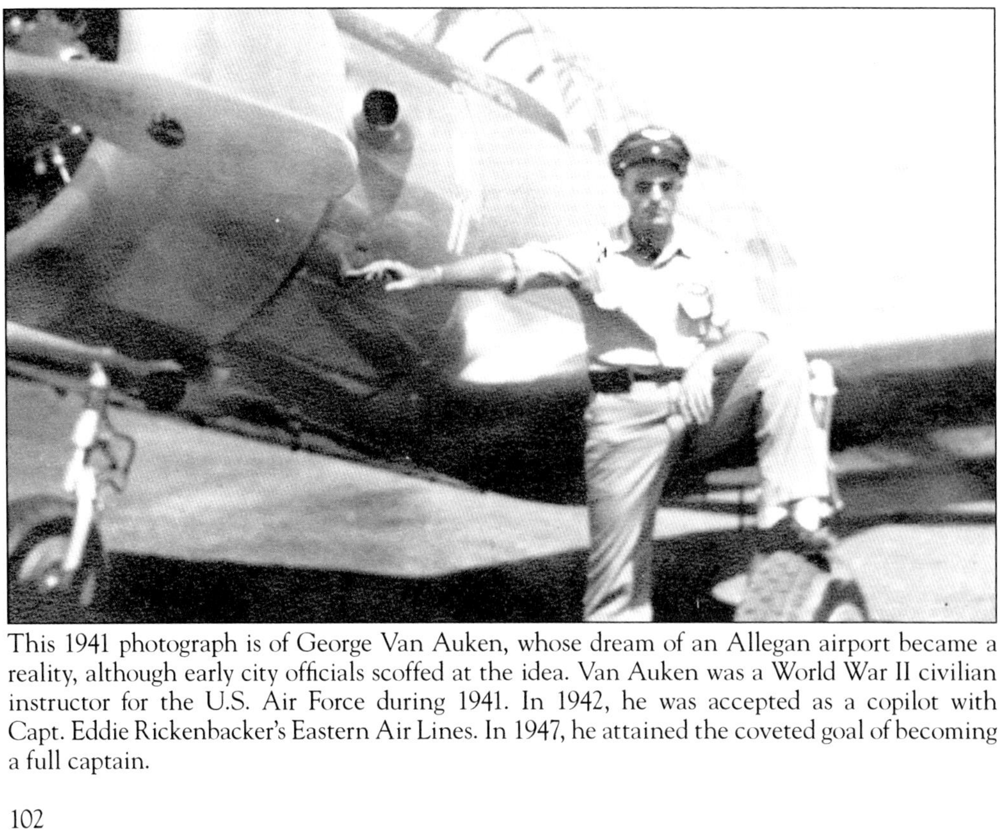

This 1941 photograph is of George Van Auken, whose dream of an Allegan airport became a reality, although early city officials scoffed at the idea. Van Auken was a World War II civilian instructor for the U.S. Air Force during 1941. In 1942, he was accepted as a copilot with Capt. Eddie Rickenbacker's Eastern Air Lines. In 1947, he attained the coveted goal of becoming a full captain.

Eight

WAR

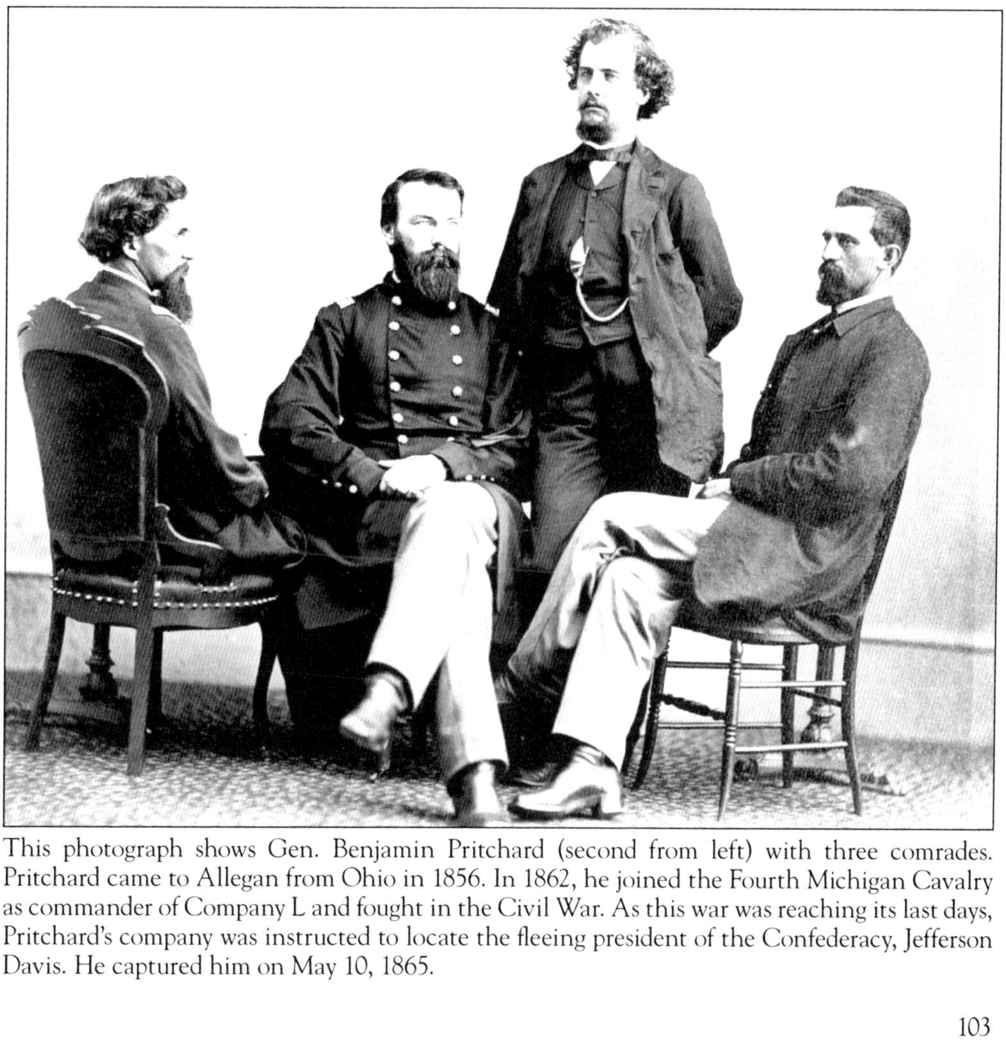

This photograph shows Gen. Benjamin Pritchard (second from left) with three comrades. Pritchard came to Allegan from Ohio in 1856. In 1862, he joined the Fourth Michigan Cavalry as commander of Company L and fought in the Civil War. As this war was reaching its last days, Pritchard's company was instructed to locate the fleeing president of the Confederacy, Jefferson Davis. He captured him on May 10, 1865.

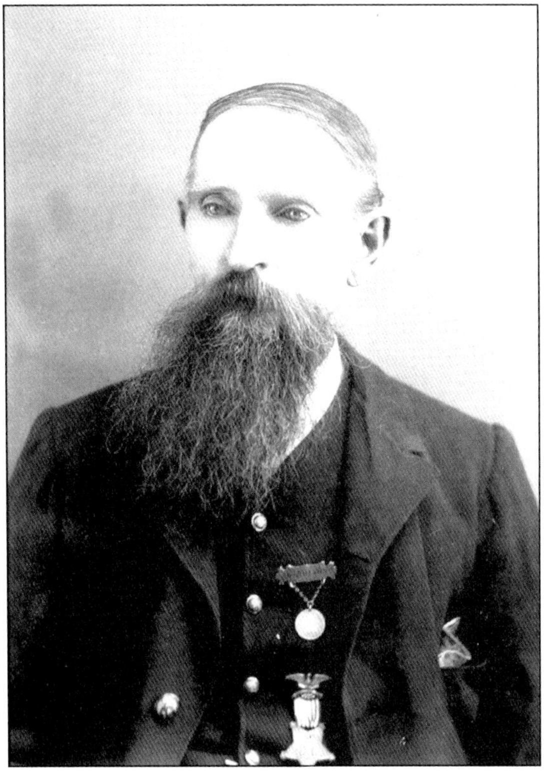

The photograph above is of Andrew Bee, a member of Pritchard's Company L. Searching for Jefferson Davis, Company L surrounded Confederate tents it located. Two women emerged and attempted to walk through Union lines and were halted. Later Bee recounted it was the large boots on Davis that gave away his attempt to flee as a woman. The clothing worn is in the U.S. War Department archives.

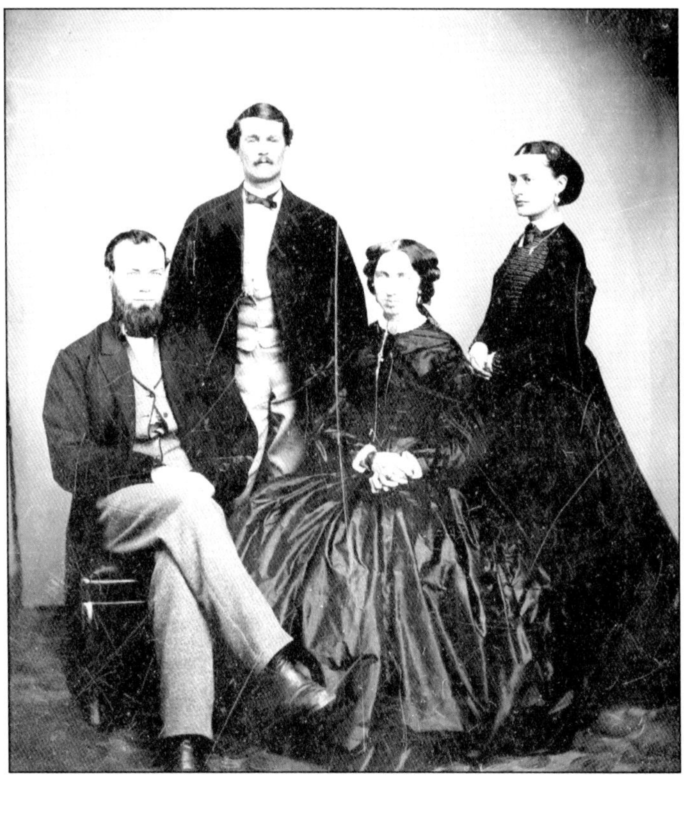

This 1866 photograph shows Gen. Benjamin Pritchard and his wife, Mary (seated), and Mr. and Mrs. Harlan Dunning (standing). General Pritchard married Mary Kent, his college sweetheart, in 1864. They had a son, Harry, and a daughter, Bertha. Mary died in 1889. General Pritchard resided in Allegan until his death in 1907, and his descendants still reside in his beautiful residence on Davis Street.

Shown above are members of the Hannah McIntosh Cady Chapter, Daughters of the American Revolution, organized in June 1909. The flag in the background was presented in 1910 by Horace Moore in honor of his daughter Winona Moore Sherwood. The first on left in the first row is Mignon Sherwood DeLano, a prominent Allegan resident whose generous gift, the DeLano Foundation, endows her hometown to this day.

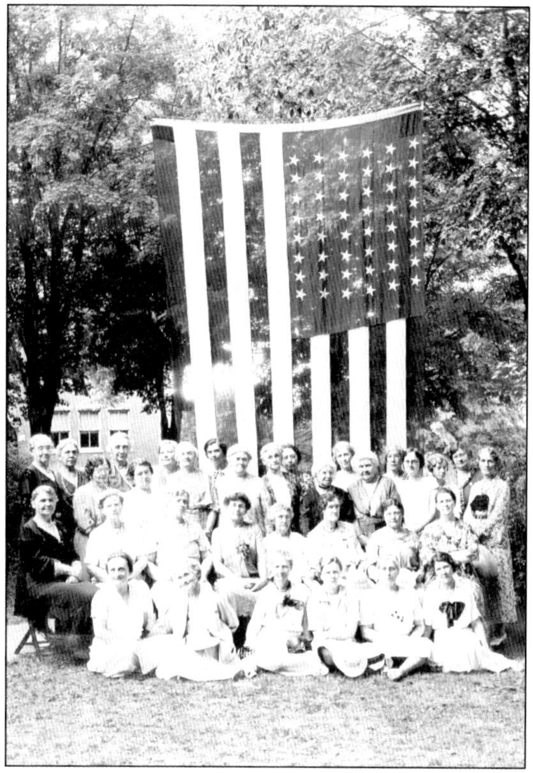

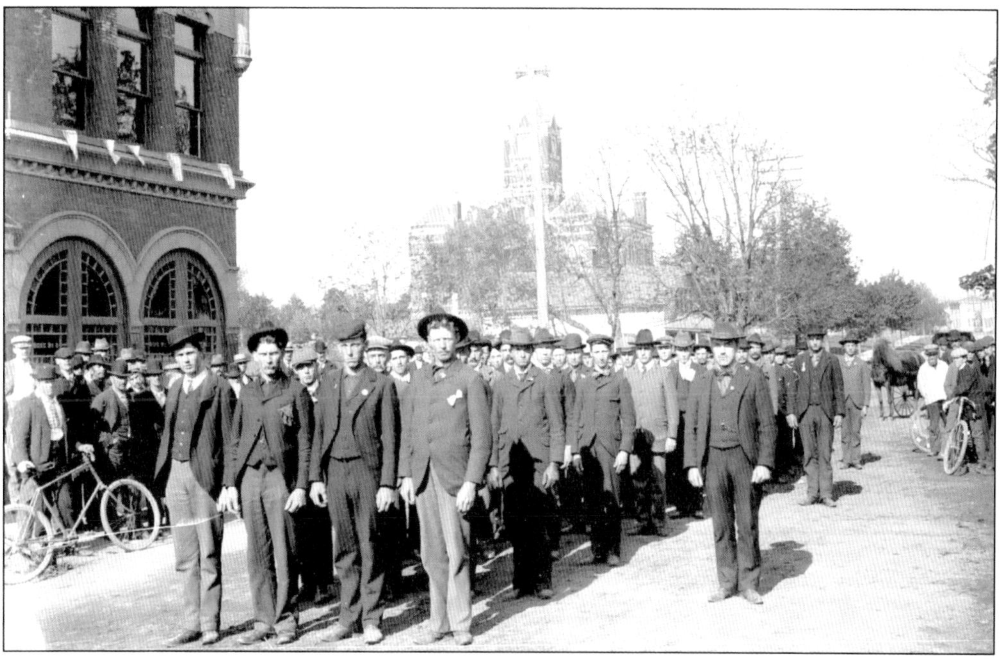

With the old courthouse in the background, gentlemen in Allegan line up in front of the fire hall on Trowbridge Street to volunteer for the Spanish-American War. They would become part of Company K-34, the regiment of Michigan Volunteers, led by Capt. Frederick Padgham, standing alone, right front, beside his men. Note the many different styles of headgear worn.

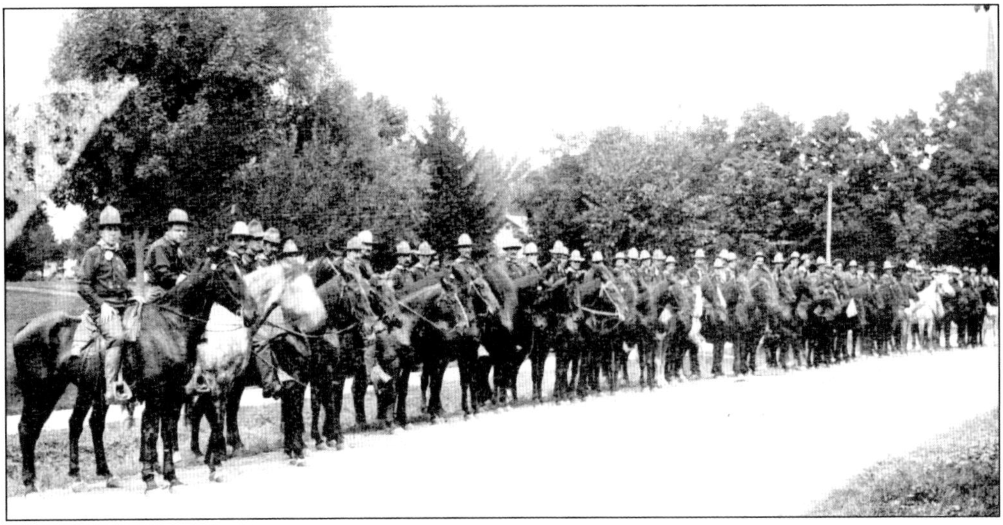

When the call went out in 1898 for a volunteer cavalry, hundreds of towns throughout the country answered. Theodore Roosevelt quickly became lieutenant colonel of the brigade, and their legend was born in the Spanish-American War. Lined up on Chestnut Street, on Courthouse Square, in 1912 are Allegan citizens replicating the famous Rough Riders.

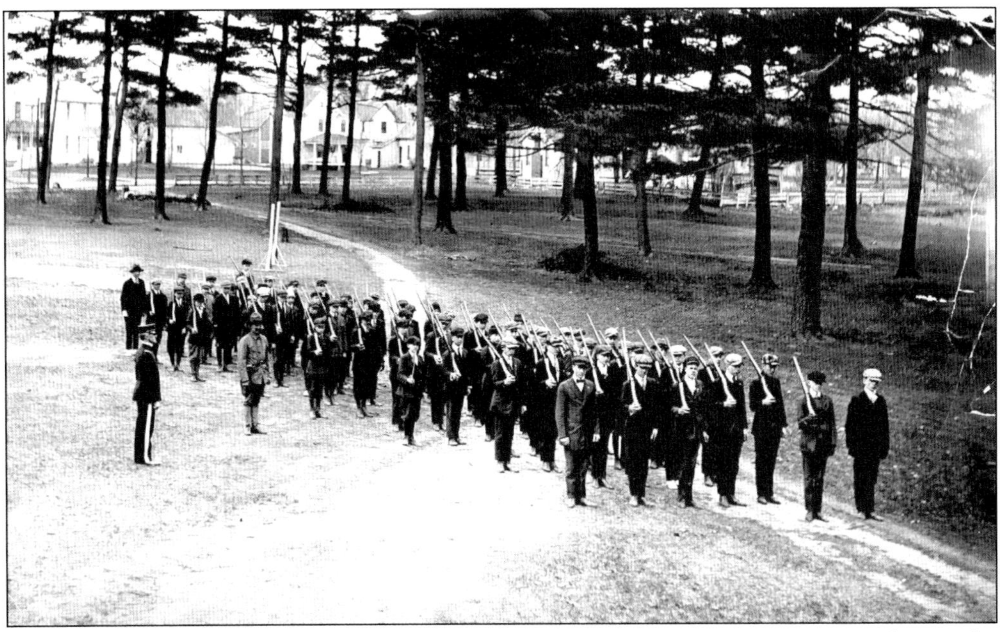

Allegan men went off to war on many different occasions. They fought in the Civil War, the Spanish-American War, World War I, and World War II. Here volunteers march on the lawn of the high school in Allegan in 1918. Shortly afterward they left to serve in World War I, "the war to end all wars," as it was called with hope.

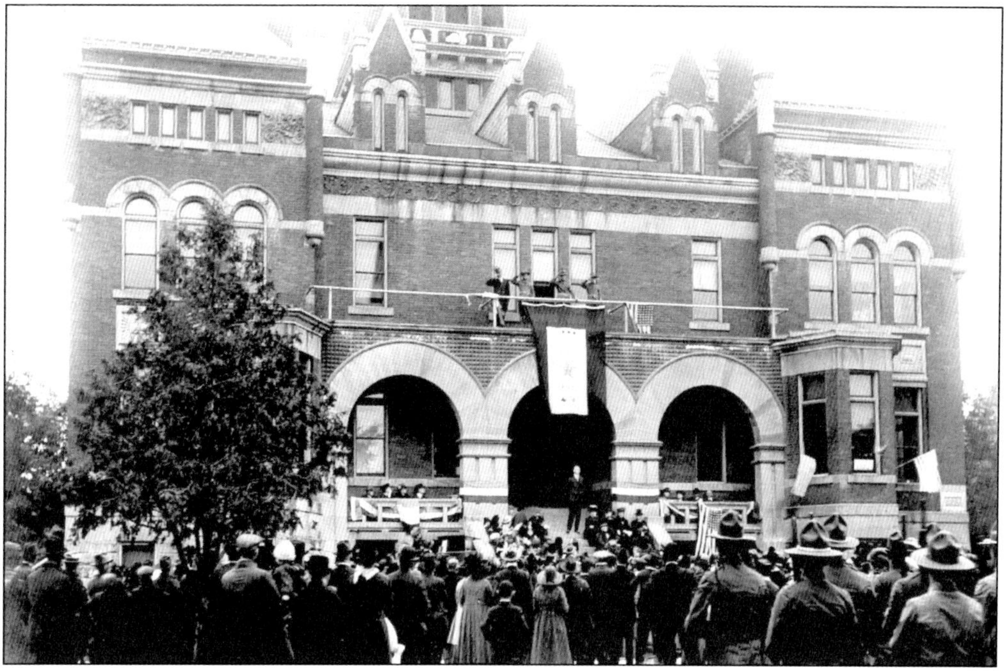

Residents and soldiers gathered on the lawn of the old courthouse to celebrate what would be known as the "false armistice." Like other towns across the country, they believed reports issued on November 7, 1918, that an agreement had been signed to end World War I. Even the New York Stock Exchange closed that day in celebration. The actual armistice agreement was signed on November 11, 1918.

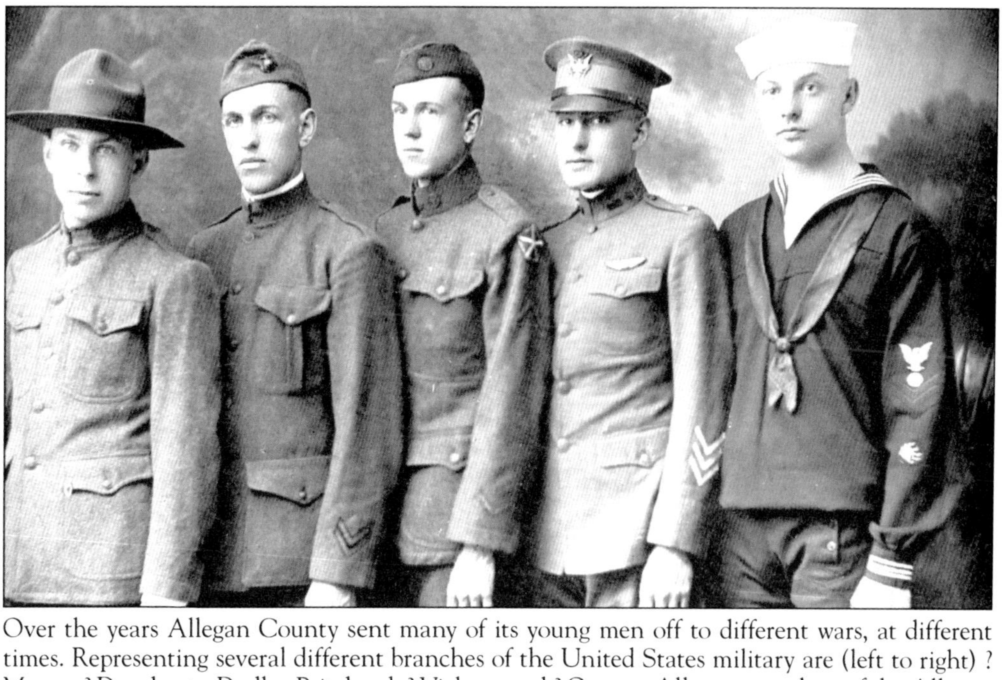

Over the years Allegan County sent many of its young men off to different wars, at different times. Representing several different branches of the United States military are (left to right) ? Moore, ? Daugherty, Dudley Pritchard, ? Vickers, and ? Osmun. All were members of the Allegan High School class of 1916. They were in service from 1917 through 1919.

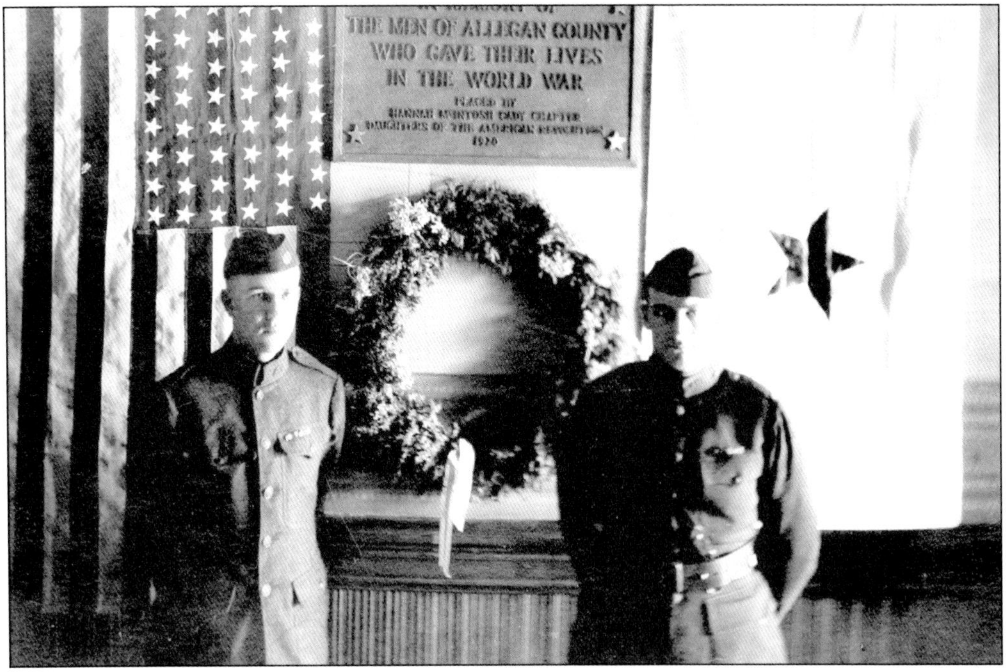

Pvt. Dudley Pritchard (left), of the 5th Corps First Army O.E.F., and Lt. Leon Chichester (right), 7th Field Artillery first Division O.E.F., stand before the bronze memorial tablet dedicated to those who gave their lives in World War I. The plaque, a gift of the Hannah McIntosh Cady Chapter of the Daughters of the American Revolution to Allegan County on May 30, 1919, is located in the Allegan County courthouse, outside the clerk's office.

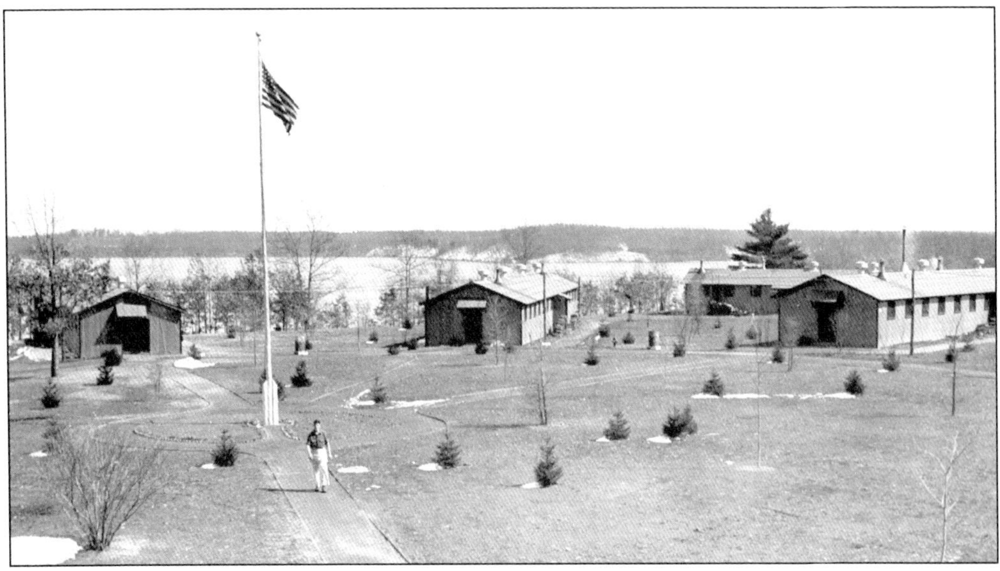

In 1944, a group of 250 German prisoners of war were sent to the former Civilian Conservation Corps camp on Lake Allegan. The prisoners helped local farmers during harvest when most of the farmworkers were off helping the war effort. Some chose to return to the area after World War II, mainly because of the kindness shown them by the people of Allegan County.

Nine

LEISURE TIME

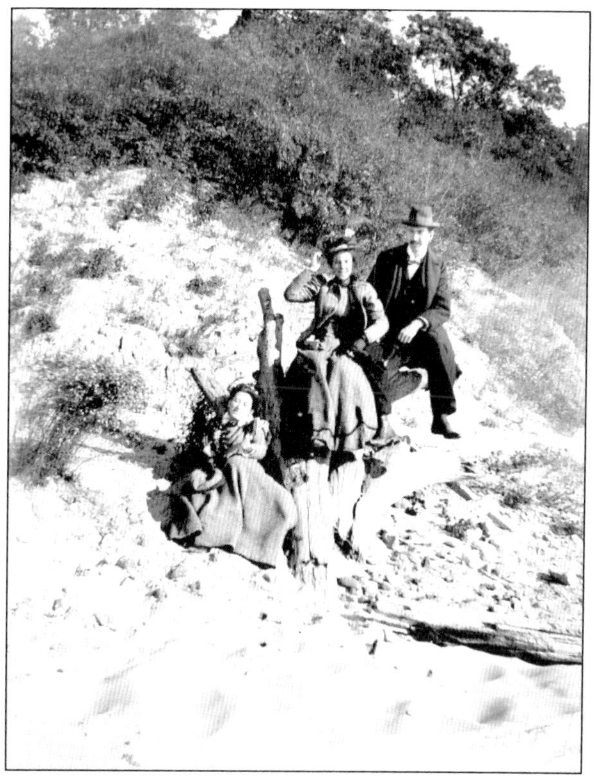

Allegan residents need not travel far to have a day at the beach, with Lake Michigan less than 20 miles west. This *c.* 1897 photograph shows the newly married Harry and Gail Pritchard and an unidentified woman posing in the sand dunes near Douglas. Gail Pritchard is holding her bonnet.

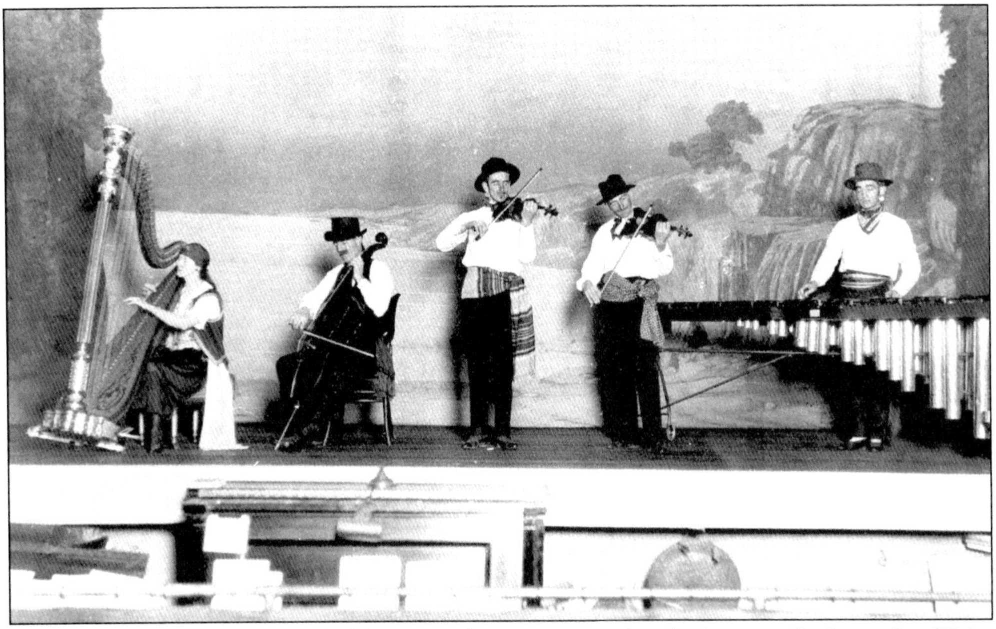

In 1920, the Regent Theater held its grand opening in what had originally been the Globe Garage on Trowbridge Street. In the 1920s and 1930s, the theater was often the scene of live entertainment. This 1922 photograph shows a performance of the Regent Theater orchestra. The members shown are, from left to right, Josephine Cady Walker, Dr. Osmun, Harry Cady, Herm Priebe, and Frank Knight.

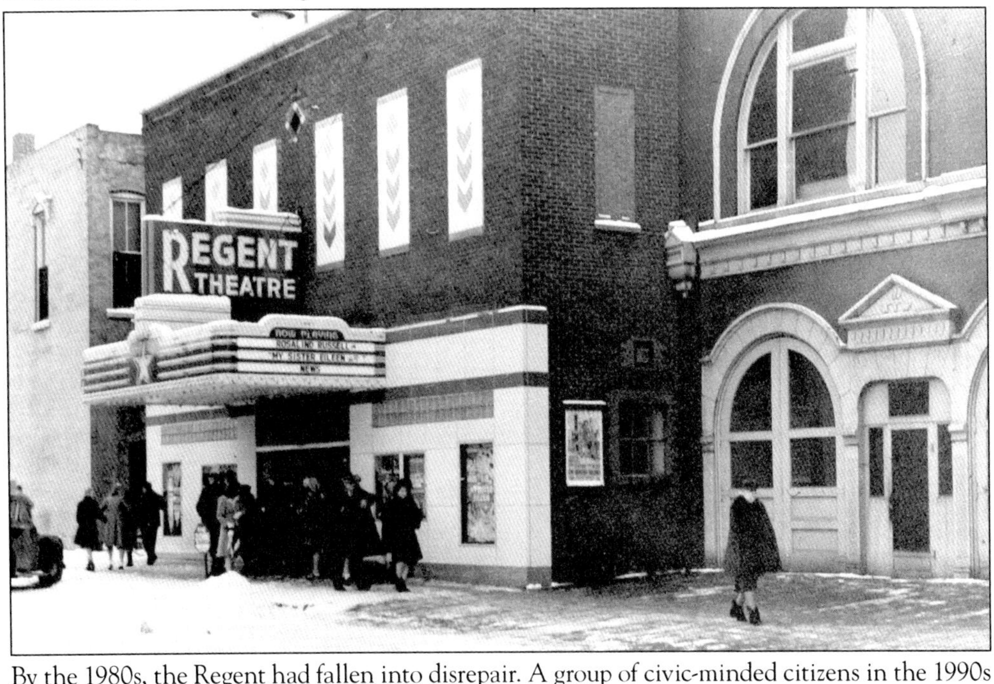

By the 1980s, the Regent had fallen into disrepair. A group of civic-minded citizens in the 1990s intervened, and this important part of leisure life in Allegan was reborn. The photograph above shows the Regent, around 1940, looking the same as it does today. The old marquee will soon be renovated, courtesy of a grant and a vote by citizens to pay the remaining costs.

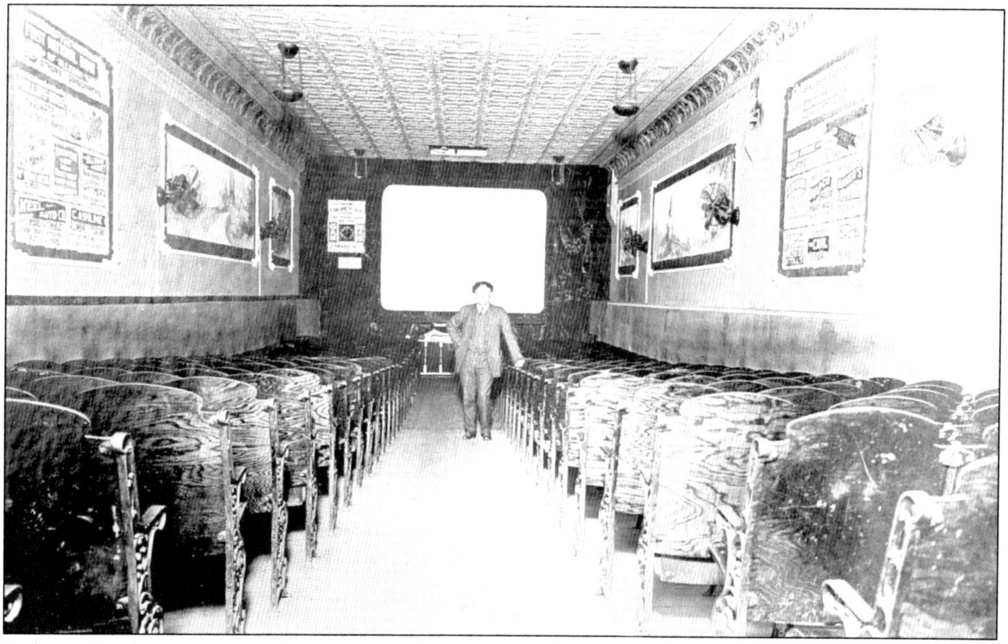

Robert Dunham poses in his new motion picture theater on Trowbridge Street in 1916. The Star Theater featured a hand-cranked projector, with Josephine Cady Walker playing the piano to accompany the silent movies. Outgrowing the 120-seat Star, Dunham purchased the Globe Garage across the street and it became the Regent. The Star Theater is now the site of Hunter's.

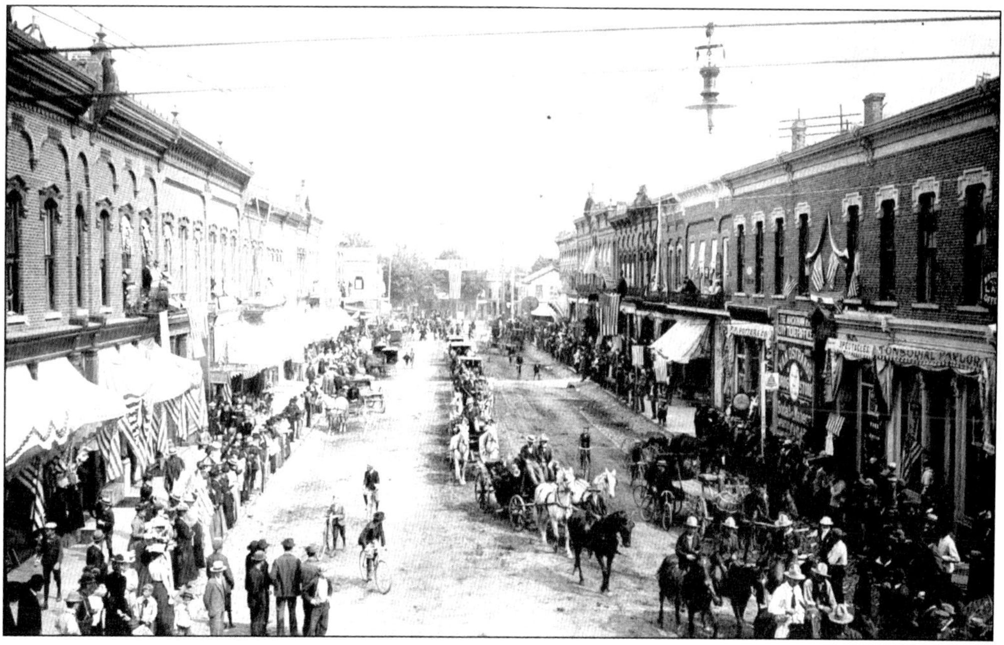

During the 1900 election campaign, the citizens of Allegan lined Locust Street to see vice presidential candidate Theodore Roosevelt. He was traveling through Michigan working for the reelection of Pres. William McKinley. They were elected in the 1900 election, beating their Democrat opponent William Jennings Bryan. In 1901, upon the assassination of McKinley, Roosevelt became president.

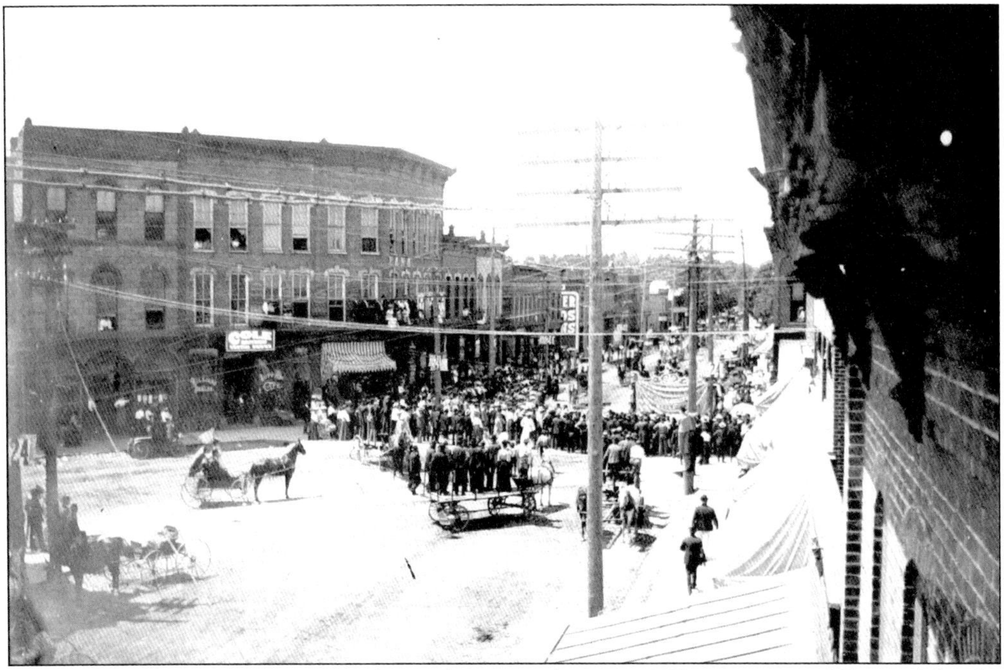

This July 1898 parade was put together with not much notice. When a meteor fell out of the sky onto Allegan, everyone felt that was as good a cause as any for a parade. Speeches were given by the city fathers of the day, and the people in town were treated to a look at this wondrous piece of rock before it was shipped off to the Smithsonian in Washington, D.C.

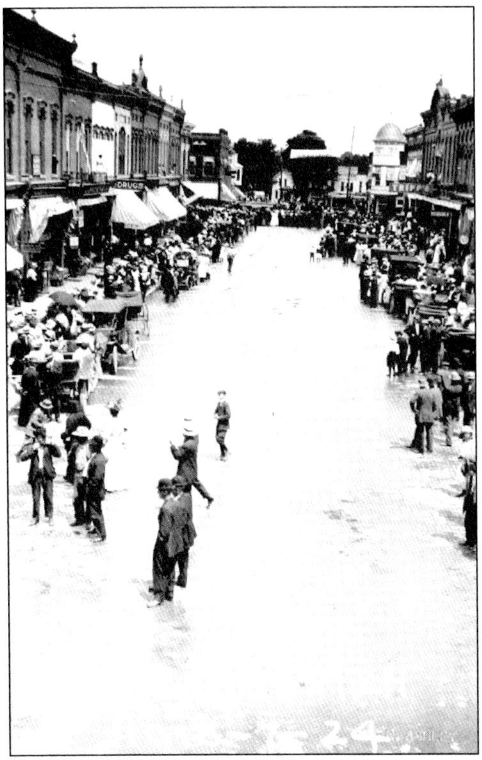

Always ready for a parade, the 1913 residents of Allegan eagerly await the arrival of Buffalo Bill and his 101 Ranch extravaganza. Following the parade to nearby Pingree Park, they would then be transported to the Wild West with a show filled with Native Americans, cowboys, and lots of shooting and showmanship.

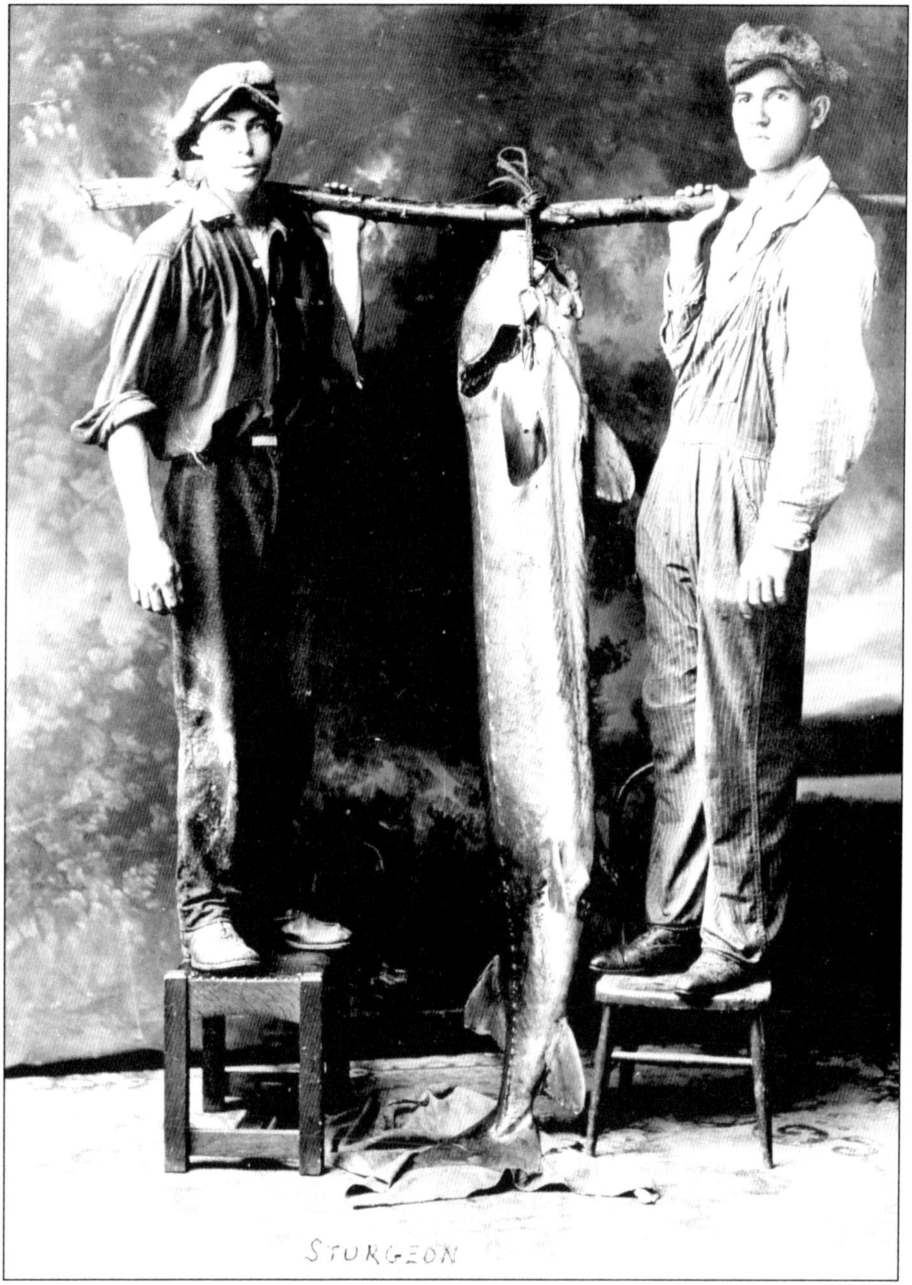

In the above 1915 photograph, Charley Wait and Wayne Bechtel pose with the 115-pound sturgeon they caught at the Allegan city dam. Knowing that it was illegal to hook, net, or spear sturgeon at the dam, the two 15-year-old boys approached the game warden to ask him if it was permissible for them to catch one by hand. The warden's response was that he was unaware of any law that made that kind of capture illegal. These two intrepid Tom Sawyer and Huck Finn impersonators jumped into the river and wrestled this seven-foot-plus fish onto the bank. Wait and Bechtel then took the huge fish to Brand's Meat Market where it was weighed and measured. Upon hearing the story, a local photographer invited the boys into his downtown Allegan studio to capture the moment with a photograph of them holding their prize catch.

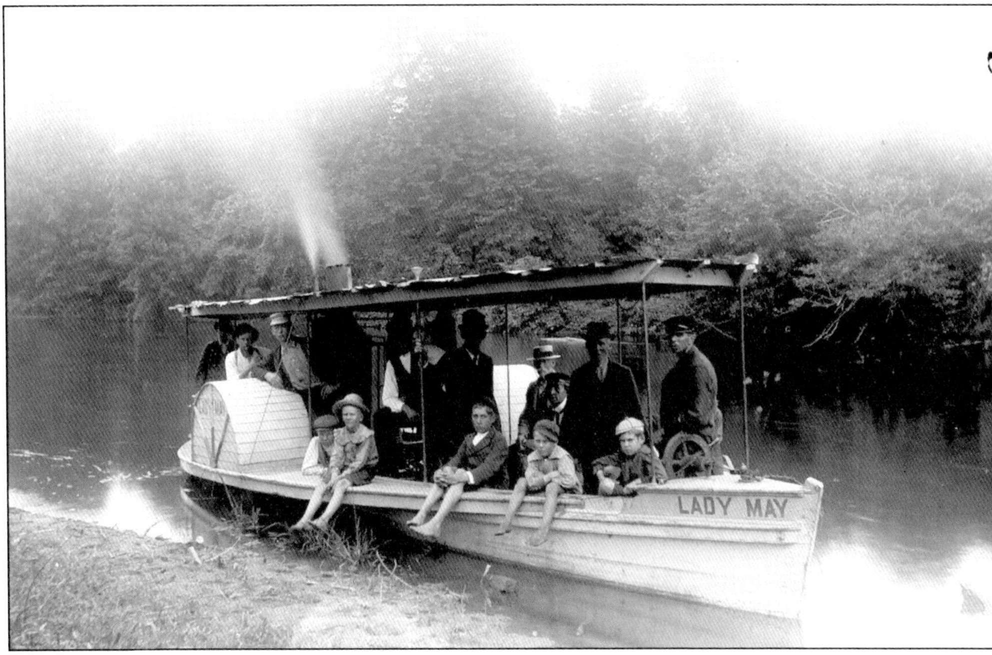

The *Lady May* churns up the Kalamazoo River with its rear paddle wheel. The river had served many functions all over Allegan over the years, as a power supply, a means of transporting logs to sawmills, a transportation system for merchandise for local businesses, and recreational boating.

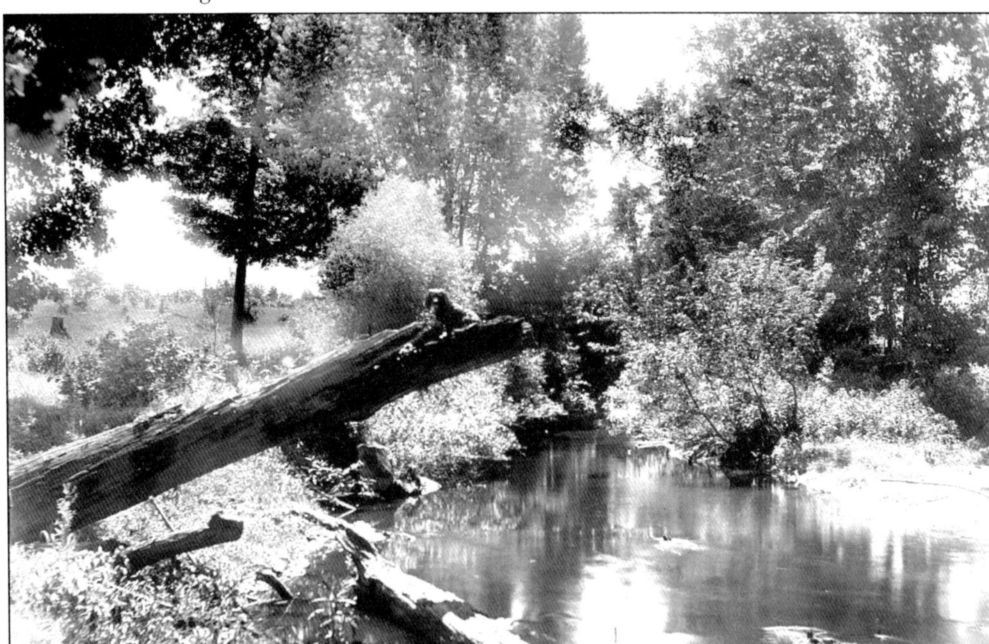

The Kalamazoo River banks offer many areas for hiking. In this c. 1900 photograph, Fritz the Second, beloved dog of Mr. and Mrs. William Vosburgh, has worked his way out onto a fallen tree overhanging the river to pose for his master. William was a jeweler and Mrs. Vosburgh occupied half of his store with her millinery shop.

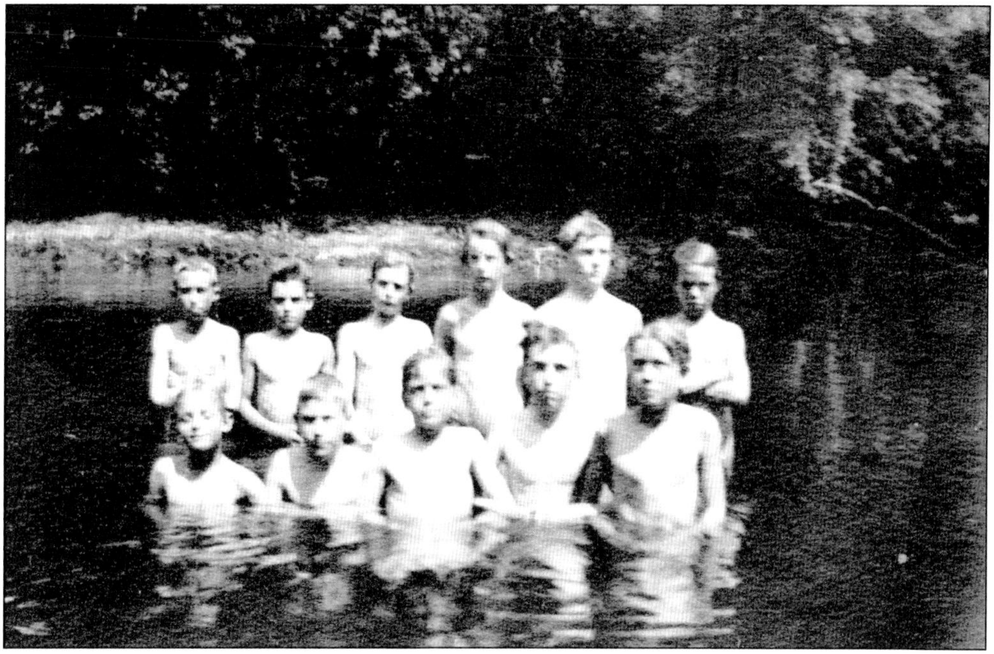

In this c. 1930 photograph, several of the young boys of Allegan are enjoying their favorite swimming hole in the bend of the Kalamazoo River they called Moore's Island. On a couple of occasions local young ladies snuck up on the bank and stole the boys' clothing. The only identified person is (front row, third from left) Harold "Bud" Tripp.

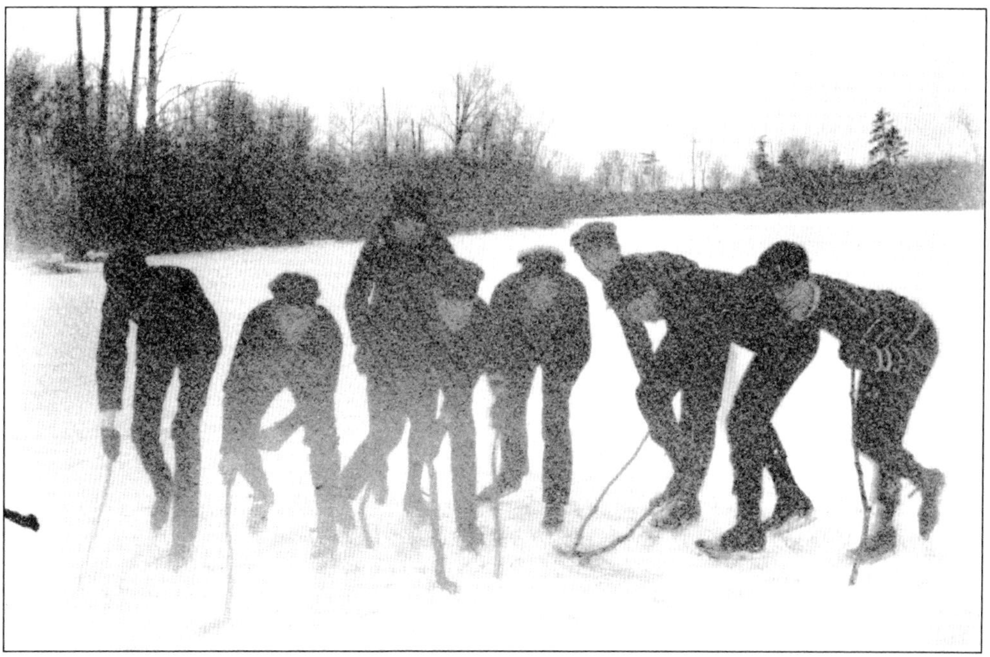

The river and the many local lakes around Allegan have always provided both summer and winter recreation opportunities. In this undated photograph a group of boys are engaged in a game of hockey. In the wintertime, the frozen lakes in the Allegan area abound with ice fishermen and their shanties also.

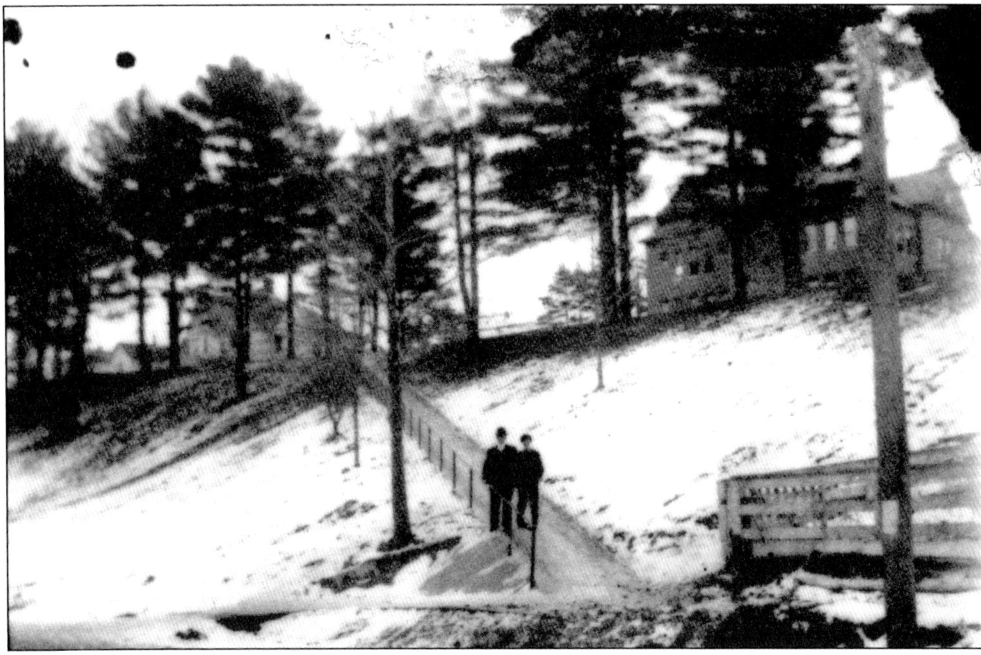

This c. 1950 photograph shows the hill coming down from the Allegan High School and Junior High School. The path ends on Pine Street, which was a very short and unbusy street. On winter days when the snow had fallen in enough abundance, this hill was very popular with the children of Allegan for sledding.

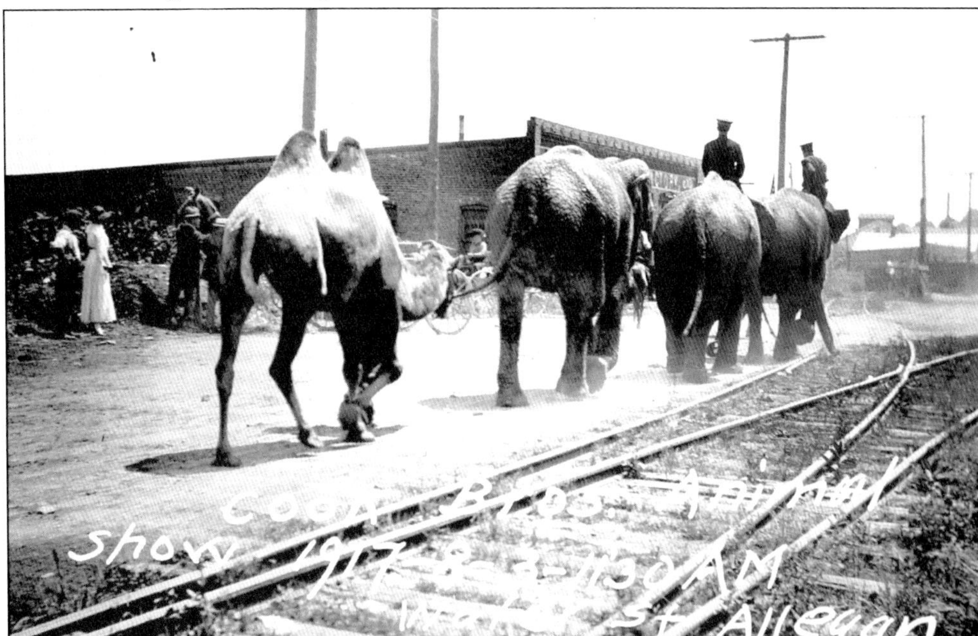

In 1917, the Cook Brothers Animal Show made Allegan one of its stops. Area residents had seen elephants on the streets of Allegan when earlier circuses came to town, but Cook Brothers brought the first, and perhaps the last, camel. In this photograph, the visiting "ship of the desert" follows three elephants down Water Street for a preshow parade.

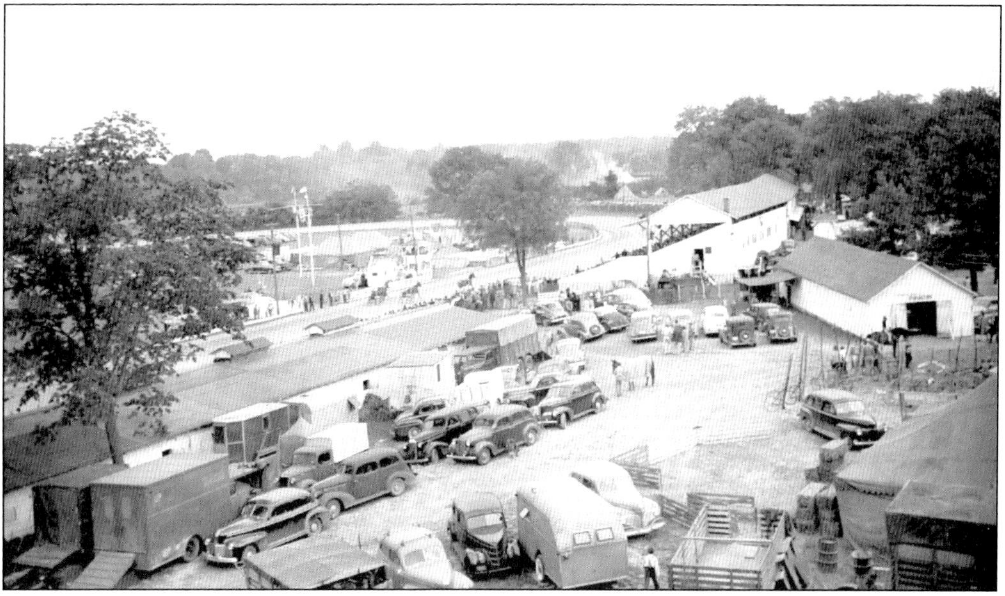

This 1945 photograph shows a grandstand crowd watching a horse race in progress. The Allegan County Agricultural Society held its first fair in 1853 in the basement of the Baptist church, also used as the courthouse. By 1856, this event had moved to an eight-acre parcel of land purchased on the river for the site of a fairground.

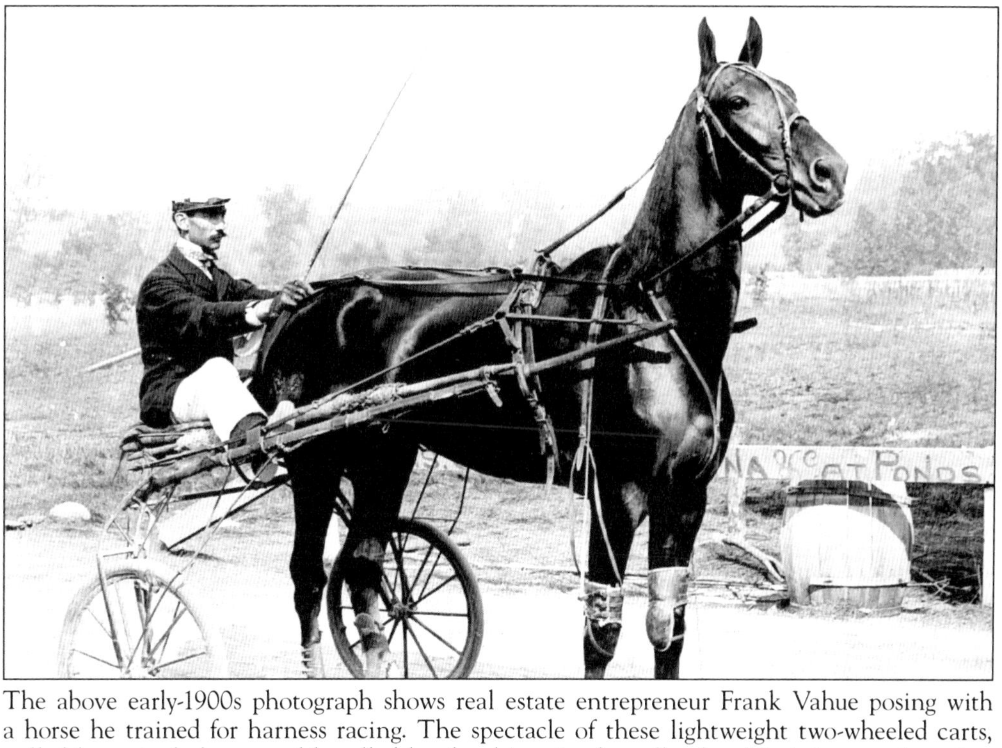

The above early-1900s photograph shows real estate entrepreneur Frank Vahue posing with a horse he trained for harness racing. The spectacle of these lightweight two-wheeled carts, pulled by a single horse and handled by the driver in the sulky, has filled the grandstand at the fair for many years. The daily harness races are still a popular event at the fair, even in this 21st century.

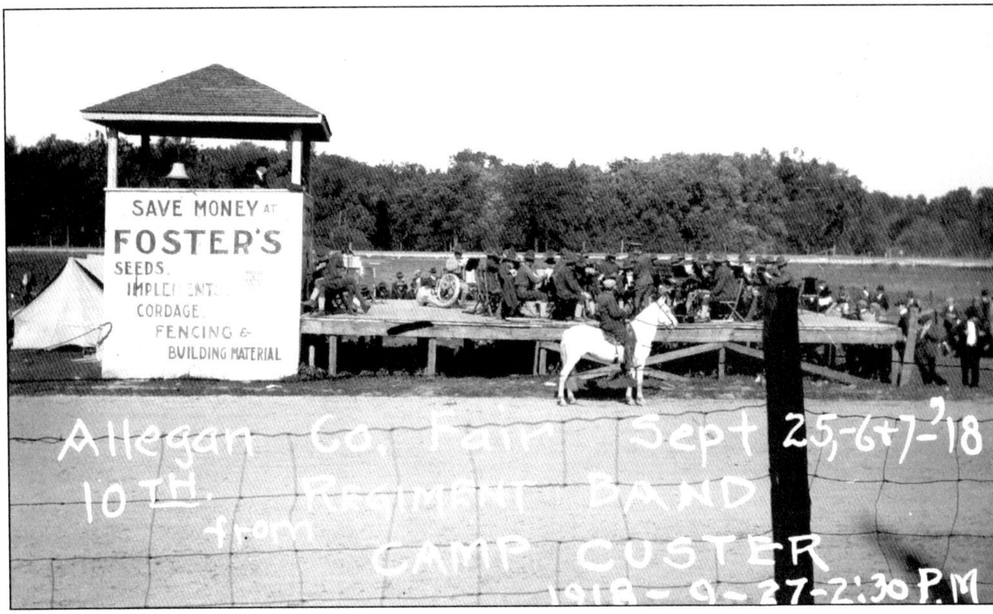

On September 27, 1918, as part of the Allegan County Fair celebration, the 10th Regiment Band from Camp Custer, now known as Fort Custer, Battle Creek, Michigan, entertains the crowd at the fairground racetrack. Today the fair board still books some of the most popular names in entertainment to perform onstage. Alton Foster, the owner of Foster's seed store advertised above, was secretary of the fair in 1899.

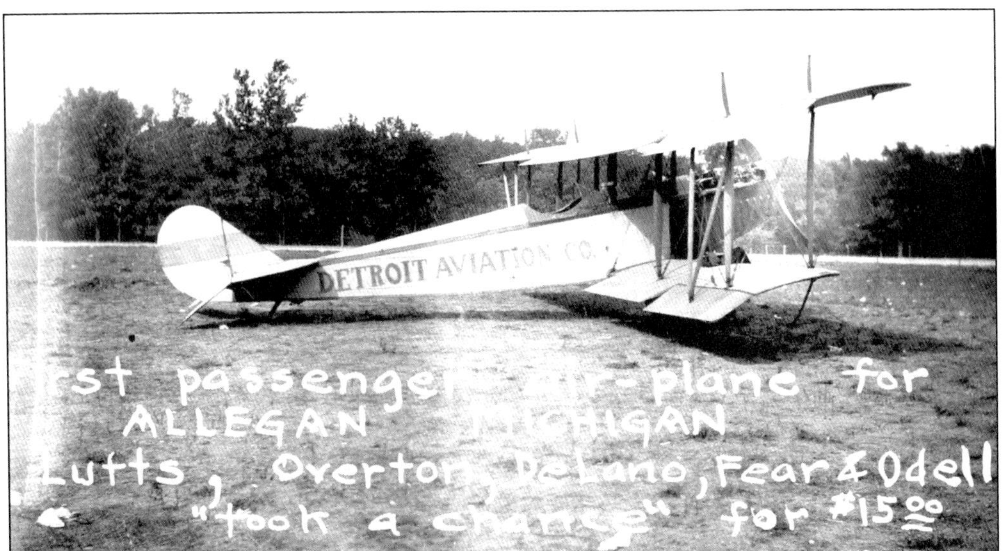

In this 1919 photograph, a new sensation arrived at the Allegan County Fair. The first passenger airplane was present and available for thrilling rides. The cost was $15, and one was taken far out over Lake Michigan. The passengers sat up front with the pilot, George E. Young.

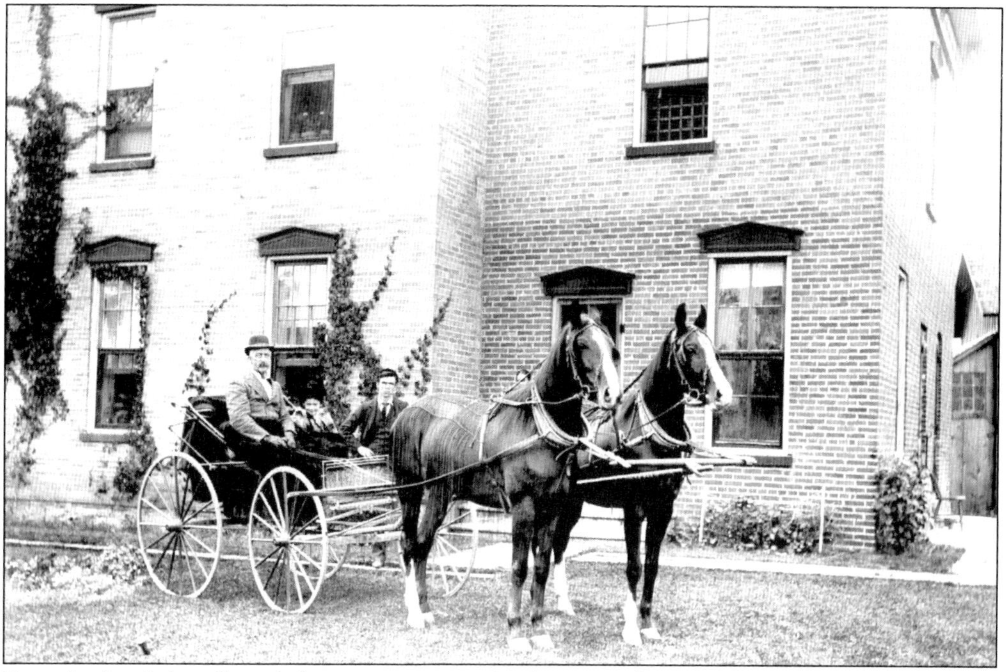

Even the local sheriff needed time to recreate. In this 1895 photograph, sheriff Joseph Stratton, seated in a two-horse hitch buggy, is ready for a pleasant ride on a nice Michigan afternoon. There are many lovely wooded areas surrounding Allegan, and they have long been the destination for pleasure jaunts and remain so today.

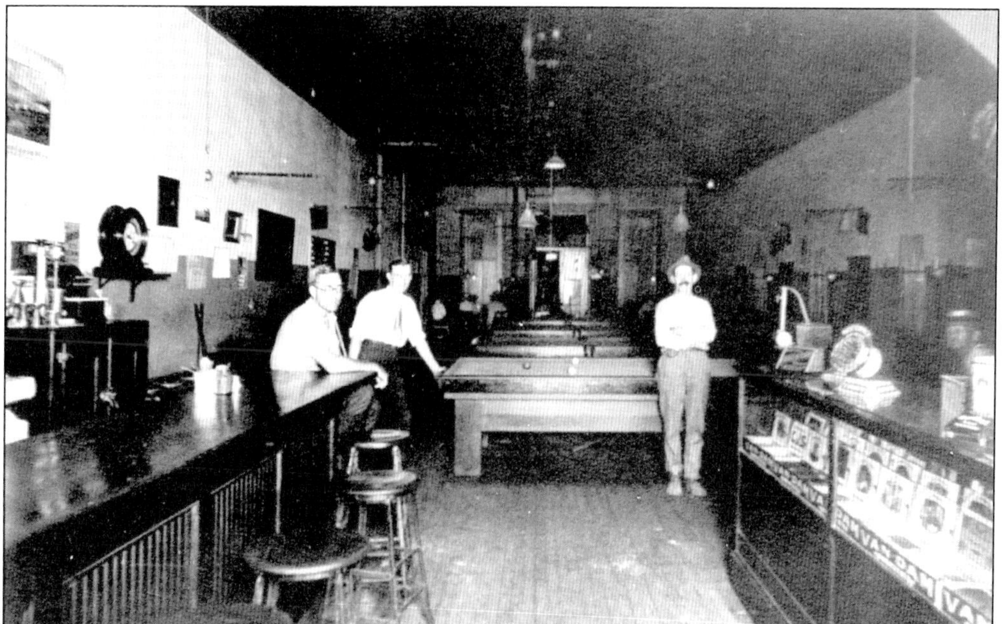

A display counter filled with cigars, a bar on the left, and a row of pool tables in the rear illustrate a typical Allegan pool hall on Hubbard Street. The gentleman with the white shirt and tie, second from left, is identified as Albert "Roundy" Maskey. The others are unidentified, and no date is given.

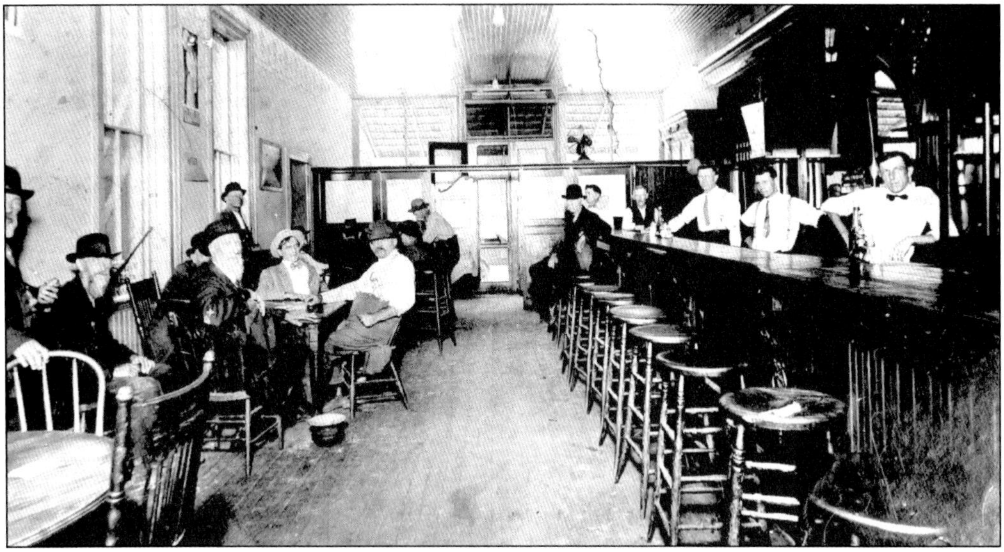

This photograph from the late 1800s shows a busy saloon in Allegan, possibly on Brady Street, with three bartenders on duty. None of the men in the photograph are identified. As was the custom of the day, each table has an accompanying spittoon on the floor and patrons were urged to aim carefully.

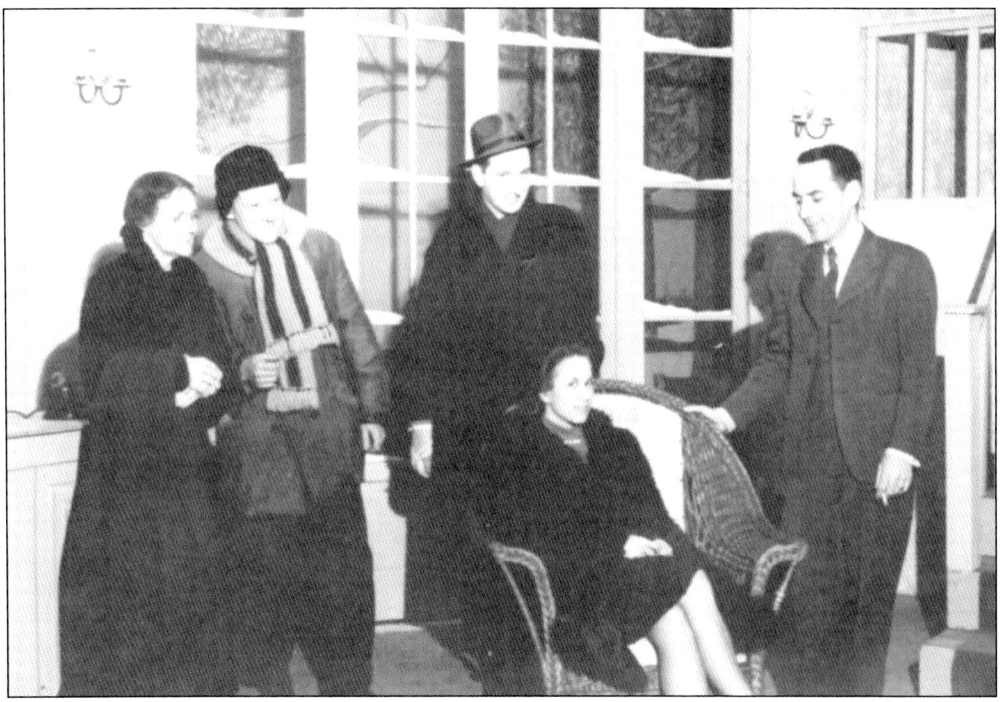

The Allegan Community Players have been a bright spot on Allegan's cultural scene since their first play at Streeter's Opera House in 1918. In 1922, they moved to the Regent Theater, and finally into the completed Griswold Auditorium. In this photograph, thespians (left to right) Marjory Newton, Walter Pierce, Ben Parker, Bette Comer, and Walter Keyes perform in *Seven Keys to Baldpate*.

The old Jewett School was in a sad state of disrepair in this 1976 photograph. The Allegan County Historical Society acquired the building, and shortly after this photograph was taken, this one-room schoolhouse made the trip from its rural home to become one of the most beloved attractions of the Historical Village at the fairgrounds.

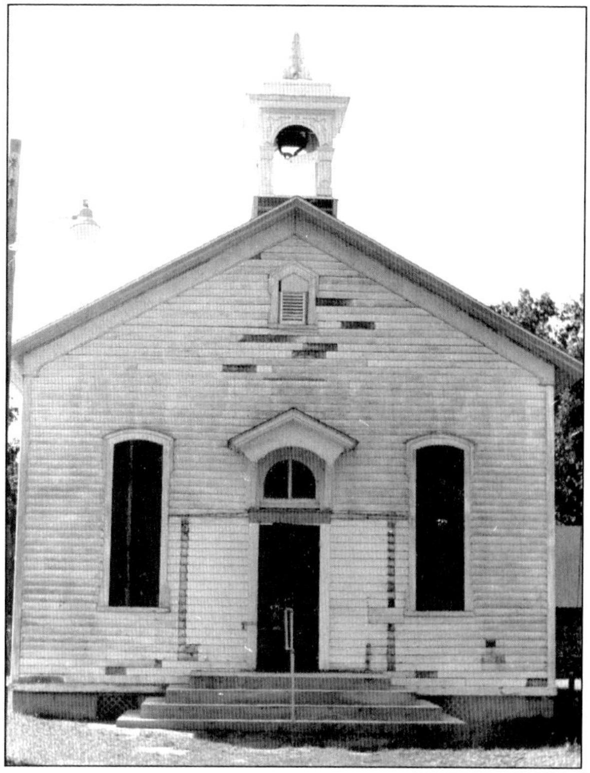

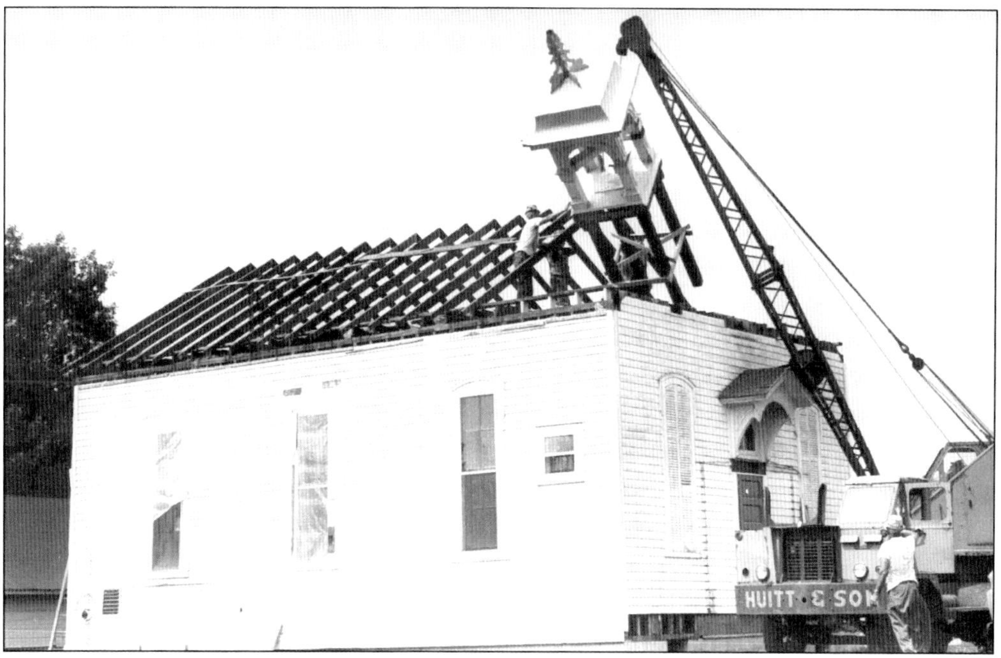

This photograph shows the careful reconstruction of the roof and bell tower of the Jewett School after it was moved to the Historical Village at the fairgrounds. The Huitt and Son crane is carefully replacing the bell tower, which was detached for the move, and a new roof will be constructed. (Courtesy Allegan County News.)

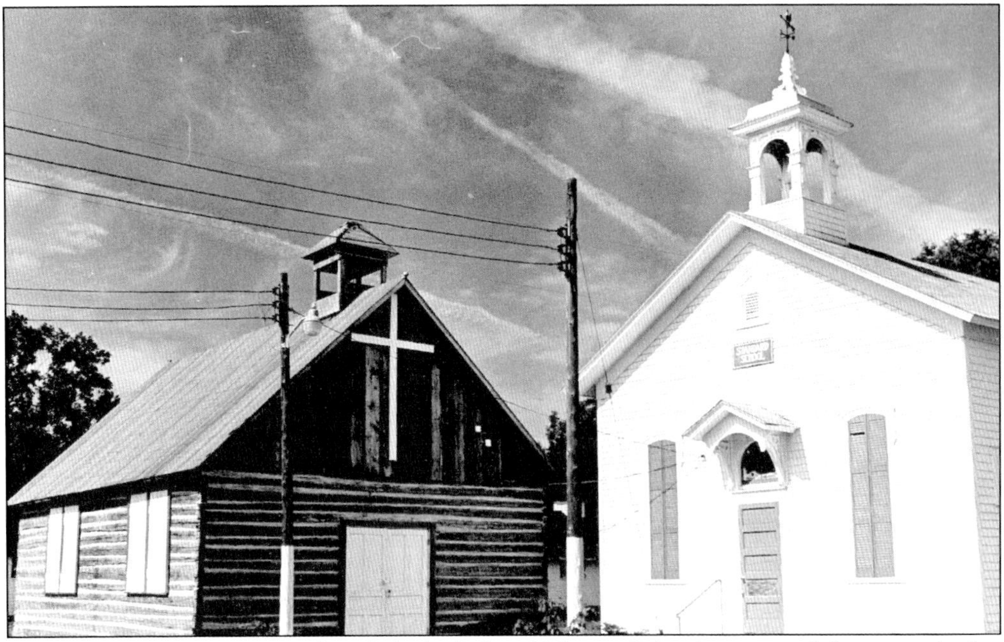

Safely transported and carefully refurbished, the old Jewett School now stands between the log church and the blacksmith shop in the Historical Village. The church is available for weddings during the summer months. During fair week, folk and gospel singing groups entertain in the old building. Classes are held in the school, with the retired teacher's association teaching area classes during the fair.

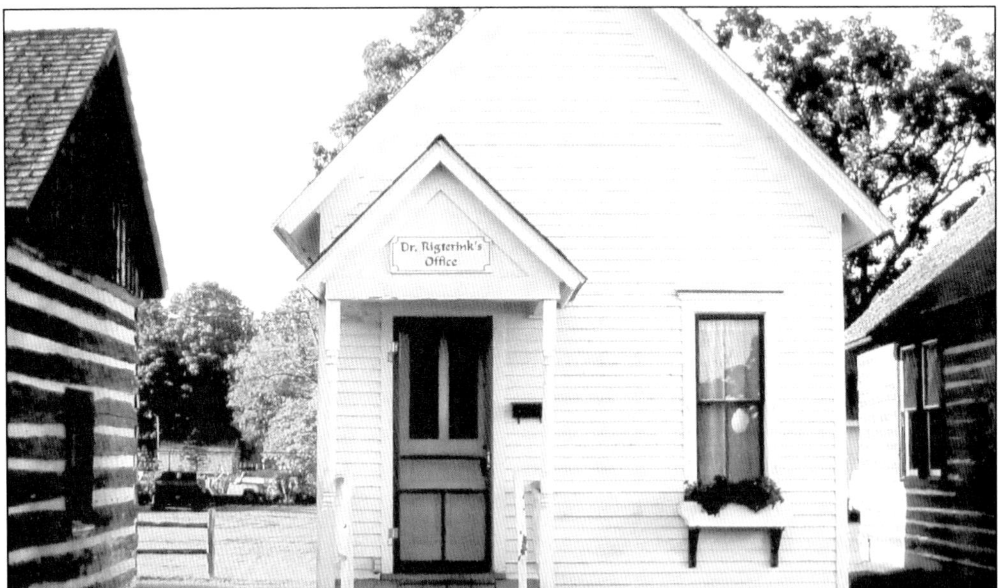

This photograph shows the office of Dr. George Rigterink at the Historical Village at the fairgrounds. Rigterink practiced medicine and dentistry in Allegan County for 52 years. In the early 1900s, he made house calls by horse and buggy. His furnished office is appointed with many of Rigterink's original furniture and medical equipment, including his ledger with patients' names and charges, which is a popular attraction.

Ten

Stormy Weather

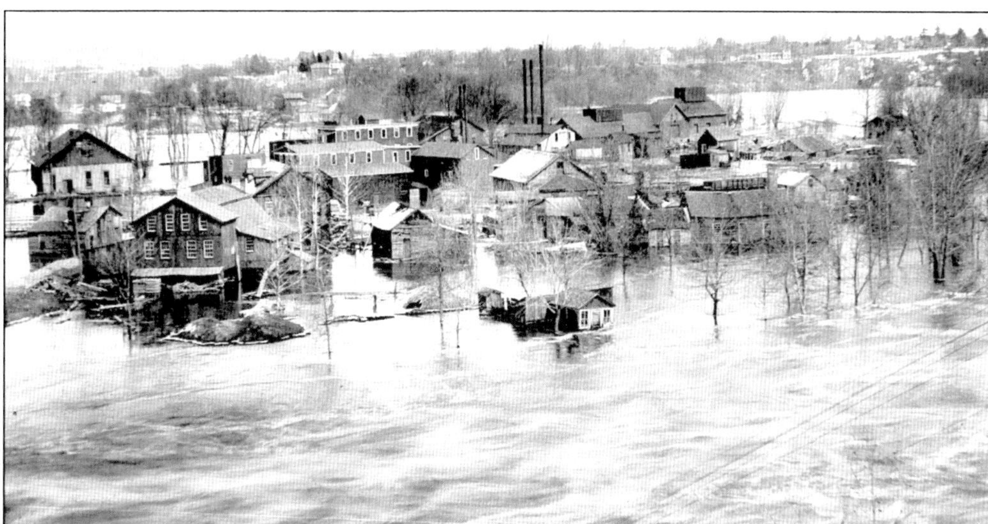

In 1909, the Kalamazoo River swept over its banks and flooded the mill district. Within the Allegan city limits there are no fewer than eight bends in the river, one of which surrounds the downtown area. Despite this proximity to the water, floods have not been a common occurrence over the years in Allegan.

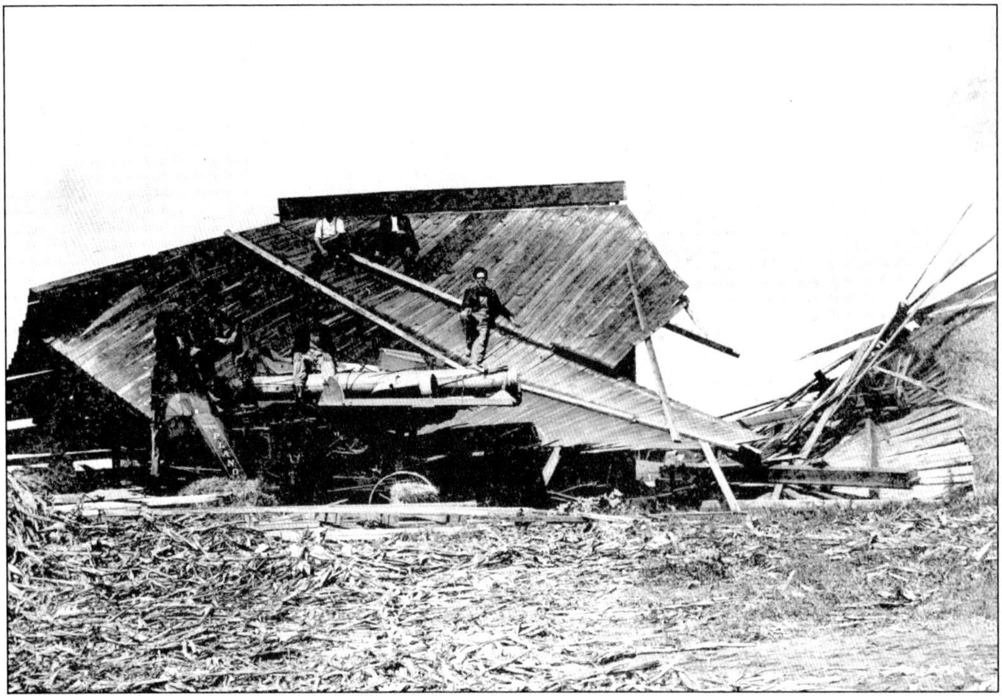

In 1897, Allegan was in the path of a cyclone, as it was called on the back of the above photograph. Alie Monteith's barn suffered major damage. Following the disaster, friends and neighbors arrived to help remove the debris. More than likely, those same friends would remain to help rebuild the barn, using some of the saved wood.

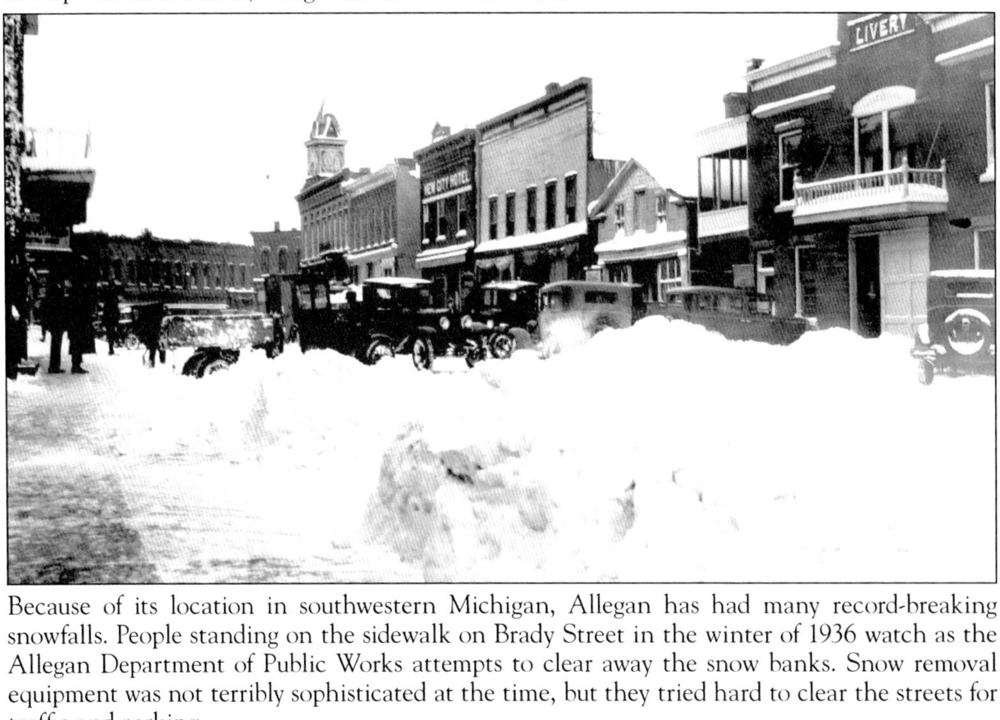

Because of its location in southwestern Michigan, Allegan has had many record-breaking snowfalls. People standing on the sidewalk on Brady Street in the winter of 1936 watch as the Allegan Department of Public Works attempts to clear away the snow banks. Snow removal equipment was not terribly sophisticated at the time, but they tried hard to clear the streets for traffic and parking.

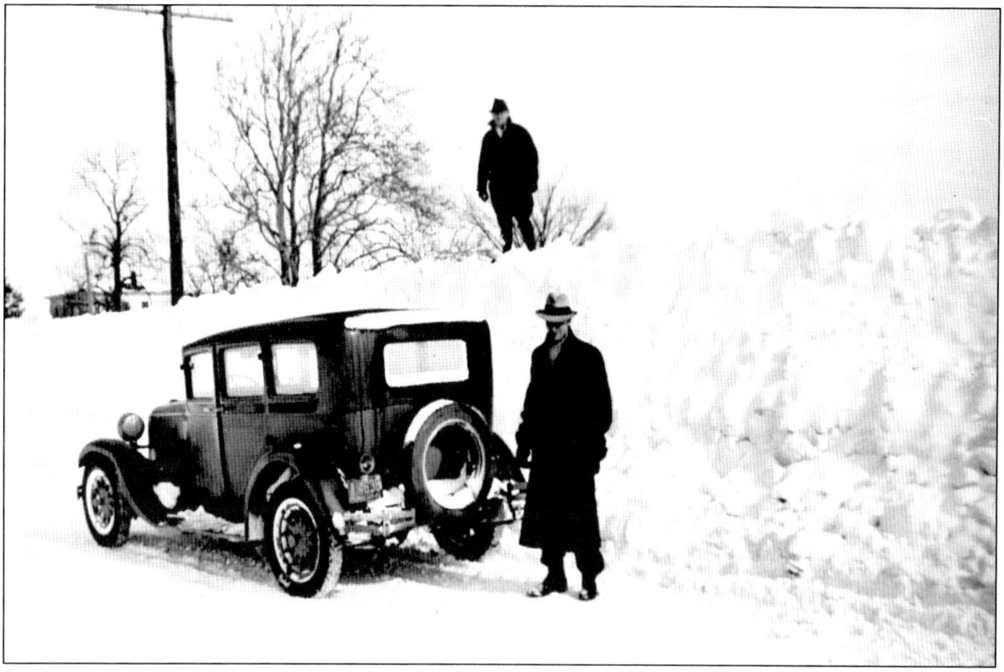

In this photograph, taken in 1936, John Katherler, towering on top of the snow bank, and Norm Bills, in the road at the rear of the car, pose for a picture illustrating the height of the plowed snow. Often it was days before the roads would be cleared, especially in rural areas.

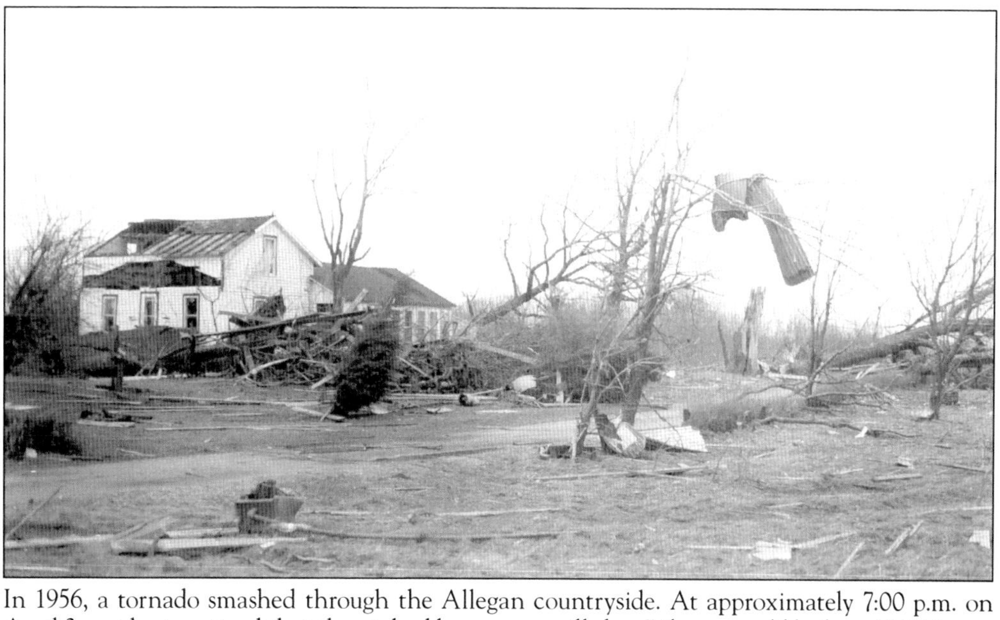

In 1956, a tornado smashed through the Allegan countryside. At approximately 7:00 p.m. on April 3, residents noticed that the air had become so still that "silence could be heard." This was followed by a roar that sounded like a train. The unidentified home above survived; however, the debris in the yard could have come from the neighbors or from miles away.

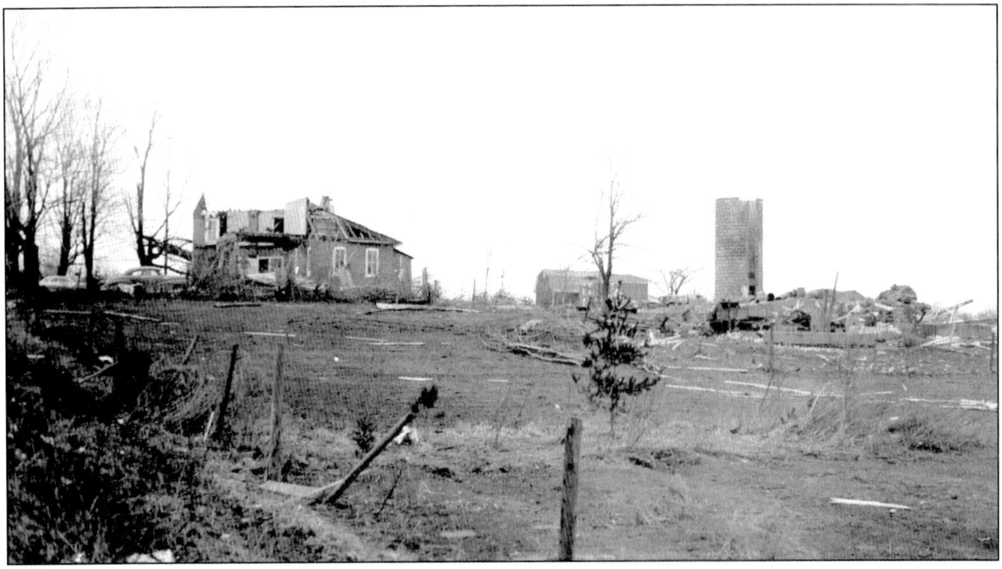

The farm of Leslie and Dorothy Miner on 118th Avenue is shown on April 5, 1956. The roof shows extensive damage, and the barn is totally gone. Their son Donald was covered with welts from flying bits and pieces of linoleum, while pieces of straw from the barn were imbedded in trees. Neighboring homes also damaged belonged to the Levett, Kent, and Spreitzer families.

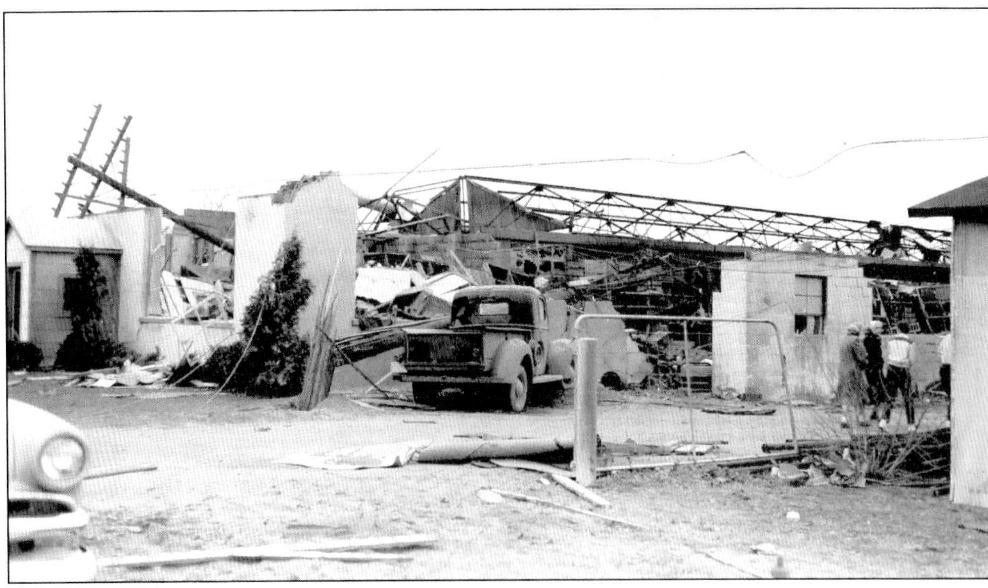

Most of the damage from the 1956 Allegan tornado was to homes; however, the Crescent Pipe Company, shown above, sustained major damage. The roof was torn off, and some of the walls collapsed. Just down the road, the heavy cement roof of the Allegan County Road Commission was completely blown off. The night of the 1956 tornado was truly a memorable one for Allegan and its residents.

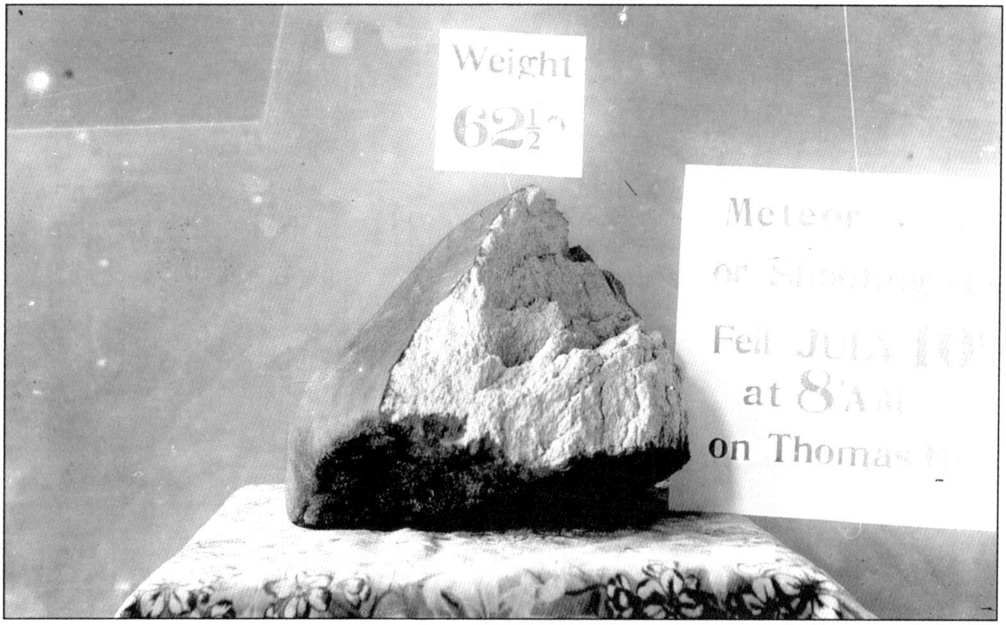

On July 10, 1898, a road construction crew on Delano Street heard a rumbling roar from the sky. They scrambled to safety as a meteor crashed to earth in front of them. The entire meteor weighed roughly 70 pounds in total, but was broken up on landing. Residents rushed to the area, and many were able to leave with a little piece of history, still warm from its fall, in their hands.

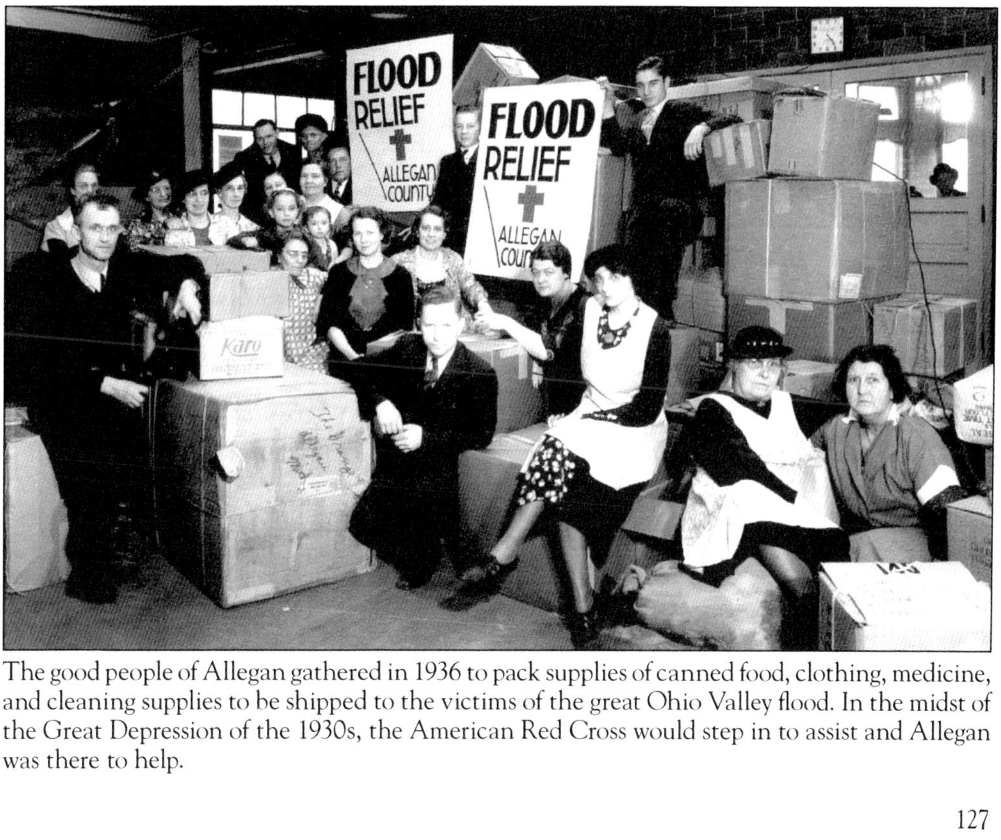

The good people of Allegan gathered in 1936 to pack supplies of canned food, clothing, medicine, and cleaning supplies to be shipped to the victims of the great Ohio Valley flood. In the midst of the Great Depression of the 1930s, the American Red Cross would step in to assist and Allegan was there to help.

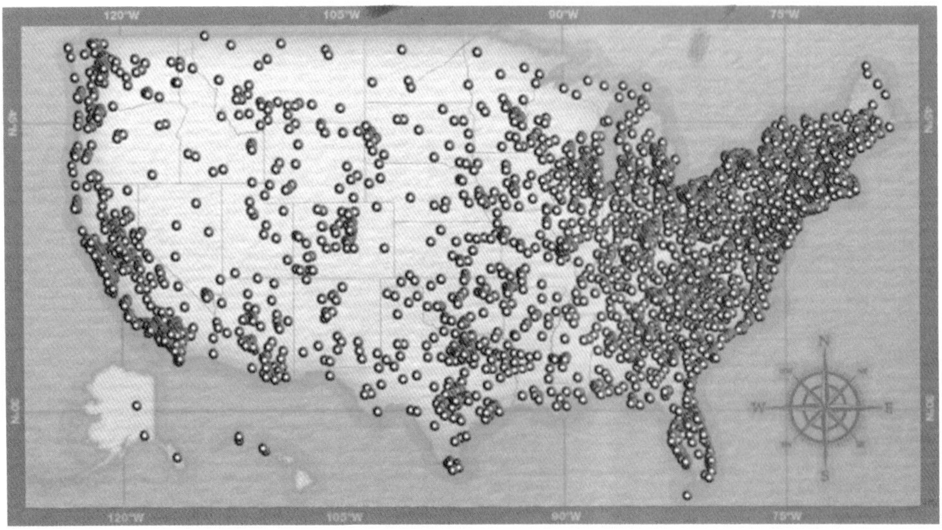